D1593030

STUDIES IN AFRICAN HISTORY · 9

Kingdoms of the Sudan

STUDIES IN AFRICAN HISTORY

General Editor: A. H. M. Kirk-Greene

St Antony's College

Oxford

1 SENEGAL: A STUDY IN FRENCH ASSIMILATION
Michael Crowder

2 SWAHILI: THE RISE OF A NATIONAL LANGUAGE
Wilfred Whiteley

3 KINGDOMS OF THE YORUBA
Robert S. Smith

4 THE MILITARY IN AFRICAN POLITICS
W. F. Gutteridge (out of print)

5 THE NIGERIAN ARMY 1956–1966
N. J. Miners

6 GHANA UNDER MILITARY RULE 1966–1969
Robert Pinkney

7 ANCIENT GHANA AND MALI
Nehemia Levtzion

8 BOTSWANA: A SHORT POLITICAL HISTORY
Anthony Sillery

R. S. O'FAHEY and J. L. SPAULDING

KINGDOMS OF THE SUDAN

METHUEN & CO LTD
11 New Fetter Lane · London EC4

~~59050~~
0504467

First published 1974
by Methuen & Co Ltd
© *1974 R. S. O'Fahey and J. L. Spaulding*
Printed in Great Britain by
Butler & Tanner Ltd
Frome and London

ISBN 0 416 77450 4 hardback
ISBN 0 416 77460 1 paperback

This title is available in both hard-back and paperback editions. The paperback edition is sold subject to the condition that it shall not, by way of trade or otherwise, be lent, re-sold, hired out, or otherwise circulated without the publisher's prior consent in any form of binding or cover other than that in which it is published and without a similar condition including this condition being imposed on the subsequent purchaser.

Distributed in the U.S.A. by
HARPER & ROW PUBLISHERS, INC.
BARNES & NOBLE IMPORT DIVISION

Contents

~~59050~~
050446

Preface

The term, *bilād al-sūdān* ('the land of the blacks'), was used by the medieval Arab geographers to describe the lands that stretched from the Senegal River to the Red Sea coast, below the Sahara but above the rain-forests, which were effectively beyond their view. Modern historians of Africa have continued this usage in their discussions of the Sudanic belt, which they have divided into three regions, western, central and eastern. The eastern Sudanic region may be regarded as falling roughly within the present-day borders of the Democratic Republic of the Sudan. This book is thus concerned with the history of the eastern Sudanic region, or the northern and western provinces, but not the southern, of the present Sudan Republic, the 'Sudan' of the title referring to the modern country of that name.

The northern and western provinces of the Sudan were, from the sixteenth until the nineteenth century, when the country was progressively conquered by Muḥammad 'Alī Pasha, Viceroy of Egypt, and his successors, dominated by two states, the Funj kingdom of Sinnār and the Keira sultanate of Dār Fūr (Darfur). Sinnār emerged at the beginning of the sixteenth century and ruled the Gezira and the Nile valley until it was destroyed in 1820 by the armies of Muḥammad 'Alī. The Keira sultanate first appears in historical records a century later and survived until 1874, when it was conquered by al-Zubayr Pasha. The sultanate was later briefly revived by 'Alī Dīnār (1898–1916) before its incorporation into the Anglo-Egyptian Sudan.

The history of the two states has been relatively neglected by comparison with the better-known states of the western *bilād al-sūdān* and indeed with other periods of the Sudan's history. Yet under their rule emerged many of the social and religious institutions, and much of the local administrative structure, of the modern Sudan.

This study is very much a preliminary account, because although notable work has been done on particular topics within the period, much fundamental research remains to be done, particularly by archaeologists and linguists, on such topics as the remoter origins of the states. It is based upon research for our doctoral dissertations (Spaulding has written part I; O'Fahey part II) and we are only too keenly aware of the speculative nature of some of our conclusions, of the many *lacunae* and of our relative neglect of the later and better documented periods, that is, Sinnār in the last fifty years of its existence and Dār Fūr on the eve of the conquest by al-Zubayr. We both hope, in the future, to produce more substantial studies of the states.

As far as possible we have ignored the colloquial Sudanese Arabic forms and have used the transliteration adopted by the *Encyclopedia of Islạm*, but with the omission of the subscript ligatures and the substitution of 'j' for '*dj*' and 'q' for 'ḳ'. For the Fur language, a modified form of the phonetic system devised by A. C. Beaton in his grammar of the language has been used.

In the spelling of place names it is impossible to be consistent and we have sometimes written the conventional anglicized form, or the arabicized form, or the form, often very inaccurate, that appears on the 1 : 250,000 Sudan Ordnance Survey maps.

Our debt to previous scholars can be seen from the bibliography. We wish to thank the Herbert H. Lehman Foundation for support for research in the northern Sudan in 1969 and 1970, and the Central Research Fund, University of London, and the Research Committee, University of Khartoum, for making possible research in Dār Fūr in 1969 and 1970. Our gratitude is also due to the Department of History, University of Bergen, whose hospitality enabled us to complete the final draft. We have profited greatly from discussions with and guidance from Professor Yūsuf Fadl Ḥasan and Dr Muḥammad Ibrāhīm Abū Salīm, who, as chairman of the Sudan Anthropology Board, gave us permission to carry out our fieldwork. We are grateful to Professors P. L. Shinnie and R. H. Pierce and the Rev. Dr A. J. Arkell for reading parts of the original draft; the errors and opinions that remain are of course ours. We owe an especial debt to our doctoral supervisors, Professor P. M. Holt and Dr Marcia Wright. Above all, we are deeply grateful to our long-suffering wives, Margaret and Karen.

I · Introduction

The geographical background

The kingdoms of Sinnār and Dār Fūr did not have rigidly defined boundaries, but each was centred in a heartland given coherence by geographical factors. Sinnār lay in the Nile valley between Egypt, the Ethiopian highlands and the swamps of the southern Sudan. It included the regions known today as the Gezira (between the Blue and the White Niles), the Buṭāna (between the Atbara and the Blue Nile) and the Bayūḍa (between the confluence of the Blue and the White Niles and the great bend of the united river further north). In the north the lateral boundaries of the kingdom extended no further than the limits of the irrigated strip along the river suitable for cultivation; in the savanna belt south of the Nile confluence the east–west boundaries were broad and fluid.

The western frontier of Sinnār, in periods of military strength, extended into Kordofan, a huge open plain, dotted with small mountain ranges in the north and dominated in the south by the Nuba mountains. For much of the eighteenth century Kordofan was disputed territory between Dār Fūr and Sinnār, until with the decline of the latter the Keira were able to occupy it at the end of the century.

The heart of the Keira state was Jabel Marra, a mountain range that rises in places to 9,000 feet, and the home of the Fur people who were the ethnic core of the state. West of the mountains, the savanna plain continued with no natural boundary between Dār Fūr and the neighbouring state of Wadai. The northern boundary of the state was guarded by the Sahara; in the south the Keira nominally ruled the Arab cattle-keeping nomads of the southern savanna region.

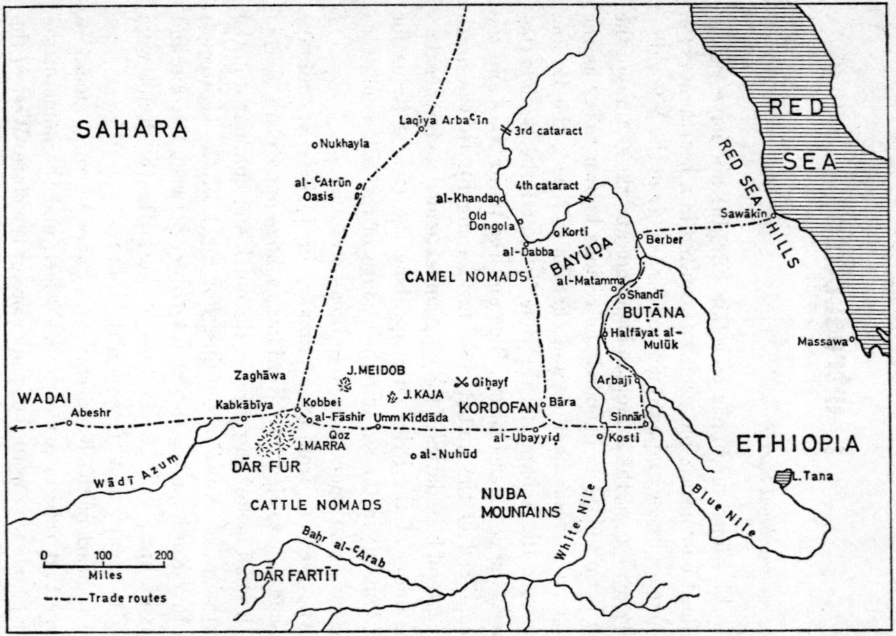

The Eastern Sudan

The Sudan is a hard land. Its geography leaves relatively few choices of life-style to those who win their livelihood there, and the economic and social patterns that arise from the land are tenacious and deeply rooted in antiquity. During the period embraced by this study no technological innovations in agriculture or animal husbandry arose to challenge or modify the inherited traditions. If one makes allowance for many local variations, the basic subsistence economies available to the people of the Funj kingdom were six: irrigated and rainland cultivation, camel and cattle nomadism, and systems of mixed farming adapted to the southern mountains and to the banks of the White Nile.[1]

The northernmost part of the modern Sudan was not included in the Funj kingdom. The rocky and thinly-populated northern riverain districts and the largely uninhabited desert on either side of the Nile formed a natural, though certainly not impermeable, boundary with Egypt.

Southward from the third cataract more cultivable land becomes available; this was worked intensively, the crops depending upon irrigation by the Nile flood or water-wheels and other mechanical devices. Irrigated fields lined the river-banks, and behind them lay a belt of date palms and the houses of the cultivators. A tenth-century visitor to the region spoke of 'narrow canals in the shade of the trees growing on the two banks',[2] and a traveller in about 1700 commented that 'along the river Nile no formed city or village is to be encountered, rather, one house stands directly next to the other, surrounded by the most beautiful palm-groves'.[3] The settlement pattern of the strip village was efficient in its exploitation of fertile land, water and labour.[4] Nevertheless the resources of the system were strictly limited, and the society that relied upon them very vulnerable to natural misfortunes and population pressures. It is not surprising that the region has a long tradition of emigration, primarily into the southern rainlands but also to Egypt, Dār Fūr and elsewhere.

At the latitude of the Nile bend occasional rains begin. A traveller in 1699 noted the transition; 'one begins to see trees and dry grass, the rains extending to this region, whereas everything up to this point was watered only by the overflow of the Nile or by machine'.[5] Dates could not be profitably cultivated south of the Nile bend, but the increase in desert vegetation made camel nomadism possible across a wide belt that included the Red Sea Hills, the Bayūḍa, and northern Kordofan and Dār Fūr. In favourable circumstances the nomads exchanged animal for vegetable foods with their sedentary neighbours, creating a symbiotic relationship. During the annual dry season, however, the nomads were forced to cluster along the Nile or migrate far to the south; in bad years they became dependent upon the cultivators for food. Politically and militarily the riverain folk usually held the upper hand.

Going south precipitation gradually increased and farmers relied to an increasing degree upon crops grown away from the rivers on rainland. At the latitude of the Nile confluence this meant planting a crop in the bed of a seasonal watercourse during the rains, a risky though occasionally profitable venture. Even further south farmers were sometimes forced to the riverbanks by drought, and irrigated cultivation extended as far up the Blue Nile as Sinnār. At that level, however, rainland cultivation was predominant. Fields were opened to cultivation by burning dense stands of thorn trees and scrub. Following several years of cultivation, the trees began to return; when young and scattered they resisted fire, and the field had to be abandoned during the life-span of the thorn-thicket. The choicest village sites were located along the rivers, but many communities were totally dependent upon shifting rainland cultivation. Land was plentiful, and an immigrant from the northern region would have found the resources of the rainlands virtually limitless.

The parts of the Sudan suitable for rainland cultivation also supported cattle or mixed cattle-and-camel nomads. The belt adapted to cattle nomadism included the southern Red Sea Hills, much of the Buṭāna and the Gezira, central Kordofan and southern Dār Fūr. The more generous southern environment reduced the dependence of the herdsmen on the cultivators and supported far greater numbers of them; unlike the camel nomads of the north, the southern groups could meet the sedentary folk on approximately equal terms. Only by a determined and sustained effort were they subordinated to the riverain kings.

Small ranges of mountains or hills dotted the plains of the Sudan in a belt extending from the Ethiopian borderlands across the central and southern Gezira and southern Kordofan. They served as refuge areas, and not uncommonly each supported a distinct linguistic and cultural group. The hill peoples usually built their villages on the hilltops for easy defence, and practised a mixed agriculture including cattle, swine, and a more intensive type of cultivation than was practised on the plains.

Along the White Nile south of the modern Kosti, shifting swamps alternated with the low banks of the river. Floods were common, and land high enough for cultivation limited. Village sites were relatively fixed, and over centuries of decay and reconstruction grew into settlement mounds. While direct evidence is lacking, it seems likely that the inhabitants of this region practised a mixed economy of cattle herding and intensive agriculture.

The region of Dār Fūr and Kordofan is a vast area of 340,000 square miles (only a little less than modern Nigeria). It is also an area of great geographical and ethnic diversity.[6] Going from north to south, three patterns of subsistence predominate, although with local variants; these largely correspond to the rainfall/vegetation boundaries. In the dry semi-desert north, where the rainfall averages less than 10 inches a year, are the camel nomads (Ar. *jammāla*); the central zone, where the rainfall ranges between 25 inches in the mountains to 12 inches on the plains, holds the sedentary rainland hoe farmers, who form the bulk of the population. The southern zone is much wetter, up to 35 inches a year, and is the home of the cattle nomads (Ar. *baqqāra*), who are more numerous than the *jammāla* of the north.

These geographically-defined patterns of subsistence do not correspond to any simple ethnic or linguistic boundaries; thus both Arabic and non-Arabic speaking peoples are to be found in all three zones, although Arabic speakers tend to dominate numerically in the camel and cattle nomad zones. Nor are the zones rigidly divided; the Fur (sedentary)/Banī Halba (cattle nomad) frontier along the Wādī Azum in western Dār Fūr is stable, although there is considerable movement of Fur across the frontier for economic reasons. There, Fur on crossing the tribal and occupational frontier leave their own way of life, and eventually language, to adopt those of the Baqqāra as being more appropriate to cattle nomadism. A similar process appears to take place on the Fur/Zaghāwa frontier in northern Dār Fūr, where sedentary farmers and cattle nomads meet.[7]

K. M. Barbour divides Dār Fūr and Kordofan into four sub-regions, Western Dār Fūr, the Semi-Desert, the *Qōz* (stabilized sand dunes) and the Nuba Mountains.[8] Western Dār Fūr was the heartland of the Keira or Fur state and repeats the pattern of the larger area. In the north of the sub-region there is little water; the population, Zaghāwa, some Fur and the Banī Ḥusayn and northern Rizayqāt Arabs keep mainly goats, sheep and some cattle.[9] In the rainy season (October to January/February) the *jizzū* grazing lands in the far north are the goal of a variety of nomadic movements; the Kabābīsh move there from northern Kordofan,[10] the Zaghāwa, the northern Rizayqāt and Meidob from other parts of Dār Fūr, and the Bideyāt and the Gura'an from Chad.

The southern part of Western Dār Fūr is better watered than the north and consequently contains the greatest concentration of people in Dār Fūr, particularly along the fertile river banks such as the Wādī Azum. The Fur appear to have infiltrated gradually into the Wādī Azum region from Jabal Marra and now live there in compact villages of 50 to 200 huts, and growing *dukhn* (bulrush millet) and *dhurra* (common millet), groundnuts, maize, sesame and onions.[11] These are sown in June/July and are harvested in November/December. Markets are held all the year round, but the trade varies with the season. To these markets come the nomads to buy grain in exchange for milk and butter.

The natural centre of Dār Fūr province is the Jabal Marra mountain range, some 70 miles long and 30 miles broad. Jabal Marra is not only the watershed between the Nile and Chad river systems, it marks, in the widest sense, a cultural frontier; the peoples to the west of the mountains have tended to look to the western and central Sudanic belt, while to the east influences from the Nile valley have predominated. This frontier had a profound importance in the history of the Keira state, which arose in the west with close affinities with the states of the Chad region, but which was increasingly drawn towards the Nile valley. The slopes of Jabal Marra are covered by a complex system of stone terraces, which give perhaps the misleading impression that the mountains supported a larger population in the past than they do today.[12] The Fur, a negroid people whose language appears to be unrelated to any other spoken in Dār Fūr,[13], regard the mountains as their ancestral home. Today, however, most Fur live to the west or south of the mountains.

The *Qōz* stretches as a vast belt from east of Jabal Marra to the White Nile. Like Western Dār Fūr, the *Qōz* sub-region has nomads in the north and south and cultivators in the centre. The latter are to be found mainly in a triangle bounded by the towns of Umm Ruwāba, al-Ubayyiḍ and al-Nuhūḍ; this is the Kordofan or Kordofal of the nineteenth-century sources. The sedentary peoples of the central *Qōz* include the Birged, who once spoke a Nubian language but who now speak Arabic, and other Arabic-speaking tribes such as the Jawāmi'a, Ḥamar, Dār Ḥāmid and Bidayrīya. It is also notable for the use made of the *tabaldī* tree (the baobab) for the storage of water; the trees form an important part of the tribal wealth.

The southern part of the *Qōz* belt is the home of the Baqqāra, whose independence and wealth in cattle was a constant lure and annoyance to the Keira sultans, as a traveller noted about 1793, 'if the tribute (from the Baqqāra) were regularly paid, it might amount to four thousand oxen per annum: but these Arabs live in tents, and consequently change their habitations frequently, and when they feel themselves united, are not much inclined to pay tribute'.[14]

In the north the *Qōz* merges into the third sub-region, the Semi-Desert, which is the home of a variety of nomad groups, the Kabābīsh, Kawāhla and, in Dār Fūr, the Zayādīya, now the only major Arab camel nomad tribe in Dār Fūr, but who in the remote past appear to have formed part of a camel nomad federation, the Fazāra.[15] The Jabal Meidob mountains, in the northern *Qōz* in Dār Fūr, are inhabited by the Meidob, a semi-nomadic Nubian-speaking people, who appear to have migrated there from the Nile valley. The Nuba peoples of the mountains in south-eastern Kordofan, with the exception of the small state of Jabal Taqali, played little part in the wider history of the area.

The sources

In the absence of a substantial body of indigenous written material from Sinnār and Dār Fūr, this history must be based on a somewhat heterogenous collection of sources, both written and oral.

The sources for the study of Sinnār include the surviving documents written in the Funj kingdom itself, the accounts of men who visited Sinnār and wrote down their experiences, and writings originating in nearby lands but containing information about Sinnār. Additional insights have been gained from descriptions of the remnants of the Funj state by visitors to the Sudan following the fall of Sinnār and from Sudanese oral traditions concerning the Funj area.

A number of Sudanese documents written during the Funj period have survived. These include a list of the kings of Sinnār written down in 1772, and a longer historical work commonly called the *Funj Chronicle*. The earlier part of the *Chronicle*, from the sixteenth up until the early eighteenth century, consists of a king-list with the accretion of a certain amount of commentary; the later portion describes in some detail the factional strife in eighteenth-century Sinnār, and some versions also treat the early colonial period. A second source is the *Ṭabaqāt* of Wad Ḍayfallāh, a collection of biographies of some prominent Sudanese holy men of the Funj period. It includes popular tales as well as accounts of historical events in which the protagonists of the biographies participated. A third set of thirty-six documents may conveniently be termed land-charters. They offer a wealth of information about the governmental structure, landholding system and legal practices of Sinnār. They assist in establishing a chronology, and give insights into the social history of the eighteenth century. Finally, a number of other minor sources from the Funj period have survived, some of them only in translation.

A second genre of source material consists of eyewitness reports by men who visited Sinnār and left written records of their experiences. Of unique significance is the account of David Reubeni, who crossed from the Red Sea to Sinnār and passed down the Nile to Egypt in 1523. Seventeenth-century accounts of Sinnār were given by an Ethiopian traveller named Zaga Christ, and the Turkish diplomat and literary figure, Evliyā Celebī, who journeyed up the Nile from Egypt to Ethiopia in 1671–2. During the first quarter of the eighteenth century numbers of Jesuit and Franciscan missionaries used Sinnār as a staging area for attempts to convert Ethiopia to Roman Catholicism. They left a substantial literature of letters and chronicles that contain comments on politics and society in the Funj kingdom. The explorer, James Bruce, spent most of 1772 in Sinnār on his way down the Nile from Ethiopia to Egypt. His *Travels* contains an account of the Funj kingdom, and much additional information may be found in the portions of his journals published by his biographer, Alexander Murray. John Lewis Burckhardt made two penetrations into the Sudan on behalf of the African Association in 1812–14. His first attempt was frustrated at the borders of Sinnār, but the second brought him as far up the Nile as the town of Shandī; there he turned east to the Red Sea.

A third type of written source material originated in neighbouring lands, but contained mention of Sinnār. Some information, particularly about the transitional age between the decline of Nubia and the rise of Sinnār, may be derived from the works of Arab geographers.[16] Ethiopian chronicles and other documents make small but significant contributions, as do the accounts of Portuguese visitors to the Red Sea area and the records of early travellers to Upper Egypt. Information about Sinnār may also be found in the Dār Fūr literature discussed below.

With the fall of Sinnār in 1821, a large number of foreigners entered the Sudan, both as private citizens and as officials of the colonial government. They observed and reported aspects of Sudanese society that illuminate earlier accounts.

A final category of source material may be called oral tradition; that is, verbal statements about the Funj kingdom made by Sudanese informants and copied in writing by a second party. In addition to comments preserved in the travellers' accounts, there exists a considerable literature dating from the Condominium period (1899–1956). More recent attempts to collect oral traditions about Sinnār have produced little new information.

The sources for Dār Fūr fall into the same general categories as those for Sinnār; the travel literature is, however, much scantier, and although the oral traditions are richer, systematic collection has scarcely begun. Unlike the riverain Sudan, few indigenous written records have been found in Dār Fūr, and certainly nothing comparable to the *Funj Chronicle* or *Ṭabaqāt*. Land-charters, similar in scope to those from Sinnār, are now being discovered in the province; so far they have come mainly from the nineteenth century, but often give information on the eighteenth. There are indications that many more land-charters are waiting to be collected.

Dār Fūr was something of a *cul-de-sac* for would-be African explorers and the sultanate is less well covered in this respect than Sinnār; thus the accounts of three travellers who did reach Dār Fūr are of great importance. The English traveller, W. G. Browne, stayed in Dār Fūr for three years (1793–6), but his book, although detailed on the commercial activities in the area, is poor on the institutions and life of the Keira state itself. The richest description we have is that of Muḥammad b. ʻUmar al-Tūnisī, who as a young man was in Dār Fūr from 1803 to 1811 when he moved to Wadai; his two books on Dār Fūr and Wadai, edited and translated by Perron, are perhaps the last major Arab contribution to the exploration of Africa in the tradition of Ibn Baṭṭūṭa and Leo Africanus. The account of another Muslim traveller, Zayn al-ʻAbidīn, is much less valuable. The German traveller, Gustav Nachtigal, at the end of a long journey through Tibesti, Kanem and Wadai, spent six months in al-Fāshir in 1874, collecting as much information as he could. His collection of oral traditions provides the essential framework for the study of Keira history.

From these accounts a rich and detailed picture of Dār Fūr in the nineteenth century can be constructed and a more tentative one for the eighteenth. But the picture thus provided is distorted; the travellers rarely strayed far from the capital or established caravan routes, they associated with the ruling classes, Muslim holy men and merchants, if they spoke Arabic, they did not speak Fur.

Although some information may be gleaned from travellers in nearby lands or from reports about the slave trade with Egypt, little more was collected during the lifetime of the sultanate. Further substantial accounts were collected only after the fall of the first sultanate in 1874. Some of the European officials of the Turco-Egyptian regime in Dār Fūr (1874–83) collected oral traditions, notably Slatin. Na'ūm Shuqayr, an official of the British administration in Cairo, collected material from a well-placed informant, the *imām* of the sultan's mosque in al-Fāshir, which he incorporated in his monumental history of the Sudan.

The Condominium officials in Dār Fūr (1916–56) collected much on the history and customs of the people of the province in which they served; the material that did not appear in *Sudan Notes and Records* can be found in the province archives in al-Fāshir. One of these officials, Dr A. J. Arkell, who spent ten years in the province, published many articles on the early history and archaeology of Dār Fūr; his papers, which he has recently deposited at the University of London, are a major source for the history of the Keira state.

PART ONE
SINNĀR

II · The transitional age in Nubia, 1300-1500

The fourteenth and fifteenth centuries were a period of change in the riverain Sudan, of adjustment to cultural and economic developments impinging from the surrounding countries, and of accommodation to two intrusive groups – the Arabs and the Nilotic-speakers, particularly the Shilluk. The unification of Nubia early in the sixteenth century may be seen as both a Nubian reaction against the invaders, and a positive response to the new economic and social circumstances that the intrusive forces had created.

The Nubian states and the Arabs

For almost seven centuries following the Muslim conquest of Egypt, an informal and occasionally uneasy truce was maintained between Cairo and the Nubian states. During these centuries small bands of Arabs ventured south into Nubia as merchants, miners, pilgrims, or nomads; though their numbers were relatively few, the early immigrants had an important impact on the border region. Well before the fourteenth century the northernmost kingdom of Maris became Muslim, fell under Egyptian hegemony, and ultimately disappeared as an independent state.

South of Maris the Nubians retained political control of the Nile valley. The kingdom of Makuria was vigorous and indeed aggressive. On 18 August 1272, the army of Makuria descended upon the Egyptian-controlled Red Sea port of 'Aydhāb. After sacking the city, executing the governor, the chief judge and the commercial supervisor, the Christians marched back across the desert and attacked Aswan. Warfare between Egypt and Nubia had rarely reached such proportions during the seven centuries, and with his attack King Dāwūd of Makuria precipitated a series of events that were to bring usurpers, puppets and Muslims to his throne. His country would be plundered, and the whole northern Sudan opened to the penetration of nomadic Arabs.

Makuria and Egypt were two parties in the dispute, and never after 1272 did the Nubians regain the initiative. When the devices of diplomacy, assassination, and the retention of Makurian royal hostages in Cairo failed to produce adequate tribute and maintain the subjection of the Nubian rulers, Makuria was repeatedly the object of Egyptian expeditions.[1] A third party was the 'Urbān, the primarily nomadic and whenever possible autonomous Arab tribes of Upper Egypt and the eastern hill country of the Sudan. The Egyptian policy of subordinating and settling the 'Urbān as peasants resulted in a long series of revolts. Escape from Egyptian rule was possible for the 'Urbān through migration, and combined with this negative incentive was the promise of rich grazing lands away in the south where the rains began. These were known through the transit of traders and pilgrims to the Red Sea ports, and also via the early arrivals in the Sudan among the nomads themselves.

Each of the various Egyptian expeditionary forces during the struggle with Makuria employed units of 'Urbān. In theory, the 'Urbān were supposed to return to Egypt after concluding the campaign, there to be settled as farmers. One article of the agreement that resulted from the expedition of 1276 provided for the extradition from Makuria of any 'Urbān who remained behind the Mamlūk army returned to Egypt.[2] In the circumstances it is not surprising that some groups of 'Urbān tried to maintain themselves in riverain Nubia, or passed beyond Makuria into the more fertile lands to the south.

By the middle of the fourteenth century, Egypt had succeeded in imposing a Muslim puppet dynasty on Makuria, now commonly called Dongola after the capital city. 'In these days', wrote Ibn Faḍl Allāh (A.D. 1331–51),

> no king is able to reign there except as a dependent of the court of the Egyptian sultans. The kings of Dongola owe a fixed tribute to the rulers of Egypt; this tribute does not consist of gold or silver, but of a certain number of slaves, male and female, of lances, and of the savage animals of Nubia.[3]

The puppet dynasty was not chosen from among the 'Urbān but from Kenzi-speaking Nubians of Upper Egypt.[4] This suggests that neither Mamlūks nor 'Urban were strong enough to impose a non-Nubian government on Dongola. Even though it was Nubian, however, this puppet dynasty was not destined to endure. A rebel Dongolāwī faction arose, enlisted its own 'Urbān supporters, seized the capital city and forced the puppet rulers north into the rocky gorge country of the third cataract. In reprisal, the Mamlūks launched what was to be their final expedition in 1365–6, but failed to recapture Dongola for their clients. Half a century later the Egyptian ruler was no longer mentioned in the Friday prayers in Dongola, and the tribute had been allowed to lapse. In correspondence with the Egyptian court, the ruler of Dongola was addressed in terms appropriate to an independent monarch.[5] The wars between Egypt and Makuria did not result in the imposition of an Arab government on Dongola; Islam, however, had come to stay.

Historians have emphasized both the Christian character of medieval Nubia and the Islamic aspects of its culture following the conversion of the rulers to Islam.[6] There is evidence, however, that both religions rested lightly over an indigenous African culture of rather a different character. In the early fifteenth century the geographer al-Bakāwī offered a revealing glimpse of the institution of kingship in the independent kingdom of Dongola, the successor to Christian Makuria.

> Dongola: (long. 43° 40′; lat. 15° 30′) A large city in the land of the Nubians. It extends along the bank of the Nile for eighty miles, although its width is very little. . . . The inhabitants are very numerous; they are Christians and they have a king named Kābīl. They pretend that the latter is descended from Himyarite kings. It is among their customs to venerate their king as a divinity, and they observe the fiction that he never eats. Thus one brings him food in secret, and if any of his subjects sees him, he is killed instantly. The king has great authority over his subjects, who attribute to him the power to make live or make die.[7]

The veneration and seclusion of the monarch, the concealment of his bodily functions, and the belief that he bestows life upon his subjects, or withholds it, are all beliefs common to the broader conceptual pattern of Sudanic kingship. The evidence of al-Bakāwī suggests that the government of Makuria and its successor state of Dongola probably resembled that of other states in the Sudanic belt of Africa. While similar evidence for southern Nubia during the medieval period is not forthcoming, it seems fair to assume that these more isolated regions experienced lesser rather than greater cultural influence from the world of Christianity and Islam. Elements of traditional African culture would have been correspondingly stronger there.

Evidence regarding the impact of Arab penetration south of Dongola is scanty. It has been customary to attribute to the Arab nomads both an immediate political impact, the decline and fall of the southern medieval kingdom Alodia, and a long-term cultural impact, the spread of the Arabic language and Islam.[8] Both of these interpretations require serious qualification; the first will be discussed below, and the second in the chapters to follow.

The decline of the kingdom of Alodia was well advanced by 1300, and therefore antedated the arrival in the Sudan of substantial numbers of nomadic Arabs. Archaeological investigations at Soba reveal that the material culture of the capital city of Alodia had fallen into decline as early as the thirteenth century;[9] towards the end of that century the geographer al-Ḥarrānī was told that the capital of the southern state had shifted from Soba to 'Waylūla'.[10] and his contemporary, the Mamlūk emmisary 'Alm al-Dīn Sanjar, found that he had to deal with nine individual rulers on his mission to Alodia.[11] The southern kingdom, it would seem, had lapsed into its constituent parts before the fall of Makuria and the major waves of Arab immigration. The small polities of the Nile valley south of Dongola were to remain fragmented for two centuries, a situation to which the incursion of the nomads undoubtedly contributed.[12] A visitor who passed through the region shortly before the rise of Sinnār reported to a Portuguese missionary in Ethiopia that the Nubians of the Nile valley had one hundred and fifty churches.

> These churches are all in old ancient castles which there are throughout the country; and as many castles as there are, so many churches do they have. . . . These lordships of the Nobiis are on both sides of the Nile, and they say that there are as many captains as there are castles; they have no King, but only Captains.[13]

Such was the political situation in the Nile valley about 1500. It remains to consider the forces that were to bring the small Nubian 'Captaincies' under a single government.

Commerce and the Nubian captaincies, 1300–1500

Commercial patterns set during the fourteenth and fifteenth centuries contributed greatly to the political unification of the northern Nubian captaincies. The most important trade route connected Upper Egypt with the Red Sea. Before the fall of Christian Makuria the principal termini for this route were the entrepot of al-Qūs on the Nile and the port of ʻAydhāb.[14] Al-Qūs was in Egypt, and the Egyptian government maintained a customs post at ʻAydhāb. The caravan route between, however, was under the control and protection of the Beja. 'It is they', wrote Ibn Saʻid (*c.* 1286)

> who conduct the pilgrims and merchants across the deserts on their camels. The security which they provide is well known in spite of the dangers on this route coming from the intrusions of the Nubians on red camels.[15]

The Nubian danger reflected the aggressive posture of Makuria in the late thirteenth century; red camels are the inferior breed of the Nile valley, while good Beja camels are white. The most prominent Beja rulers from the fourteenth through the eighteenth centuries were the Ḥaḍāriba, a section of the Bishārīn[16] who claimed ideologically fashionable Arabian ancestors.[17] Although the Ḥaḍāriba occasionally proclaimed their loyalty to Egypt when an Egyptian army or fleet was at hand, in ordinary circumstances they held the food-and-waterless island ports such as ʻAydhāb, and later Sawākīn at their mercy. In return for their protection the Beja rulers expected not only fees from individual merchants and pilgrims, but also a substantial share of the customs revenues of ʻAydhāb. In earlier times their share had ranged from one-half (*c.* 1165)[18] to most of the revenue (*c.* 1183)[19]; in Ibn Baṭṭūṭa's day (*c.* 1350) they were receiving two-thirds.[20] This apportionment of revenues between the Ḥaḍāriba and the Egyptians seems to have been a relatively constant feature of the history of ʻAydhāb.

As Makuria declined during the fourteenth century the primary trade route from the Nile to the Red Sea shifted south. This was caused largely by the desire of the Ḥaḍāriba to evade Egyptian control, and was facilitated by the removal of the hostile Christian regime in Dongola. The port of ʻAydhāb

59050

faded, the victim in part of capricious Egyptian policy, as did the old Nile entrepot of al-Qūs.[21] On the Nile the new trading centre of al-Tīn arose. It lay on the west bank, evidence that its trade was directed south via Dongola, not directly east.[22]

The focus of the new commercial pattern was the Ḥaḍāriba port of Sawākīn, which lay to the south of ‘Aydhāb along the Sudanese Red Sea coast. Ibn Faḍl Allāh's excellent mid-fourteenth-century account is worthy of quotation:

> Then there is the Shaykh of the Ḥaḍāriba Samra b. Malik, who disposes of great numbers and a redoubtable force, with which he makes incursions against the Abyssinians and the peoples of the Sudan, which brings him a rich booty. All the rulers of the interior as well as other Arabs have been commanded in writing to render him aid and assistance and to accompany him in his military expeditions whenever he desires. He has received the investiture of the countries that he has conquered, and has been granted the supreme authority over the Arabs of the interior from al-Qūs to the furthermost limits of where he has planted his standard.[23]

The account of Ibn Faḍl Allāh suggests that the Ḥaḍāriba came to exercise political as well as commercial influence over much of the northern Sudan east of the Nile before the rise of Sinnār. Some of the riverain captaincies seem to have been included, perhaps even Dongola, for they alone among the peoples of the northern Sudan practised a distinctive type of investiture.[24] The pretence of Egyptian overlordship may be ignored.

The immigrant Arabs of the area were incorporated into the Ḥaḍāriba state as warriors subject to the Beja king. Ibn Baṭṭuṭa, who was shipwrecked on the Sudanese coast in the mid-fourteenth century, observed that the Ḥaḍāriba monarch commanded a mixed force of Beja and Arabs of the Juhayna and the Awlād Kāhil. The latter, he added, were ‘intermingled with the Bujah and know their speech’.[25]

Repeated campaigns towards the southern interior, wrote Ibn Faḍl Allāh, were a profitable aspect of Ḥaḍāriba policy. There were sound commercial incentives for expansion in this direction, for in addition to the transit trade discussed above, the Sudan itself offered materials highly desired on the international market – gold, gum, ivory, frankincense, civet, perfume, rhinoceros horn, medicines, condiments and slaves. Camels and surplus grain had a regional export market in Egypt and Arabia. Of these goods, only camels came from the region north of the Nile confluence; the others had to be procured from the south. If it was therefore clearly in the interest of the rulers of Sawākīn to secure political and commercial beachheads in the southern regions, the Ḥaḍāriba port in turn offered a relatively convenient outlet to the world market for the peoples of the southern interior. While Arab writers emphasized the activities of Arab merchants in the area,[26] it is also significant that the first merchant from southern Nubia itself to enter the historical record did so in the age of Ḥaḍāriba expansion. Al-Ḥājj Farāj al-Fūnī was a Muslim Funj trader familiar with Egypt, the Ḥijāz and the Muslim states of eastern Ethiopia.[27] He exemplified the increasing involvement of southern Nubians in international commerce during the fourteenth century.

The fifteenth century brought an even higher level of prosperity to the Ḥaḍāriba state, for the wars of the Timurids disrupted overland trade routes in Central Asia and Iran, making a southern passage to Egypt via the Red Sea particularly attractive to merchants.[28] By virtue of their control over one of the main routes from the Red Sea coast to Egypt, the rulers of Sawākīn were in position to profit from this upsurge; the accounts of visitors to Sawākīn in 1470 and 1482 testify to the independence and vitality of the port.[29] It is not surprising that the rise in wealth and power of Sawākīn during the fifteenth century also had repercussions among the interior peoples associated with the Ḥaḍāriba.

The fourteenth-century accounts of Sawākīn by Ibn Faḍl Allāh and Ibn Baṭṭūṭa described the westerly and southerly expansion of the Ḥaḍāriba state, which employed soldiers from among the Juhayna and the Awlād Kāhil. They provided the context for a discussion of the career a century later of ʻAbdallāh, called Jammāʻ, the ʻGatherer', to whom Sudanese traditions credit the unification of the northern Nubian region.[30] While the traditions are often confused or contradictory, a few themes may be extracted with some confidence.

Traditions assign ʻAbdallāh Jammāʻ various pious Muslim ancestors, but agree that he inherited his political power from his links to the Juhayna, or more specifically to a ʻking in the east'.[31] One need not doubt that he was a gifted leader ʻof ancient and honourable lineage, the descendant of the chieftains of his own clan', and a family relationship with the Ḥaḍāriba king is not implausible.[32] One tradition mentions warfare near Sawākīn early in his career,[33] and a second that he entered the Sudan (more probably the Nile valley) via Sawākīn after his rise to power in the east.[34] The ʻking in the east', it was said, had appointed him governor; chiefs and captains flocked to his standard or were compelled to join him, so that he marched with ʻforty kettledrums of red copper'.[35]

Having consolidated his position on the Nile, tradition asserts that ʻAbdallāh Jammāʻ established his capital at Qarrī on the east bank a little below the confluence. He then turned his attention to the south. His immediate neighbours in that direction were the people of Soba, the ʻAnaj, who occupied the area around the confluence and the northern Gezira.[36] They were Christians; initial attempts at peaceful relations proved to be futile, and after protracted warfare the victory went to ʻAbdallāh Jammāʻ.[37] He received great booty including, according to one tradition, ʻthe bejewelled crown of the Anaj kings, and a famous necklace of pearls and rubies'.[38] More importantly, his merchants advanced one step further into the wealth-producing regions of the south. Proof of the accelerated commercial activity in the former 'Anaj kingdom late in the fifteenth century may be seen in the rise of the new town of Arbajī on the Blue Nile, probably after the victory of 'Abdallāh Jammā' over Soba.[39] That was to mark the southern limit of the penetration, however, for at Arbajī the forces of 'Abdallāh Jammā' encountered the other founders of the Sinnār sultanate, the Funj.

The coming of the Funj

The Funj were a southern Nubian people whose homeland lay along the White Nile below the great swamps; like their northern neighbours, they were heirs to the ancient cultures of the riverain Sudan. Under the pressure of attacks by the Shilluk in the south and confronted by the advance of the northerners up the Blue Nile, the early sixteenth-century Funj leader 'Amāra Dūnqas crossed the Gezira and challenged the army of 'Abdallāh Jammā'.[40]

III · The age of unity in Sinnār, 1500-1611

Funj and 'Abdallāb

The sixteenth century opened with a confrontation between the Funj and the 'Abdallāb. The outcome was the founding of the Sinnār sultanate, an event which traditional sources place in the year 910/1504–5.[1] The account of James Bruce offers the best information about the initial relations between the Funj and 'Abdallāb. Before the coming of the Funj, Bruce learned, the whole northern riverain Sudan had been ruled by the prince of Qarrī – 'the Shekh of all the Arabs', as he put it, whose title was 'Welled Ageeb', or 'Wed Ageeb' for short.[2] In order to reconcile Bruce's nomenclature with that of this study, it is merely necessary to replace the title Welled or Wed Ageeb – an anachronism[3] – with a more general term such as 'the 'Abdallāb ruler', and Bruce's 'Arabs' with the less specific "Aballāb and their followers'.

Bruce's initial discovery of a Funj victory over the 'Abdallāb came as he inquired about the origin of the 'relations of the king and great men at court'; who 'are, as they are called, Funge, that is, Shangalla converted to Islamism, of the country [unknown to Bruce] whence those Shangalla came who drove out the Arabs ['Abdallāb] under Wed Ageeb [the 'Abdallāb ruler]'.[4] Later Bruce received confirmation that this victory had taken place at the beginning of the dynasty and was related to the founding of Sinnār. 'The Mek Ismail', he learned, 'is the twentieth king of the Funge in Sennaar, since the [Funj] conquest over the Arabs ['Abdallāb]'.[5] Bruce's final account was influenced by his belief that the Funj and the Shilluk were one and the same:

> In the year 1504, a black nation, hitherto unknown, inhabiting the western banks of the Bahar el Abiad [White Nile], in about latitude 13°, made a descent, in a multitude of canoes, or boats, upon the Arab provinces [ʻAbdallāb territory], and in a battle near Herbagi [Arbajī], they defeated Wed Ageeb [the ʻAbdallāb ruler] and forced him to a capitulation, by which the Arabs [ʻAbdallāb] were to pay their conquerors. . . .[6]

Half a century after Bruce, Cailliaud took down traditions in Sinnār that tended to confirm Bruce's account of the battle at Arbajī.[7]

Following the victory of the Funj, said Bruce, the prince of Qarrī 'became, as it were, their lieutenant',[8] and Funj rule was extended to include the former kingdom of ʻAbdallāh Jammāʻ. David Reubeni, who passed through Sinnār later in the reign of ʻAmāra Dūnqas, found that the authority of the first Funj sultan was respected not only south of the Nile confluence but also in the Jaʻaliyīn country and as far north as Dongola. Royal messengers and units of cavalry led by sons of the king could be found throughout the former ʻAbdallāb kingdom, and any province might be obliged to act as host to the sultan's roving court.[9] For the time being, both the ambitions of local rulers in the north and the particularistic tendencies of their subjects were contained.[10]

Sawākīn, it would seem, was also associated with the new Funj kingdom, for the Ḥaḍāriba divided the customs revenues with the Funj.[11] The town was at the height of its prosperity early in the sixteenth century. It had become one of the major ports of the Middle East, and an enthusiastic Portuguese chronicler who saw it in 1541 said that it could only be compared to Lisbon! Gangplanks stretched from merchants' warehouses to ships at anchor, whose bowsprits projected over the waterfront streets. They discharged cargoes from India, Burma, Malaya and less remote lands as well.[12]

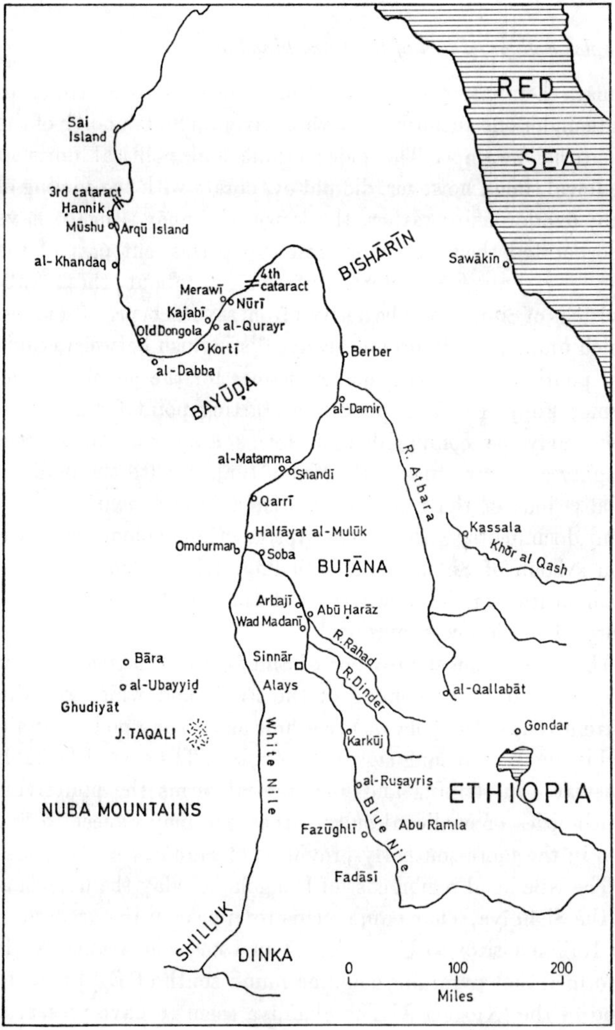

The Kingdom of Sinnār

0504467

Peoples and provinces of the Funj kingdom

'Amāra Dūnqas was the first ruler since Meroitic times to unite under one authority the whole riverain Sudan north of the equatorial swamps. The older ethnic and political units of medieval times, however, did not evaporate with the coming of Funj overlordship; rather, the kings of Sinnār seem to have incorporated them as an integral and permanent part of the new governmental system. Information about these subdivisions of Sinnār may be derived from several types of sources, which unfortunately do not always distinguish between ethnic and political units. The modern names for the peoples of the former Funj heartland provide a starting point for analysis; these may be compared with terms appearing in sources roughly contemporary to the rise of Sinnār, with the political subdivisions of the heartland as listed in eighteenth-century Funj documents, with the descriptive ethnic colour classification system of Sinnār, and with linguistic evidence. Several ambiguities remain, however, and the conclusions proposed must be considered provisional.

The northernmost province of Sinnār was Dongola, a name that antedated the coming of the Funj, and which remains current today. Dongola was an ethnic as well as a political unit, and its distinctive language is still spoken. The case of Dongola illustrates in striking and unequivocal terms the underlying continuities of medieval culture that one may expect to find also in the more southerly provinces of Sinnār.

The Nile bend region east of Dongola is today the homeland of the Shāīqīya. That name seems to appear in the account of an Italian visitor to Upper Egypt in 1529, who was correctly informed that pyramids could be found south of Egypt in the land of the 'Xiogeia'.[13] The Shāīqīya seem to have preserved their pre-Arabic language until the relatively recent past; it was either still spoken or a living memory as late as the early nineteenth century.[14]

In 1523 Reubeni passed through the 'kingdom of Al Ga'l' on his way down the Nile from the confluence to Dongola; this seems to be an early reference to the Ja'aliyīn, the modern inhabitants of the region.[15] Like the Shāīqīya, the Ja'aliyīn preserved their pre-Arabic language into the nineteenth century; Russegger found that they were generally known in the city of Sinnār as 'Berabra' or northern Nubians, a name that they shared with the people of Dongola, the Shāīqīya, and Egyptian Nubians.[16]

Before the rise of Sinnār the area around the Nile confluence was the home of the 'Anaj, or people of Alodia. After Soba fell to 'Abdallāh Jammā' the people of this region came to be known as the 'Abdallāb, a term commonly used throughout the Funj period. As late as the nineteenth century, however, Brun-Rollet heard the term 'Anaidj' applied to the people of the 'Abdallāb homeland,[17] and some of them, even in the present century, observed the custom of swearing oaths by 'Soba, the city of my ancestors'.[18]

Arbajī marked the approximate border between what Evliyā Celebī called 'Berberistan' to the north and 'Funjistan' to the south. The Funj heartland was subdivided into several political districts along the Blue Nile including Khashm al-Baḥr, Bayla and al-Qarbayn. The pre-Arabic language of the Funj heartland was noted by Celebī in the seventeenth century,[19] and again by Russegger in the nineteenth;[20] a few fragments seem to survive in the form of titles in later Funj documents.[21]

Three other provinces with sedentary populations were permanent parts of Sinnār. South of the latitude of Arbajī along the White Nile lay the province of Alays, while east of the Blue Nile were Atbara and al-Tāka, situated respectively around modern Qallabat and Kassala. Certain nomadic groups were associated with Sinnār, and various peripheral regions were also incorporated; these will be discussed below.

Another approach to the problem of the ethnic composition

of Sinnār may be found in the system of colour classification used by the Sudanese and recorded by Cailliaud.[22] The population of Sinnār, Cailliaud learned, was composed of 'six classes, so distinct that there is not one individual who does not know to which he belongs'. Five of these classes were identified by colours – blue, green, yellow, green and yellow mixed, and red. To some degree these colours were believed to indicate the hue of the skin, but Cailliaud's description reveals that other physical and cultural traits were involved. The groups differed to such an extent that Cailliaud felt justified in calling each a 'race'.[23]

Three of Cailliaud's classes may be directly associated with groups mentioned above. The first of these he called 'El-Soudan-Azraq', or the Blues. 'Their colour is copper', wrote Cailliaud; 'they are the Funj.'[24] The Greens were rather similar, wrote Cailliaud; 'they have hair like that of the Funj, and their traits compare very closely to those of Negroes'.[25] Modern 'Abdallāb are commonly considered to be Greens, and the historical identification may be confirmed by the tradition that the great 'Abdallāb leader 'Ajīb I was a Green.[26] Cailliaud called a third group 'El-Kat-Fatelolem', probably a corruption of *khātif lūnayn*, 'of two colours mixed'. 'The individuals of this class . . .', wrote Cailliaud, 'are half yellow and half green. . . . The blood-strain which predominates in them is that of the Ethiopians – an agricultural people whose colour resembles that of the Abyssinians. . . .'[27] By 'Ethiopia' Cailliaud meant Meroë, the Ethiopia of classical antiquity; modern Ethiopia he called Abyssinia. Cailliaud explored the Meroitic remains near modern Shandī, and it is probably to the contemporary inhabitants of the old Meroitic heartland, the Ja'aliyīn, that his description applied.

The other three classes did not belong to the heartland of Sinnār. The first of these were the Yellows.

> They are the least coloured, and belong to the tribes of nomadic Arabs. They have straight hair. This race crosses

> only rarely with the others. . . . It is easy to recognize, not only from the traits of their visage, but from the purity with which they still speak the Arabic language.[28]

Another marginal group were called the *'abīd* or Nuba, derogatory terms for the slaves imported into Sinnār from the south and west.[29] A final group was identified to Cailliaud as the Reds.

> These have a reddish complexion, reddish woolly hair and reddish eyes also. Perhaps this race derives its characteristic nuance from the original inhabitants of the Sudan. It is the least numerous.[30]

The Reds were the Prenilotic-speaking folk of the Blue Nile south of Sinnār and the southern mountains. It is not surprising that they appeared 'red' to their neighbours, for many of them observed the custom of smearing the hair and body with ochre.[31]

In summary, the main peoples of early Sinnār seem to have been, from north to south along the Nile, the speakers of Dongolāwī, of Old Shāīqī, of Old Ja'alī, possibly of 'Anaj, of Funj, and of Berta. In the absence of adequate information it is difficult to ascertain the degree of similarity among these languages or among the cultures of these who spoke them. Under the Funj, however, they all came to share a distinctive set of political institutions, and a common national destiny.

The conversion of the Funj

Bruce was told that the Funj were pagans at the founding of Sinnār; an 'Abdallāb tradition asserts that 'Amāra Dūnqas began his career as a Christian.[32] The two accounts are not mutually exclusive, for even if the early Funj were nominally Christian that need not imply that their culture was heavily influenced by that of any other Christian state. The conversion of the Funj rulers to Islam was an accomplished fact by 1523; Reubeni, disguised as a *sharīf*, received great honours.[33] At about the same time travellers in Ethiopia began to hear tales of the 'bad black Moors (Muslims)' of Nubia.

Several motives have been suggested for the Funj rulers' conversion. The least credible asserted that they did so out of fear of the Turks.[34] The objection to this interpretation is that the Turkish government contemporary to 'Amāra Dūnqas never sent forces anywhere near the Sudan and could hardly have threatened the Funj, while the later Turkish government that did seize the Red Sea coast and Egyptian Nubia and waged war against Sinnār did so decades after the Funj conversion.[35]

An 'Abdallāb tradition claimed that 'Abdallāh Jammā' imposed conversion upon 'Amāra Dūnqas as the price of peaceful relations: 'The Sudan is a simple land,' he said, 'and it is narrow. It will not bear two religions, the Christian creed and the creed of Muḥammad. Become a Muslim or face death!'[36] In view of Funj supremacy in the days of 'Amāra Dūnqas it would seem unlikely that the 'Abdallāb leader was in any position to make good his threats, if indeed he made them. Yet both the legends of Funj conversion for political motives contain a core of truth. The fall of the 'Anaj kingdom of Soba removed the last major non-Muslim state in the north and left the Funj isolated; in these circumstances conversion to Islam was in practical terms a precondition to effective rule over Muslim subjects.

Bruce was told that the Funj became Muslims in order to facilitate trade with neighbouring lands, particularly Egypt,[37] and circumstantial evidence lends plausibility to this interpretation. The early sixteenth century was a time of increasing commercial activity in the Sudan, as indicated by the foundation of Sinnār and Arbajī, and by the accounts of visitors to Sawākīn and Upper Egypt.[38] 'Amāra Dūnqas made Sinnār the seat of his treasury, though not the capital,[39] which suggests that the royal institution was already concerned with trade. Most of Sinnār's trading partners were Muslim; even the trade of Christian Ethiopia was in Muslim hands.[40] Probably the merchants among the Funj, such as al-Ḥājj Farāj, had been Muslim long before the founding of the sultanate. The commercial incentive combined with the strategic motive thus provided a strong impulse for the conversion of the Funj.

A process complementary to the choice of Islam as the Funj royal cult and its subsequent spread throughout Sinnār was a gradual increase in the use of Arabic as the *lingua franca* of administration and trade. The various ethnic groups of Sinnār had no language in common, but most provincial courts were in contact with the nomadic immigrants and Arabic-speaking merchants from neighbouring lands. Sudanese Muslims, of course, held Arabic in great esteem for religious reasons. Simple rural folk were conservative, however, being isolated from both Islam and from foreign trade, while the court society of Sinnār, even after the adoption of Islam, preferred to speak Funj. Only in the eighteenth century did state documents in Arabic appear, and at the fall of the kingdom some provincial lords still could not speak Arabic.[41]

Sinnār and her neighbours

The rise of Sinnār was an event of international significance which neither Egypt nor Ethiopia, her powerful neighbours, could view with equanimity. In the first place, the Sudanese interrupted communications between the two powers. From about 1480 to 1516 no official correspondence or envoys were able to reach Egypt from Ethiopia.[42] This was considered highly irregular in Egypt, but was a matter of particular concern to the Ethiopians, who needed a new bishop.[43] The successful Ethiopian mission of 1516, however, did not mark an end to the difficulties. From Portuguese accounts it would appear that the Ethiopians came directly into conflict with Sinnār. Upon arriving at the Ethiopian coast late in 1519, a Portuguese embassy could not get permission to land because the governor of the Ethiopian coastal province was away campaigning against the 'Moors'.[44] Subsequent information revealed that the governor's expedition had been directed 'towards Egypt', and that he had lost his son and four hundred horsemen in battle.[45]. Further provocation came in the spring of 1520 as the caravan season opened; a group of merchants and pilgrims observing what had hitherto been acceptable diplomatic protocol was massacred on the crossing from Sawākīn to Upper Egypt.[46] The governor of the coast then appealed to the emperor for aid, proposing an invasion of Sinnār to settle once and for all with the apostate Christian 'Nobiis'.[47] The Ethiopian attitude was expressed succinctly by the monk Antonio of Urvuar; 'On the way beyond the (Blue) Nile going to the province of Nubi they are bad people, robbers and murderers, and most of all in the province of Nuba'.[48] But Ethiopia was beset with internal problems, and the day of reckoning with Sinnār was postponed.

The rise of the Sinnār sultanate also presented difficulties to the newly-established Ottoman rulers of Egypt. From an Egyptian perspective it would have been undesirable in the best of circumstances to leave the trade route from the Red Sea to Upper Egypt in foreign hands. The massacre of 1520 showed what could happen if the new power in the south was unfriendly or uninterested in maintaining security for caravans. Moreover, the Portuguese expedition of 1540–1 demonstrated that the Europeans were willing and able to use the African ports of the Red Sea for their own purposes. Finally, the expansion of the Funj held a subversive potential for Egypt itself; there was no inherent reason why it could not have spread north of Dongola into Egyptian Nubia. These were probably the factors that led the Turks to pursue a forward policy in the south.

Following the Portuguese incursion of 1540–1, Özdemir Bey occupied the Red Sea littoral, including Sawākīn and Massawa.[49] The Turkish garrison at Sawākīn was very vulnerable, for the island city was dependent upon the mainland for fresh water and food. But both the Turks and the Sudanese had common interests in stimulating trade and excluding the Portuguese so the Ottoman conquest ended in a state of compromise: on the Nile, the border between Upper Egypt and the Funj remained fluid. If the account of Evliyā Celebī may be believed, Özdemir was also active on the Nile, and in 1528–9 occupied Sai Island, an advance that led to repeated Funj attacks.[50] According to traditions collected by Burckhardt, the ruler of Dongola tried to extend his influence north into Egyptian Nubia, whose peoples were divided and weak. Two parties developed, and the anti-Funj faction, facing defeat, appealed 'to Constantinople'.[51] The Turks chose this occasion to intervene, and in 1576 appointed an officer to bring the border area firmly under Ottoman control.[52] Thirteen years later a traveller in Upper Egypt learned that the Turks, intending to capture Dongola from the Funj, had marched south with many boats.[53] The Funj army met them at Ḥannik, near Arqū island, and a battle ensued. 'Abdallāb tradition maintained that though the Turks had many guns, it was insufficient to gain them the victory.[54] Natural disasters took their toll – or provided an excuse – and in any case only one boat returned to Egypt.[55] Although the Turks failed to conquer Dongola, they planted garrisons at Aswān, Ibrīm and Sai, thus consolidating their hold on Egyptian Nubia and effectively blocking the northward expansion of the Funj. The tomb of a holy man was later constructed on the site of the battlefield; it remained the border between Egypt and Sinnār until 1821.[56]

'Ajīb the Great

Of the sultans who followed 'Amāra Dūnqas during the sixteenth century little is known except their names, dynastic relationships, and regnal dates that are more suggestive than exact. This information is derived from several king-lists of

Sinnār, of which the earliest and probably the most accurate was written down in the capital city for James Bruce by the *sīd al-qūm* Aḥmad.[57] 'Amāra Dūnqas, according to this source, reigned for thirty years following the foundation of Sinnār and died in 940/1533-4.[58] He was succeeded by his son Nāyil, who ruled for seventeen years until 957/1550–1.[59] A second son of 'Amāra Dūnqas, 'Abd al-Qādir I, succeeded to the throne in that year and reigned for eight years until 965/1557–8. Then 'Amāra II b. Nāyil, called Abū Sakīkīn, reigned for eleven years until 976/1568–60. Dakīn, a second son of Nāyil, reigned from 976/1568–9 to 994/1585–6, and was succeeded by his son Dawra, who was deposed in 996/1587–1588.[61] Then Ṭayyib (or Ṭabl) b. 'Abd al-Qādir I reigned until his death in 1000/1591. Ṭayyib was succeeded by his son Ūnsā I, who reigned until his deposition in 1012/1603-4. Ūnsā was replaced by his son 'Abd al-Qādir II, who was in turn deposed in Rajab 1015/December 1606. The next rulers were 'Adlān I b. Ūnsā, who was deposed in 1020/1611–12, and Bādī I b. 'Abd al-Qādir II, 'Adlān's *sīd al-qūm*, who ruled until 1025/1616–17.

With the reigns of Dakīn and his successors, greater information is available concerning the political affairs of the rulers. For towards the end of the sixteenth century, Sinnār experienced an upheaval that resulted in a major reorganization of the kingdom. Instrumental in effecting this change was a prince of Qarrī named 'Ajīb, who thus became one of the most prominent figures in the historical traditions of Sinnār.

The span of 'Ajīb's career may be dated with a fair degree of accuracy; he may have come to power as early as the reign of 'Amāra Abū Sakīkīn,[62] and was definitely a contemporary of 'Amāra's successor Dakīn.[63] He died at the battle of Karkūj in 1020/1611–12.[64] Since the Funj seem to have administered northern Nubia directly before the reign of 'Ajīb, he probably began his career as a minor provincial king. As in the case of 'Abdallāh Jammā', only a few themes may be extracted with a reasonable degree of certainty from the traditions concerning the life of 'Ajīb. One tradition recalled a war early in his reign either near Mushū, the Funj frontier post in northern Dongola, or yet farther north in Maḥas.[65] These traditions suggest that 'Ajīb was a participant in the attempted expansion of Sinnār into Egyptian territory, and that his first major test was the Turkish invasion of 1576. This interpretation is confirmed by a second tradition which seems to credit 'Ajīb with the Turkish defeat.[66] The victorious northern campaign would have given 'Ajīb an excellent opportunity to build up his military forces and increase his influence throughout the northern Funj kingdom. The contemporary sultan Dakīn, meanwhile, had been defeated at Abū Ramla in a border campaign,[67] and when he returned, or 'came from the east', he conceded to 'Ajīb the right to appoint judges at Arbajī, Abū Ḥarāz, Nūrī and in the Jamū'īya country.[68] This would approximately delineate 'Ajīb's sphere of influence at that stage of his career.

'Ajīb was not content with greater political autonomy, however, and would seem to have had no less an objective than the conquest of the whole Funj kingdom. A long period of Funj-'Abdallāb hostility followed. 'The cause of the war,' concluded one very realistic appraisal, 'was simply land and (the question of) roya lauthority.'[69] As 'Ajīb's power increased, he forced sultan Ṭabl to marry his daughter, an act, which, according to Funj dynastic marriage practice, had the effect of making Ṭabl his vassal. Probably Ūnsā I, the offspring of this union, was also 'Ajīb's puppet.[70] The conflict between the Funj and 'Abdallāb reached crisis proportions during the reign of 'Abd al-Qādir II. 'Ajīb's armies swept south towards Ethiopia, driving the king before them. 'Abd al-Qādir was declared deposed in December 1606; the next April he sent a gift of horses as a symbol of submission to the Ethiopian emperor, and before Christmas 1607 he paid homage in person to Susenyos and sought refuge at his court. With him was one 'Alī wad 'Ajīb, probably a son of the 'Abdallāb ruler and 'Abd al-Qādir's nominee for the throne of Qarrī once 'Ajīb's ambitions were contained.[71] 'Ajīb, for his part, founded mosques near Ruṣayriṣ and at Fādāsī on the Ethiopian border.[72]

'Ajīb's conquests extended from Ethiopia to Dongola, but he was not yet the uncontested master of the whole Funj kingdom. Partisans of the Funj invested a new sultan, 'Adlān I, who continued to resist the 'Abdallāb. Advancing age hindered 'Ajīb, and he was defeated in two decisive battles, first near Sinnār, and again at Karkūj, where he was killed. The sons of 'Ajīb fled to Dongola, pursued by the forces of 'Adlān. But while he was in the north, 'Adlān in turn was deposed, and his *sīd al-qūm*, son of the defeated 'Abd al-Qādir, was invested in his place as Bādī I.

Further fighting was averted by diplomacy, and the settlement between the Funj and the successors to 'Ajīb was destined to shape the next two centuries of the history of Sinnār. The intermediary who brought about the reconciliation between the sons of 'Ajīb and Sultan Bādī was the *faqīh* Idrīs wad al-Arbāb. He was well qualified for the role of mediator, being both a holy man and the son of a nobleman.[73] The terms of the treaty he arranged have been preserved in 'Abdallāb tradition as follows:[74]

> *Article I.* Sheikh Mohd. el Agail (Shaykh Muḥammad al-'Ajayl b. 'Ajīb, successor to the throne of Qarrī) to possess 'the land which his father ruled' with all its boundaries.

This was not strictly true; the territories allotted to al-'Ajayl more nearly reflected the Funj-'Abdallāb *status quo* as of the reign of Dakīn. Arbajī, moreover, was transferred to Funj jurisdiction.[75]

> *Article II.* The Mek of the Fung to possess the Gezira and the country south of it, and all Arabs belonging to the sheikhship of Gerri living in the Gezira to pay taxes

> through the sheikh of the *dar* [tribal homeland], who is under the 'Abdallab.

The Nile confluence was for practical purposes the southern limit to 'Abdallāb jurisdiction, with the proviso that nomadic groups ('Arabs' or Yellows as opposed to Greens, Blues, Ja-'aliyīn, and Reds) who spent the wet season in 'Abdallāb territory would be considered tributary to the 'Abdallāb kings.

> *Article III*. If the daughter of the Fung Mek cultivates the land east of the (Blue) Nile she must pay dues to the people of the Sheikh of the 'Abdallab.

The Buṭāna, or land between the Blue Nile and the Atbara, was primarily a nomadic region, and most of its inhabitants would have been tributary to the 'Abdallāb under Article II. Article III implies that some rainland cultivators of the Buṭāna were politically subject to the Funj sultan, but that their tax revenues should go to the 'Abdallāb. The peculiar phraseology will be considered below. Articles IV and V are straightforward:

> *Article IV*. If the Sheikh of the 'Abdallāb goes to Sennar no drum shall be beaten there during his stay except his nahas.

> *Article V*. If any enemy invades 'Abdallab country, the Sheikh of the 'Abdallab is to fight him, and the Mek of the Fung is to help him. . . .[76]

While the settlement was undoubtedly disappointing to the more fervent supporters of 'Ajīb's ambitions, it would seem to have satisfied many, for there followed a long period of peace and stability in Sinnār.

In summary, the era of direct Funj rule throughout the kingdom was over. The provinces of 'Berberistan' north of the

Nile confluence were thereafter subordinate in the first instance to the prince of Qarrī, and only indirectly to the sultan. The new northern rulers called themselves ‘Abdallāb, looking back to the pre-Funj kingdom of ‘Abdallāh Jammā.[77] But significant changes had taken place in northern Nubia during the century between ‘Abdallāh Jammā‘ and ‘Ajīb; the old system had been decapitated when the Ottomans seized Sawākīn, and the Nubian town of Qarrī on the Nile had replaced the port on the Red Sea as the centre of political power. ‘Abdallāh Jammā‘ had been an Arab, a ‘Yellow’, subordinate to the Ḥaḍāriba ‘king in the east’. ‘Ajīb was a Green; ‘the kingdom of the son of ‘Ajīb’, as the new polity was often termed,[78] was in essence a reassertion of the kingdom of Alodia under a Muslim name.

IV · State and society in Sinnār

The ruling institution

One evening in 1699 the king went from the palace to a country estate for dinner, and a European visitor described the occasion as follows:

> Between three and four hundred horsemen, mounted upon fine horses, make the first appearance. After these comes the king, attended by a great number of footmen and armed soldiers, who with a loud voice sing forth his praises and play upon the *tabor*, which makes no unpleasant harmony. Seven or eight hundred young maids and women march together with these soldiers, and carry upon their heads great round baskets of straw, of different colours and finely made. These baskets, which represent all sorts of flowers and the covers whereof are pyramid-wise, are filled with copper dishes tinned over and full of fruit and several meats ready dressed. These dishes are served before the king, and afterwards are distributed amongst those who have the honour to attend upon him. Two or three hundred horsemen follow in the same order as those that went foremost, and close the whole march.[1]

The public appearance of the Funj sultan was accompanied by much pomp and ceremony, for the mere display of the ruler before the people was itself a notable event. Funj kings spent most of their reigns secluded within the palace walls, and though the degree of isolation might vary with the ruler's personality, he was at all times set apart from casual contact with lesser men. Tradition asserts that the sultan was 'veiled to his subjects',[2] a usage confirmed by Poncet: 'the king never appears in public but with his face covered with a silk gauze of several colours'.[3] Indeed the last sultan continued to wear the veil even after the fall of Sinnār.[4] Those who were granted the privilege of a royal audience were led through the labyrinth of the palace complex to the throne room. There they would find the king seated upon a raised earthen dais, surrounded by court officials, attendants and armed guards. Stones placed in the floor delineated a precinct around the royal presence; beyond these the petitioner must not step.[5] Upon entering the throne room the subject was obliged to lower to his waist any garment he might have around his shoulders. He announced his name and title, after which the king repeated his name only, and the subject replied the equivalent of 'My Lord'.[6] He might then receive permission to kiss the royal hand and be seated on the ground below the throne.[7] Court sessions of the sultan were invariably interrupted at mealtime, for it was considered unseemly for the king to be seen eating. In Dongola, the strict rules of the medieval kingdom as described by al-Bakāwī had been relaxed somewhat by 1699; Poncet was given a dinner by the king who, however, sat 'at a table apart'.[8] The last reigning heir to the throne of Dongola refused to be seen eating.[9]

In the evening at sunset the royal drums were sounded; these could be heard throughout the capital and into the countryside across the river.[10] They marked the time for the daily ceremony of obeisance to the king, a rite that was probably limited to royal intimates in the capital, but which was open to the whole populace at the provincial courts. At Qarrī, for example, the citizenry was assembled each evening by royal agents bearing a staff symbolic of the king's authority. Gathered before their lord, each man performed obeisance in the manner described above, and praised the ruler as 'the most mighty, the most just, the richest, and (with) a hundred titles of honour of a similar sort'.[11] The people of Sinnār, wrote one observer, would 'extol in the most hyperbolized terms the merits of their great men'.[12] It was also an occasion for boasting on the part of the king, involving such formulas as 'I am a bull, the son of a bull, and will die or conquer!'[13] In short, the kings of Sinnār were treated by their subjects with the respect due to one who wielded the power to 'make live or make die'. Even the amulets prepared in the capital city were believed to derive special merit from the proximity of the sultan.[14]

Although the Funj sultan was very influential, his power was far from absolute. Decisions of state were taken in council, when the king was surrounded by his court – the 'twenty old men' observed by Poncet.[15] Every person at court knew his allotted place, for the kings undoubtedly continued the practice attributed by the *Funj Chronicle* to Dakīn: 'to such as were wont to be seated in his presence he gave a definite order of precedence when they were so seated in the council chamber'.[16] Deliberations of the council were orderly and followed a set procedure. One visitor to a Funj provincial court commented that 'greater harmony could not exist in any assembly: the highest in rank expresses his sentiment on the subject first, and the others almost invariably coincide with him'.[17] The authority to speak before the king was symbolized by a small staff, called *ḥaddātha* in Arabic and *gambagagui* in Dongola; this the king handed in turn to those present, in descending order of rank.[18] Similarly, when the Funj government began to use written documents during the eighteenth century, the court officials affixed their signatures in descending order of precedence. These lists of titles make it possible to give some description of the court hierarchy, though many ambiguities exist, and the following discussion must be considered provisional.

Visitors to Sinnār in about 1700 were impressed with the importance of a minister whom they called the Vezir at the sultan's court and the 'Secretarius, who governed everything' at the contemporary court of Qarrī.[19] This chief minister may perhaps be identified with the first signatory to the Funj documents, who commonly used the title *amīn* or *amīn al-sulṭān*. The title *amīn* may well have also carried military connotations, for on several occasions this official personally led the army in battle. The second-ranking signatory was entitled the *jundī*; the titles of *amīn* and *jundī* were both hereditary within a family of the freeborn nobility.[20] The *jundī* presided as master of ceremonies at the coronation ritual.[21] His more mundane activities included supervision of the market – hence his variant title *jundī al-sūq* or 'market *jundī*' – and command of the state security forces. These latter were divided into two sections: one was delegated to the charge of a slave official who led the military units dispatched to hunt down runaway slaves and ferret out thieves, while the *jundī* himself was the head of a second organization that combined the functions of a police force with those of a political and military intelligence unit.[22]

Another court official, according to Brocchi, was the *manamalecna* or *sīd al-kalām*: he was the court 'interpreter' and regulated the market.[23] Perhaps the term *manamalecna*, although it could be literally translated as *sīd al-kalām* ('Master of Speech' or something similar), was the original Funj term for the *jundī* – who was responsible for the peace of the market, and whose role in the coronation ritual resembled that of the 'linguist' at other Sudanic courts. This evidence is rather circumstantial, and the *manamalecna* may simply have been a Funj–Arabic interpreter.

The accounts of Bruce and Brocchi emphasized the importance of a high court official called the *sīd al-qūm*. Like the *amīn* and the *jundī*, the *sīd al-qūm* was a freeman of the high nobility, and indeed was chosen from among the closest relatives of the sultan. He served as royal bodyguard in peace and war, and in theory was expected to remain in the sultan's presence at all times. He was the only person in the kingdom authorized to shed royal blood, and he performed the executions of state.[24] In the first instance it would seem strange that the signature of this important official does not appear on any of the sultanic documents of Sinnār.[25] It is known, however, that because of his role as executioner, the *sīd al-qūm* was barred from all court deliberations that concerned the fate of the king; perhaps it was considered improper for him to sign even a land-charter.[26] Further hints are provided by the rather strange signature that usually followed those of the *amīn* and the *jundī* on sultanic documents; this was the 'deputy from the court of the maternal uncle of the king'.[27] Since Funj dynastic succession was matrilineal, it would follow that the maternal uncle of the king would be a very important person. He would be the sultan's superior within the royal family, though not necessarily in the sphere of national politics. Tentatively, one may propose that the maternal uncle of the king was the *sīd al-qūm*. Being the one man in the kingdom technically superior in rank to the king, his role as the lawful executioner of monarchs would become plausible; though usually barred from attending court in person, he was represented there by a deputy. Finally, though their role in government is veiled, both the mother and the sister of the sultan seem to have been politically important.

'Slavery in Sennaar', wrote James Bruce, 'is the only true nobility.'[28] While that statement was an exaggeration, it accurately underscored the importance of slave officials at the Funj court. One was the treasurer or *karalrau*; a second was the keeper of the royal seal.[29] Many of the slave officials were entitled *muqaddam*, and their roles in government may conveniently be considered in various contexts below. In the list of charter signatories the *amīn*, the *jundī* and the deputy of the *sīd al-qūm* were followed by the subordinate provincial princes, the *muqaddams*, military officers and holy men. Before examining the structure of government in the provinces and the army, however, it would be profitable to observe the whole court in the exercise of one of its most important functions – the choice of a new king.

Upon the death of a Funj sultan, the court assembled to elect a successor. Often the council simply ratified the right to accession of the heir-apparent; this was the first son of the late sultan born 'in the purple', whose mother had then been honourably rusticated so that she would not bear rivals to the first-born. If the heir-apparent had died or fallen into disfavour, the court enjoyed considerable latitude in selecting the next king from among the other sons – usually very numerous – of the late sultan. In either case, once the choice was made all the other sons were executed by the *sīd al-qūm* in order to remove potential rivals to the new ruler.[30]

The election of a sultan was followed by his formal investiture. The *jundī* conducted the preparatory rituals, which culminated in the candidate's coronation with the two-horned cap distinctive of Funj royalty. A typical crown was

> made out of red velvet with yellow tufts and trimmings, and covered with colourful pieces of material. It has a round shape similar to that of a low hat. Two long ends of the otherwise-narrow border are bent out like a brim and stand up like horns on either side of the head.[31]

Following the coronation the candidate was seated upon a carved wooden stool called the *kukur*, and all present performed obeisance. The next stage of the ceremony was the marriage of the new sultan to a woman of the royal clan, the Ūnsāb. In the words of the *Funj Chronicle*, 'so, at the time when they appointed a new sultan, they would cause him to marry from among the descendants of that woman (the ancestral mother of the Ūnsāb). . . .'[32] Only through a woman of the royal clan could the sultan produce a noble and legitimate heir; in this respect the status of nobility descended from mother to son.[33] The royal couple were secluded for about forty days in a house especially prepared, in the hope of conceiving an heir early in the reign. Upon emerging the new king underwent a rite of purification; as the *Funj Chronicle* described the practice, 'then they would go out with him to a place known to them, in which there was water coming out to them from the ground; they partook of it as it was coming out, and forboded ill if it was lacking'.[34] It was probably also at this time that the new king was obligated to plough a field with his own hand, from which the common royal name or title Bādī, meaning 'farmer', was derived.[35] The exact purpose of this ritual has been lost, but it may have been intended to assure a fruitful reign.[36]

Court control over the new sultan did not end with his investiture. Every year there was a month-long festival of anarchy, during which the government was considered not to exist.[37] It was probably at this time that the court exercised its prerogative of judging the king, and of replacing him with another if found undesirable. Deposed kings were executed by the *sīd al-qūm*.[38] In the similar festivals that took place at the provincial courts, the populace also participated in the judgement of their local ruler.[39]

The Funj kingdom was divided into a number of provinces, over each of which there ruled a *mānjil* or king. Some of the provinces, notably the 'Abdallāb kingdom, were subdivided into subordinate kingdoms of tertiary rank, whose rulers were commonly titled *makk*, meaning 'lesser vassal' rather than literally 'king'.[40] Kings at all levels imitated the court and dynastic practices of the sultan; the set of relationships that bound *makk* to *mānjil* was analogous to those that linked the provincial lords to Sinnār, and one description may serve for both. The historical source materials for Sinnār emphasize wars and revolts – in which the provincial lords figure prominently – over times of peace and order.[41] This bias has led some to conclude that Sinnār was merely a chaotic collection of tribes, an impression that vanishes, however, once the bonds between lord and overlord in the Funj kingdom are understood.[42]

Vassal kings such as the 'Abdallāb *mānjil* were careful to

describe the location of their own domains as 'in the Funj territories';[43] they were not likely to forget, for a member of the royal clan sat beside them, exercising the power of the *sīd al-qūm*, and couriers of the sultan and units of cavalry rode imperiously throughout the kingdom, demanding hospitality and great deference. 'In these lands whole villages and towns quiver before such royal messengers, for they are obliged to provide horses and camels for him and his servants, along with whatever they need or demand.[44] Every year the provincial kings had to appear before the sultan to perform obeisance, account for their behaviour, and deliver the tribute charged to their provinces.[45] When at court the provincial lords were assigned a certain order of precedence. The 'Abdallāb *mānjil* ranked first, followed by the king of Alays, the rulers of the Blue Nile provinces, and of outlying regions. If a vassal failed to pay tribute, an army was dispatched to collect it.[46]

The most important ties binding lord to overlord in Sinnār were dynastic, a fact that may at first seem difficult to reconcile with Bruce's observation that the founders of Sinnār had a practice of making 'the prince of the state they have conquered their lieutenant in the government of his own country afterwards'.[47] The apparent contradiction is resolved if one examines the process by which lesser kings became legitimate vassals of Sinnār. Brought to the capital, they underwent a ceremony of investiture identical to that of the sultan himself, except that the vassal's own *jundī* presided, and the overlord placed the crown upon his head.[48] A vassal was then required to take a wife from the royal clan, for only through her could he produce legitimate heirs.[49] The vassals' royal wives, observed Bruce, were 'spies upon their husbands, and keep up the consequence of their birth in their husband's house, even after they are married. . . .'[50] Funj marriage practice made every vassal the son-in-law of his superior, and certain taboos governed that relationship.[51]

In the riverain Sudan it was the custom that a wife, upon

becoming pregnant, return to her mother's family until the child was born and weaned. In the case of Funj princesses married to vassal rulers, that meant that the heirs of the vassals were born and raised in Sinnār under the watchful eye of the central government. Together with the sultan's own sons, they formed a distinct community at the court of Sinnār; 'locked up tighter than the cloistered nuns of Christendom', they served as hostages for the good behaviour of their fathers.[52] In his account of Christian Makuria, Ibn al-Furāt mentioned the captive princes at court, called *sawākira* in the language of Makuria.[53] A slave official at the Funj court called the *muqaddam al-sawākira* may thus be identified as the caretaker of the princes, and one may infer that the marriage policy of Sinnār did not differ greatly from a similar practice in Christian Nubia. On the death of a vassal the overlord would select his successor from among his heirs. Since it was desirable for the sultan to preserve in confinement potential rivals to each subordinate ruler, it would seem that systematic executions did not take place. The princes bore the title *arbāb*, and usually lived out an idle and powerless existence at court, supported by the largesse of the ruler.[54]

Government in the provinces

The provincial lords of Sinnār lived in smaller, fortified versions of the palace complex of the sultan. In Dongola and the Shāīqīya country these castles were often built of unshaped stones, and sometimes older structures were incorporated. The most characteristic type of Funj castle north of Sinnār, however, was built of earth; rectangular in outline, it had one or more three- or four-storey towers with gently inward-sloping walls. In the rainy region south of the capital, both kings and commoners lived in thorn-hedged compounds of thatched huts (*tukuls*), but the rank and wealth of the nobles was easily visible in the large size of their compounds.[55]

In addition to the king and his family the castle was

inhabited by the slave retainers who formed his army and civil service. The royal community usually numbered several hundred. The people of the castle formed a distinct, caste-like group; they monopolized the right to govern and to fight, and avoided family ties with the people of the kingdom. Royal marriages were contracted with the overlord's family, or the ruling houses of other provinces – royal concubines were slaves, not local free women. Freemen of the kingdom were forbidden to marry even servile members of the royal household;[56] they in turn disdained such relationships.[57] Casual intercourse between female slaves of the royal household and freemen, however, was tolerated and even encouraged;[58] offspring of such unions joined the royal household as slaves.[59] All illegitimate children of free women were considered slaves, and property of the king.[60] 'The result of the system', concluded Hoskins, 'was, that the Melek (king) had always a large force of slaves and dependents, besides those of the Meleks his kinsmen, who were also implicitly devoted to his will, and deeply interested in maintaining the peace and security of the kingdom.'[61]

The king delegated the administration of parts of his kingdom to his free-born sons, and sometimes daughters.[62] 'Each of the sons of these petty kings', wrote Hoskins, 'had estates assigned to him; but they all acknowledged the head of the family, that is, the reigning Melek, contributed to his support and defence, submitted to his laws and commands, and served him in war.'[63] The lord placed each village of his territory under the supervision of a trusted and experienced slave, entitled *mankarūkan*, authorized to punish minor infractions by beating.[64]

The kings of Sinnār received a wide variety of taxes and services from their subjects. The basic tax for sedentary folk was a levy on crops traditionally known as *jabāya*,[65] but sometimes interpreted as the Islamic *'ushr*.[66] In those parts of the kingdom that were irrigated by waterwheel, each wheel was assessed a fixed amount, and the men who owned and farmed the land behind the wheel then distributed the burden among themselves according to various traditional arrangements.[67] Crops grown on rainland were also taxed. Tax records were kept at the castle: 'when we entered', noted Hoskins, 'the *melek's* cash-keepers were counting the money they were receiving from the peasants, and settling their accounts with the assistance of their strings of beads'.[68] The crops collected as taxes were stored in or near the castle, often in great subterranean bins called *matmuras*. Grain from the royal *matmuras* supplied the palace community, and might also be placed on the open market in times of seasonal scarcity.[69]

In addition to the tax on crops, the peasants were also obliged to supply unpaid labour to the king for such projects as building a castle or a reservoir.[70] They had to supply oxen and labour to till the private estates of the lord. Several obligations were related to the provisioning of royal agents and soldiers or the lord himself when travelling. These included right of way or of access, hospitality, and food and lodging for the visitors and their mounts. The cotton-weavers had to contribute a percentage of their production in taxes,[71] and similar regulations probably applied to other craftsmen. If the lord became involved in a blood-feud the peasants had to contribute to an absolving weregild. Finally, the lord could expect to receive substantial presents from his subjects on special occasions. This list of customary obligations is representative, but may not be complete.

The Funj king was responsible for the administration of justice among his subordinates; 'every day', wrote David Reubeni, 'they hold courts of justice'.[72] Symbolic of this royal duty was the throne before the palace gate where, on occasion, the king's justice was available to the people.[73] Krump observed legal proceedings on several occasions at the court of Qarrī:

> In the morning and afternoon the Shaykh held public court, in which both the plaintiff and the defendant chose advocates

> from among those present. The plaintiff's attorney would state what was held against the defendant, and then the defendant's representative would refute the charges and justify him. As soon as the two parties had presented their cases, all present joined in, pro and con, after which the Shaykh pronounced sentence, which is without appeal.

Beating was the most common form of punishment; it was administered by all present at the command of the king, until he gave the order to desist.[74]

The nomadic peoples of Sinnār lived in a world apart, maintaining only a minimum of contact with sedentary society. Periodically dependent upon the cultivators for food, the nomads accepted the suzerainty of Sinnār, which was ordinarily exercised through the 'Abdallāb *mānjil.*[75]

The army of Sinnār

At no time was the social distance between lord and subject in Sinnār more clearly expressed than when a simple peasant family was confronted by an armed nobleman demanding hospitality for himself and his men. Russegger described typical Funj warriors:

> these black chieftains appeared clad in chain mail tunics with spiked iron helmets on their heads, while their horses were enveloped in quilted blankets to protect them from lance-thrusts, and were equipped with large copper head-guards.[76]

It is possible to recapture some of the chivalric flair and bravado that characterized the nobility from traditional stories of their exploits. Tales abound of heroic cavalry charges, incidents of personal valour, sudden reverses of fortune, and much boasting, omens-taking and exchange of insults. They reveal that combat among armoured knights was not too deadly a business; one hero, determined to die in battle, first had to remove his helmet and mail.[77] Unarmed folk of town and countryside undoubtedly found the soldiers deadly enough, for their part, as did even the far-from-defenceless nomads. Some of the armour worn by the knights of Sinnār was imported, but Sudanese craftsmen were also skilled in manufacturing mail.[78] The Funj nobility was a true aristocracy of the sword; blades were blessed by holy men, cherished by their owners for their magical powers, and passed on as treasured family heirlooms. No other weapon enjoyed such emotional allegiance.[79] The long Funj broadsword was an appropriate weapon for the customary style of fighting, which usually involved a crushing, overpowering cavalry charge. The sword was also compatible with the toe-ring stirrup used in Sinnār; the leather loops around the horseman's big toes gave him a reasonably firm seat in hand-to-hand combat, but did not permit him to transfer the energy of his charging mount as did the foot-stirrup and seated lance of the European knight.

The horse used by the cavalry of Sinnār was bred with care. For battle it was fitted in armour of quilted cotton, with metal head and breast plates and sometimes trappings of beaten silver and many little bells. The saddle rose high at the pommel and behind the rider to make it difficult to unseat him. Horses were trained to kneel so that a man in armour could mount without difficulty.

The burden of fighting in Sinnār did not rest exclusively upon the hereditary nobility; each lord, according to his means, maintained a professional army of slaves. At the smaller courts this force might number less than one hundred, not all the soldiers being equipped with horses and armour. The major provincial kings and some of the court officials, however, kept fully-equipped armies numbering several hundred. The smaller forces were bivouacked in the lord's castle, while the larger armies were kept in garrison settlements in the countryside. The typical soldier wore a tunic of leather or quilted cotton, and over it a suit of chain mail. His helmet was of iron or copper, and he carried a shield, preferably of elephant, buffalo or giraffe hide. Heavy leather gloves protected his hands. His arms typically consisted of the long, two-handed sword, several armour-piercing javelins of iron, a hooked throwing knife, and a long thrusting lance with a leaf-shaped blade. Firearms were not unknown, but rare, and unreliable in battle. Each unit of cavalry was commanded by a slave officer of court rank entitled *muqaddam al-khayl*.

At the pinnacle of the local and provincial forces was the sultan and his court officials. Their own armies were usually the strongest in the kingdom, and it was they, in times of national need, who summoned the whole fighting force of Sinnār. Each of the great provincial lords would send units of cavalry, either commanding them in person, or entrusting them to a relative or the *muqaddam al-khayl*. Sometimes the sultan himself led armies in the field; more commonly, however, he would appoint a commanding general. On various occasions the sultan's *amīn*, *muqaddam al-khayl*, *sīd al-qūm*, and the 'Abdallāb *mānjil* served as the field commander, or *amīn al-jaysh*.[80] The nomadic groups tributary to Sinnār also sent men to join the sultan's army. The fighting men of each tribe would assemble and choose a leader – usually not the tribal shaykh – called the *qā'id* or *'aqīd*.[81] When the nomadic warriors joined the national army, they were placed under the command of the sultan's general of nomad auxiliaries, the *muqaddam al-qawāwīd*.[82]

The sultan and the economy

The sultan of Sinnār exercised theoretically unlimited rights over the natural resources of his kingdom and the material possessions of his subjects. He alone could make grants of land anywhere in the kingdom, and his permission was required to visit or settle within Sinnār.[83] The sultan reserved the right to confiscate arbitrarily the property of any subject.[84] Though our knowledge about them is at present vague, he had at his disposal a corps of tax-collectors, among them the *muqaddam al-qawwāriya.*[85] The economic relationship between ruler and subject extended to the most intimate matters; for example, government officials regulated the amount of wealth to be given over at marriage.[86] In practice, of course, the broad powers of the sultan were tempered by custom and circumscribed by the strong political pressure that the court officials, the provincial vassals and the army could bring to bear.

A comparatively well-documented aspect of the economic life of Sinnār is the structure of the trading system. The sultan played a central role in the organization of long-distance royal commerce in luxury or strategic items of low bulk and high value. This royal trade conformed quite closely to the pattern described by Karl Polanyi as 'administered' commerce, an 'archaic' or pre-bourgeois system in which the procurement of exotic articles from abroad by the king provided the primary incentive, rather than the abstract profit motive *per se.*[87]

At the heart of the commercial system of Sinnār and the fiscal powers of the sultan was the gold trade. All gold mined within the kingdom belonged to the central government; the larger nuggets automatically became the property of the sultan, while those of lesser size fell to the high court officials. Gold dust also passed first into the hands of the court, but was then released onto the open market.[88] By tightening or loosening the flow of gold dust out of the royal treasury according to the fluctuating demands of the market, the sultan could effectively control the value of the gold ounce, the 'currency' of Sinnār.[89] The value of the gold ounce was high relative to the market price of most articles of trade in Sinnār, and the actual circulation of gold must have been restricted to comparatively large exchanges. For the economy at large the most important function of the gold ounce was probably that of a 'fictitious currency' or standard of evaluation for the commonplace goods that actually changed hands. While the use of the gold ounce has been only imperfectly documented, slaves, camels, and even units of salt, cloth or grain were employed as 'fictitious currencies' in the manner described during the later years of the kingdom when the powers of the sultan over the gold trade had collapsed. It seems reasonable to infer that the gold ounce served a similar purpose prior to 1700, when it was the generally acknowledged 'currency'. Notable was the total absence in Sinnār of a circulating coin currency minted – or officially recognized – by the central government.

A second major source of wealth available to the sultan were slaves. Each year a government slave-hunt was organized by a special court official, the *muqaddam al-salaṭīya.*[90] Of the slaves captured, one-half belonged to the king.[91] Though many of these slaves were undoubtedly incorporated into the army, the bureaucracy or the *ḥarīm*, others were sold abroad. Along with gold, the surplus slaves formed the bulk of the exportable wealth of Sinnār that lay in the hands of the king.[92]

Finally, during the heyday of Sinnār the sultan had the exclusive right to sponsor caravans to the outside world, particularly Egypt. The royal merchant caravans were led by emissaries bearing kettledrums symbolic of kingship, and in later years a written *laissez-passer* from the sultan.[93] Funj consular agents, often relatives of the king, were stationed in Egypt (and perhaps elsewhere) to entice persons with valuable skills or merchandise to Sinnār.[94] These latter would join the caravan of royal merchants on its return to the Sudan. When the caravan reached the capital, the sultan's goods were placed on the market first while the demand was greatest and the prices highest; later the private traders from abroad might offer their wares.[95] While in the capital each foreign trader was assigned to one of the court officials, who gave him lodging, policed his activities, represented him at court, and probably secured for him the services of a broker skilled in arranging exchanges in the commodities he had imported. Noteworthy was the restriction of the caravan trade to agents of the court and their foreign allies; a caravan of private Sudanese gold or slave merchants was unthinkable.

V · Funj and 'Abdallāb, 1611-1718

Chronology of the kings

Sultan Bādī I died in 1025/1616–17. The internal peace that followed the failure of the revolt of 'Ajīb the Great endured for many years, and Sinnār entered a period of expansion, prosperity, and increasing contact with the outside world. The long reigns of the sultans Rubāṭ I (1025–54/1616–17 to 1644–5), Bādī II, called 'Abū Diqn' (1054–92/1644–5 to 1681) and Ūnsā II b. Nāṣir b. Rubāṭ (1092–1103/1681 to 1692) were dotted with memorable events; the defeat of a major invasion from Ethiopia, the conquest of Kordofan, the great famine of 1684, and the rise to prominence of Muslim Sudanese holy men. Other important themes in the history of the era were less conspicuous; the increasing pressure of Nilotic-speaking immigrants along the southern frontier, renewed tension between ambitious provincial princes and the central government, and the impact of military, social and economic influences from abroad. During the reign of Bādī III, called 'the Red' (1103–1128/1692 to 1716), the sultan's forces successfully contained a major outbreak of renewed civil strife, but the restive elements reasserted themselves during the reign of his successor Ūnsā III (1128–32/1716 to 1719–20).[1] These two revolts shattered the long calm of the seventeenth century, and revealed that the conservative ruling institution of Sinnār was ill-prepared to govern a kingdom transformed through a century of intimate relations with Islamic culture and the money economy of its neighbours.

Funj conquests in the southern borderlands

Both Ethiopia and Sinnār were anxious to assert their authority over the rugged borderlands between the kingdoms of highland

and plain. Control of the routes, passes and fords of the frontier region gave both a military and commercial advantage; the area was itself a source of ivory, civet, slaves, and particularly gold. The initial Funj penetration into the borderlands during the first half of the sixteenth century was directed northeastward against Ethiopia. Portuguese accounts indicate that shortly after the founding of Sinnār Funj soldiers had crossed the Buṭāna and were probing the western defences of the Ethiopian emperor's provinces in the Eritrean hills. With the defeat of Aḥmad Gran, however, the emperors established a new permanent capital at Gondar in the northwestern highlands and consolidated their control over the adjacent frontier regions. Further Funj advances in the northern border area became more difficult, and the efforts of Sinnār were diverted towards the south.

Bruce was given an account of the Funj conquest of the two most northerly of the hill peoples of the Gezira, believed to have taken place about the middle of the sixteenth century. At that time the hill folk were not yet Muslim, and their kings fiercely resisted the armies of the Funj. After a long siege, however, the sultan

> forced them to surrender; and, having fastened a chain of gold to each of their ears, he exposed them in the public market-place at Sennaar in that situation, and sold them to the highest bidder, at the vile price of something like a farthing each. After this degradation, being circumcised, and converted to the Mahometan religion, they were restored to their government, as slaves of Sennaar, upon very easy conditions of tribute, and have been faithful ever since.[2]

One by one the other mountains of the southern Gezira succumbed and were incorporated into the Funj state. In each case the rulers became Muslims, entered into dynastic marriages with Sinnār, and came to regard themselves as Funj. They retained many pre-Islamic customs such as the use of pork, however, and often continued to speak the language of their subjects.[3] The final major outpost of Funj authority in the southern borderlands was Fāzūghlī on the left bank of the upper Blue Nile. An Ethiopian chronicle mentioned Funj military activity at Abū Ramla (slightly northeast of Fāzūghlī) during the reign of Dakīn,[4] and Fāzūghlī itself fell to the Funj after prolonged resistance during the reign of Ūnsā II.[5]

Early commercial ties between the southern borderlands and Sinnār were probably established by the nomads whose patterns of seasonal migration encompassed both regions. The extension of Funj authority over the southern mountains introduced the new system of royal 'administered' trade, and a new type of merchant entered the borderlands:

> Those concerned (the merchants) are the people who ordinarily live in the land situated between Ruṣayriṣ and Fāzūghlī, who are often kinsmen or allies of some *makk* (king) of those countries. Their relations with the *makks* of the mountains through which they travel give them a certain security within the dependencies of these kings: the only danger for them lies on the route from one mountain to another.[6]

The danger lay in banditry, particularly by nomads who did not welcome commercial rivals; a few items of trade, such as ivory, probably remained largely in nomad hands.

Relations with Ethiopia

The campaigns of Dakīn and his successors in the southern borderlands seem to have brought the Funj directly into conflict with the Ethiopians; there followed a period of strained relations, culminating in a general campaign against Sinnār by the emperor Susenyos in 1618–19. Information about this conflict is derived almost exclusively from the emperor's own chronicle, which greatly exaggerates the successes and virtues of the Ethiopians and says little about the Funj response.[7] It is possible to correct some of this bias by reference to conditions in Sinnār itself.

At the dawn of the seventeenth century the whole of Sinnār was convulsed by the attempt of ʻAjīb to overthrow the Funj dynasty. In these circumstances it is understandable that the embattled Funj sultans tried to conciliate the Ethiopians in order to avoid creating a powerful new enemy on a second front. Presents were exchanged between the monarchs, and if Ethiopian traditions recorded by Bruce are to be believed, the Funj sultan accepted from Susenyos a royal kettledrum that could be interpreted as a sign of submission and homage.[8] When the deposed sultan ʻAbd al-Qādir II fled to Ethiopia in 1607 and performed obeisance to Susenyos, it seemed to offer the emperor a golden opportunity to intervene in the affairs of Sinnār.

The death of ʻAjīb and the re-establishment of order in Sinnār must have come as a disappointment to Susenyos. If he had hoped that the successors to ʻAbd al-Qādir would continue to honour that sultan's submission to Ethiopia, he was rudely awakened when Bādī I, in return for a golden bracelet and a chair ornamented with gold, sent Susenyos in return two old, lame horses. Funj princes began to raid Ethiopian posts along the major road from Sinnār to Gondar, and gave asylum to rebellious Ethiopian border chiefs. Tension between the two states was exacerbated by the fact that during Bādī's reign Ethiopia had to procure a new bishop from Egypt. The appointed candidate, Abba Yeshaq, had the misfortune to be passing through Sinnār when Bādī died; roads to the outside world were closed during the interregnum,[9] and by the time Rubāṭ I was properly invested and normal conditions restored, the bishop had followed Bādī to the grave.

Susenyos then decided to devote the campaign seasons of 1618 and 1619 to operations against Sinnār. Numerous raids were carried out by Ethiopian border princes while the bulk of the emperor's army was being mustered along the frontier. At one point an Ethiopian force advancing down the main road from Gondar to Sinnār fought a pitched battle with a Funj army dispatched to the front by Rubāṭ. The Ethiopian chronicle described the battle as a victory for Susenyos, but since the Ethiopians immediately retreated, this interpretation is questionable. The next year the Ethiopians crossed the frontier in force and raided some of the provinces east of the Blue Nile. They captured many head of cattle, but avoided contact with the riverain provinces of Sinnār and the Funj army. Following the fighting of 1618–19 relations between Ethiopia and Sinnār remained cool; the major trade routes were soon reopened, however, and fighting on a large scale between the two powers did not occur again for over a century.

The Dinka invasions

The expansive energies of the Nilotic peoples were by no means exhausted with the penetration of the Shilluk into the Funj homeland. A second wave of conquest was carried out by the people generally known today as the Dinka; first mentioned in Shilluk traditions that may be roughly dated to about 1630, the Dinka continued to expand into the southern Gezira at the expense of Sinnār throughout the seventeenth and particularly the eighteenth century. The Dinka were versatile and adaptable, and formidable fighters in the terrain offered by the southern Gezira; their 'citizenry at arms' far outnumbered the small professional armies of the Funj. Since the Dinka lacked a central political institution, however, their energies were often dissipated in internal feuds, and large-scale co-operation among the clans was impossible to maintain for long. For this reason the Dinka were never a mortal peril to Sinnār, but their increasing presence gradually but decisively shifted the balance of power against the Funj in the south.

The invasion of the Dinka threatened both the Funj and the Shilluk, who during the seventeenth century confronted each other along the White Nile.[10] Though traditions of hostility between the two groups still ran deep, time and mutual contact had blunted the sharpest animosities, while the new common enemy provided a powerful incentive for rapprochement. After their initial wave of conquest had been contained, the Shilluk had come to regard the Funj with respect. While some undoubtedly cherished the memory of the early victories and hoped to press on northward,[11] there arose a considerable body of opinion that considered such adventures to be unwise. For example, one oracle who spoke for Nyikang, ancestral father of the Shilluk, warned his people not to invade Funj territory:

> Am I not Nyikang?
> Can I not do whatsoever I will?
> This I say to you:
> The Funj will throw you back!
> Let me make this clear:
> The Funj will throw you back!
> Thus saith the Lord.[12]

The establishment of more peaceful relations between the Funj and Shilluk resulted in some acculturation. Some of the northern Shilluk, for example, adopted the use of the *raḥat* (thong skirt) for unmarried girls,[13] and towards the end of the seventeenth century Reth Tugo introduced a new coronation ritual and perhaps other reforms that seem to have owed much to the corresponding practices in Sinnār.[14] The Shilluk Reths seem to have used both the circumstance of the Dinka threat and the example of Funj institutions to reinforce the royal role among their own people.

To oppose the Dinka the Funj sultan Bādī II and the Reth Duwat (*c.* 1635 to *c.* 1650) formed an alliance,[15] and fighting on the southern front continued sporadically throughout the century. The alliance was renewed by succeeding Shilluk leaders, particularly Reth Tokot (*c.* 1670 to *c.* 1690), a contemporary of the sultans Bādī II, Ūnsā b. Nāṣir and Bādī III.

In the time of Tokot units of Shilluk soldiers served in the army of the Funj; they campaigned in Kordofan under Bādī II, and during the civil strife of the late seventeenth and early eighteenth century fought for the central government against the rebellious northern provinces.

The combined efforts of the Funj and Shilluk succeeded in containing the expansion of the Dinka to the north and west, and the main thrust of the newcomers was diverted northeastward into the hill country of the Ethiopian borderland. The Dinka contested the Funj hegemony in this region throughout the eighteenth century, and carried their raids to the gates of the capital city itself.[16] In the course of time, however, the Dinka like the Shilluk before them began to enter into less hostile relations with the people of Sinnār; units of Dinka mercenaries served the *makks* of the southern Funj provinces, while Dinka merchants became important suppliers of the slave trade of Sinnār.[17]

Expansion into Kordofan

West of the White Nile lay Kordofan, a rich source of gum, horses, slaves and gold. The earliest direct evidence concerning Funj authority in northern and central Kordofan is an ʿAbdallāb document of 1736, in which the *mānjil* of Qarrī guaranteed security of passage to pilgrims between Sawākīn, Ethiopa, Aswān and al-Kāb in northwestern Kordofan.[18] While that may have been a somewhat optimistic assessment of Funj authority west of the Nile, it probably had some basis in fact. The document would suggest that Funj influence in northern Kordofan was exercised by the *mānjil* of Qarrī in his capacity as supervisor of nomad affairs. Probably the government of Sinnār was able to exercise the greatest influence over those groups who, like the Ḥasanīya and Kabābīsh of modern times, spent part of the year not far from the Nile. There is little reason to believe that Funj authority in northern and central

Kordofan was newly established in 1736, though evidence from earlier periods is not at hand.

West of the Funj province of Alays in the eastern Nuba mountains was the kingdom of Taqalī. Taqalī, according to tradition, had been created during the latter part of the sixteenth century and the first half of the seventeenth by a series of Muslim kings, the first of whom was the offspring of a local princess and a pious 'Wise Stranger' from the Nile.[19] These early kings seem to have used Islam and the Arabic language to overcome the ethnic divisions and parochial loyalties of the mountain peoples, and they attracted the services of some of the leading Muslim holy men of seventeenth-century Sinnār – notably the 'Irāqī *faqīh* and Qādirī missionary Tāj al-Dīn al-Bahārī.[20] The kings of Taqalī also borrowed extensively from the political institutions of Sinnār; one is told, for example, of the *jundī*, a court official who controlled access to the king and played an important role in naming his successor, and the '*sokarawi*', perhaps a reference to the institution of the *sawākira*.[21] It is indeed possible that the kingdom of Taqalī was older than the traditions indicate, having been associated with the Funj before the rise of Sinnār and the adoption of Islam by the Funj, for it was said that the office of *jundī* in Taqalī antedated the arrival of Islam there.[22]

By the seventeenth century Taqalī had established commercial links with the Funj kingdom. On one occasion, according to the *Funj Chronicle*, the king of Taqalī seized some goods from a 'friend' of Bādī II – probably a royal merchant – and this precipitated an invasion of Taqalī by Bādī and his Shilluk allies.[23] After crossing the White Nile and the thorn desert to the west, the Funj laid siege to the mountain fortifications of the king of Taqalī. They took many captives, but were unable to storm his stronghold. The king of Taqalī made peaceful overtures, and after a time Bādī accepted them; he withdrew his army, leaving Taqalī in peace at the price of a yearly tribute. It may well have been on this occasion that Taqalī was incorporated into the traditional Funj dynastic marriage system; certainly in later years the ruling elite of Taqalī, like their counterparts on the Nile, regarded themselves as Funj.[24] Taqalī became a typical province of Sinnār; as one observer put it, 'just as was the government of Sinnār, so was that of Taqalī'.[25]

Upon his return from Kordofan, according to the *Funj Chronicle*, Bādī

> built a village for each different race of prisoners; and these villages surrounded Sennar like a wall to the east and west, and the inhabitants acted as troops for the aid and protection of the realm, and they bred and multiplied until the fall of the kingdom.[26]

Over a century later Bruce passed through the circle of garrison settlements surrounding Sinnār. He found that the original population had been supplemented by purchased slaves and by later captives, both from the southern mountains and the Nuba hills. Many were not yet Muslims, though Bruce thought that 'the generality of their children' were converting to Islam.[27] Those who had occasion to spend time in the capital city learned Arabic, but most continued to speak their native tongues. Their role and status in the society of Sinnār was fixed and limited; 'few of them', wrote Bruce, 'advance higher than to be soldiers and officers in their own corps'.[28] They were not, however, a restive element; Bruce observed that 'having settlements and provisions given them, as also arms put in their hands, they never wish to desert, but live a very domestic and sober life. . . .'[29] Bruce estimated the number of fighting men among the garrison settlements at twelve to fourteen thousand, who 'fight naked, having no other armour but a short javelin and a round shield, very bad troops, as I suppose'.[30] Indeed lightly-armed infantry could not be expected to stand against the Funj cavalry on the plains, and the garrisons played no conspicuous role in the later history of

Sinnār. 'They are very quiet,' concluded Bruce, 'and scarcely ever known to be guilty of any robberies or mutinous disorders, declaring always for the master, that is, the great one set over them.'[31]

The northern provinces

The defeat of 'Ajīb the Great and the settlement of Idrīs wad al-Arbāb brought almost half a century of peace to the 'Abdallāb kingdom, during which the sultans chose the ruler of Qarrī from among the sons and grandsons of the Great Mānjil.[32] Remote from Sinnār, the northern kings were proud, and their subjects divided from the southerners by language. If the 'Abdallāb overlord became weak, or if dynastic rivals in Qarrī sought to turn the particularistic tendencies of the northerners to their own advantage, the authority of the central government in Dongola would be in grave danger. These disruptive possibilities were realized in the crisis that erupted in about 1659.

The spark that ignited the revolt was a dynastic dispute between two heirs of 'Ajīb. The *mānjil* Ḥammad b. al-'Ajayl, a grandson of 'Ajīb, had a son named 'Uthmān who seems to have cherished the title for himself. Upon the death of the *mānjil* Ḥammad, however, the sultan invested a cousin named 'Ajīb II b. al-'Arayb, and when 'Ajīb II was succeeded by his brother Mismār, the disgruntled 'Uthmān withdrew to the Shāīqīya country and revolted. 'Uthmān had the backing of the northern nobility,[33] and he also sought popular support. Robing himself in the rough wool of a *faqīh*, he won over two of the leading northern holy men; 'Awūḍa b. 'Umar and Shaykh al-A'sir reassured the populace that 'the short, pale, bald man' would emerge victorious.[34]

Meanwhile the sultan was organizing a campaign against 'Uthmān, and appointed Mismār the commanding *amīn*. Undismayed by omens that foretold his impending deposition in favour of the son of ʿUthmān, Mismār marched north into Dongola. The *amīn* enjoyed initial success; ʿUthmān was driven up into the fourth cataract and besieged on Dulga Island. There he made a stand, and defeated Mismār in battle.[35] The victory was decisive; 'the armies parted, and the horses parted, tail to tail'. ʿAlī, the son of ʿUthmān, 'sent to king Bādī b. Rubāṭ and informed him of the defeat and demanded of him the (ʿAbdallāb) kingdom'. The sultan was forced to consent, explaining to his court and soldiers that he had been forewarned of the defeat by Shaykh al-Aʿsir, who had appeared to him during the midday siesta and threatened him should he send an army into the Shāīqīya country.[36] ʿAlī b. ʿUthmān was invested as *mānjil* in place of the unfortunate Mismār.[37]

The successful revolt of ʿUthmān established a dangerous precedent, and the sultans soon took measures to consolidate their hold over the north. They dispatched a substantial force under a Funj *mānjil* to found a colony between Dongola and the Shāīqīya country, including al-Dabba and Korti. In Hoskins' words:

> The Sultan of Sennaar, as some call him, sent here a detachment of the tribe called Funge, to which he belonged, to keep this country under his subjection. . . . Ibrahim was the first [*mānjil* of the Northern Funj], and was succeeded by his son Musnet.[38]

Ibrāhīm and his son 'sent considerable quantities of corn, oxen and horses to Sennaar',[39] and undoubtedly strengthened the sultan's control over the north. By the end of the seventeenth century, however, the settlement began to decline; as Hoskins was told, 'the descendants of Musnet enjoyed less authority over their subjects, and the tribute to Sennaar was less regularly paid'.[40] This impression was confirmed by the missionary Brevedent, who passed through Korti early in 1699 and enjoyed the hospitality of the reigning *mānjil* Qandīl. 'Once very rich', observed Brevedent, 'he is now rather decayed, but full of generosity and kindness'.[41] Even in decline the colony of the Northern Funj served as a useful base for the sultan's military operations in the north,[42] but it was resented by its neighbours, and the colony proved to be no more than a temporary solution to the problem of the north.

Foreign influences in seventeenth-century Sinnār

European visitors to the Funj capital at the end of the seventeenth century found a large foreign community and a receptive, cosmopolitan atmosphere. 'This is a free city,' wrote Krump, 'and men of all nations and beliefs may live in it without hindrance.'[43] The foreigners in Sinnār included Muslim and Coptic Egyptians, Turks, Ethiopians, Arabians, Jews, Portuguese, Greeks and Armenians. Most were merchants, although some practised crafts. The military, commercial and religious influences brought by the foreigners to Sinnār were to have a profound impact upon the kingdom. The full significance of the cultural innovations, however, was felt only in the eighteenth century.

During the seventeenth century the Funj became increasingly aware of the changes in armaments and military organization that had been taking place in neighbouring states, particularly Egypt. Towards the end of the century Bādī III attempted to reform the Funj army; firearms and cannon were introduced, and the cavalry began to practise Mamlūk drills. The French consul in Cairo during the 1690s learned that quantities of powder, lead, and even cannon had been dispatched from Cairo with the royal Sinnār caravan. He also reported that numbers of Europeans were believed to have entered the service of the Funj court to establish a cannon foundry and drill the troops.[44] Even a passing missionary was pressed into service as a drillmaster,[45] and by 1700 Bādī commanded a corps of two hundred musketeers.[46] But Bādī's attempt to introduce firearms into Sinnār on a large scale was a failure.

Cannon were impractical in a land where wheeled transport was not used; there is no indication that the Funj ever fired one in combat. Smaller firearms were difficult to maintain in working order, and craftsmen to repair them were rare. The Funj did not learn the technique of manufacturing gunpowder, while imported supplies were both expensive and uncertain. One suspects, however, that the greatest barrier to Bādī's military reforms was political. The provincial kings would have viewed the new corps of musketeers in the capital with great suspicion; equipped with arms imported through the unique mercantile prerogatives of the sultan, it threatened to reduce the relative power of the conventionally-armed provincial forces. Following the reign of Bādī III, the Funj kingdom entered a time of troubles; neither the sultan nor his rivals were able to maintain a significant supply of firearms, and the partisans of all factions reverted to traditional weapons as the kingdom disintegrated.[47]

The prosperous foreign trading community in Sinnār in 1700 testified to the hospitality of the Funj government, and to the success of its commercial initiatives abroad. 'One should know', wrote Krump, 'that in all Africa . . . Sinnār is near to being the most distinguished trading city. Caravans are arriving continually from Cairo, Dongola, Nubia, from over the Red Sea, from India, Ethiopa, (Dār) Fūr, Bornu, Fezzan and other kingdoms'.[48] Though the commercial boom of the later seventeenth century brought prosperity to the towns and luxuries to the royal court, it also brought the potential for profound conflict. While direct evidence is in most cases lacking, one may reasonably infer that the traders from abroad chafed at the restrictions imposed on them by the Funj court. The main complaints would have been the requirement that they sell their imported goods at a disadvantage after the sultan's wares had blunted the demand, and that they purchase gold, slaves, and perhaps other commodities from the sultan at royally-regulated prices. Other grievances probably included the close supervision of the Funj brokers and the court officials who served as merchant patrons, as well as government searches and seizures intended to prevent smuggling, and the restrictions on travel within or out of Sinnār, that sometimes bordered on extortion.

In addition to the channel provided by the expatriate community in Sinnār, foreign influences also returned to the Funj kingdom with the numerous individuals from Berberistan, and particularly Dongola, who migrated to Cairo and Alexandria to seek employment for a period of years. A visitor to Egypt in mid-seventeenth century noted that the Nubians commonly took service as household servants, being regarded as exceptionally astute and trustworthy. The members of the Nubian community in Egypt, he noted, 'acted towards each other as brothers'.[49] The Nubian workers were quick to learn foreign languages such as Turkish and Italian, and carried on a petty trade in Sudanese exotica.

As the number and influence of the foreign merchants in Sinnār grew, it became increasingly difficult to enforce the trading prerogatives of the sultan. By 1700 the merchants were discovering a partial solution to many of their complaints – the introduction of coin currencies. As the use of currency became generally known in some of the major trading centres of Sinnār, the power of the sultan to regulate prices in terms of the gold standard evaporated. Once removed from the prying eyes of the king, the market value of gold like that of other commodities could be reckoned by private traders in terms of currency.[50] In short, the gradual penetration of coin currencies into the Funj kingdom implied also the introduction of the unregulated market system, and the corresponding collapse of royal control over commerce – and ultimately over the economy as a whole.

It is difficult to document the penetration of coin currencies into Sinnār prior to 1700, but the accounts of early eighteenth-century visitors offer more substantial information. Firstly, the use of any sort of money was unknown except among those who participated in the royal caravan trade, the high nobility, and in the commercially-sophisticated capital city. As Krump expressed the situation, ʻalthough no coinage (is) current among the common people of this land, nevertheless it has value among the merchants and other nobles'.[51] The royal traders and their foreign allies still did much of their business in terms of the royal gold ounce, but coin currencies were also in use.[52] Poncet mentioned the use of an Ottoman silver *faḍḍa*,[53] and Krump a silver coin of uncertain provenance that may well have been the same.[54] The supply of coins in the capital city seems to have been inadequate to meet the demand, particularly for coins of small denomination. Private merchants manufactured small iron coins for use in the capital; ʻwhoever so desires may make these iron coins', wrote Krump, ʻand one may make them large or small, thick or thin, narrow or wide, long or short.'[55] Twelve, sixteen or twenty of them, depending on their size, were equal to a silver penny – possibly the Ottoman coin mentioned by Poncet.

One may conclude that the impact of coins and the money economy upon the commercial system of Sinnār was not very great prior to 1700; royal authority over the gold ounce and the ʻadministered' caravan trade remained substantially intact. Nevertheless the narrow end of the wedge had been inserted; coins were becoming known and their use understood among the Sudanese, and the Funj court was unable to suppress their use – if indeed it appreciated the danger. The heterogeneous and irregular character of the coins in Sinnār in 1700 probably reflects the fact that their use was a relatively recent innovation, and that no coinage had yet found general acceptance among the trading community. It is not surprising that the merchants in Sinnār soon adopted a single standard currency, the Spanish dollar. ʻAt present', noted Krump in about 1700, ʻthey are beginning to accept the piece of eight.'[56] By the end of the eighteenth century the Spanish dollar had become the standard currency throughout Sinnār; only vestiges of the sultan's fiscal and commercial authority remained.[57]

A final set of foreign influences that assumed new significance in Sinnār during the seventeenth century were religious; there is reason to believe that only in this century did the new faith of Islam take firm root among the people of Sinnār. This interpretation is based upon examination of the careers of Muslim holy men of the Sudan as recorded in the *Ṭabaqāt* and the *Funj Chronicle*,[58] the *fuqarā'* to whom Sudanese scholarship has justly ascribed the major responsibility for converting the Sudan.[59] The conversion of the Funj, Yūsuf Fadl Ḥasan noted, 'was bound to attract teachers from *Dār al-Islām*'.[60] Though this was undoubtedly true in the long run, it would seem that very few teachers indeed were attracted to Sinnār during the first century after its nominal conversion. The presence of some may be assumed rather than documented, but it is difficult to avoid the impression that before the seventeenth century Islam in Sinnār remained an exotic royal cult, committed to a language unfamiliar to the Sudanese, and primarily associated with traders from abroad and visiting dignitaries such as the *soi-disant* descendant of the Prophet, David Reubeni.[61]

If the historical perspective of the *Funj Chronicle* may be trusted in this instance, it would seem that the reign of 'Adlān I and the early seventeenth century saw a marked increase in the number and significance of Muslim missionaries in Sinnār. Some came from abroad; men such as Tāj al-Dīn al-Bahārī, who introduced the Qādirīya brotherhood to Sinnār, and the formidable organizer of men, Ḥasan wad Ḥasūna. At about the same time the first holy men of Sudanese nationality appear in the historical records of Sinnār: Maḥmūd al-'Arakī, who returned to the Sudan from Egypt and began missionary work sometime after 1551; Idrīs wad al-Arbāb, whose role as a conciliator in the troubles of 1611 has been mentioned above; and Ibrāhīm al-Būlādī, who brought the first standard textbooks of Islamic law to the Sudan during the reign of ʿAdlān I, and helped the Mālikī *madhhab* win general acceptance among the Muslims of Sinnār.[62] The contribution of these holy men must have achieved a great advance for Islam over the conditions that had obtained during the previous century, and it is highly significant that some of them were Sudanese. However, they were still few in number, and all seem to have been dependent upon training abroad.

By about the middle of the seventeenth century a new stage was achieved in the advance of Islam into Sinnār. Beginning with the generation of holy men who succeeded Idrīs wad al-Arbāb and Ibrāhīm al-Būlādī, the great majority of holy men whose lives appear in the *Ṭabaqāt* were men of Sudanese origin who received their training within the Funj kingdom. Though still the faith of a small minority, Sudanese Islam had become self-sufficient, drawing both its leaders and followers from among the people of Sinnār. Symbolic of this situation was the construction of the first mosque in Sinnār during the reign of Bādī II.[63]

The form of Islam that permeated seventeenth-century Sinnār reflected the duality of mode that prevailed at that time throughout the wider Muslim world. Islam in the Funj kingdom bore two faces – the orthodox and the ecstatic. Each brought a distinctive set of institutions, though individual Muslims might reconcile in their own lives the modes of feeling, expression and thought of both traditions.

The primary goal of the orthodox school was conformity to the corpus of Islamic law, and more specifically the interpretations of the Mālikī *madhhab* as embodied in the *Mukhtaṣar* of Khalīl b. Isḥāq and the *Risāla* of Ibn Abī Zayd.[64] The orthodox approach emphasized the institutions of the mosque and the school; in Sinnār, this implied that its appeal was largely restricted to well-to-do townsmen who could spare the labour of their sons during the years of education, and who appreciated the practical value of literacy in Arabic.

The ecstatic or Sufi school emphasized the quest for mystical union with the higher powers, to be achieved through ascetic practices and spiritual exercises. Sufism brought to the Sudan the *ṭarīqa* or religious brotherhood, a new form of social organization. Authority in a Sufi community was vested in a leader who possessed *baraka,* roughly translatable as supernatural power; the leader received his *baraka* from his own teacher and spiritual master, and would in turn pass it on to a successor, not uncommonly his son. Brotherhoods met periodically for worship, and adherents often preferred to live close together; the organization was adapted to both urban and rural settings. The Sufi brotherhoods in Sinnār functioned effectively only on the local level. though most owed broader allegiance to the Qādirīya. The system of brotherhoods was open to men with little training in the doctrines of the orthodox, and had the potential for easy syncretism with older pre-Islamic practices and beliefs.

The revolt of 1705–1706

Bādī III, noted the *Funj Chronicle,* was 'the first Funj king against whom a section of his [own] people revolted'.[65] Born about 1680, Bādī received the royal title in June 1692,[66] and was about twenty years old in 1699 when numbers of European missionaries arrived in his kingdom on their way to Ethiopia. At that time Bādī, described by his guests as 'black, but well shaped and of a majestic presence', had not yet personally assumed the reins of power.[67] The government was in the hands of the court; the Jesuit missionaries' adviser in Cairo, the canny French consul De Maillet, had been careful to send diplomatic gifts to the Queen Mother and a high court official whom he called the '*wazīr*' (possibly the *jundī*), as well as to Bādī himself. Upon their arrival in Sinnār the missionaries confirmed that Bādī was 'yet a youth, and under the tutelage of a wazir',[68] who seemed to have the power of a 'viceroy', and whose name was 'Alī al-Ṣughayyir (Ali Zugoyer).[69] Events were to show, however, that the young sultan could not be kept under tutelage indefinitely. When the Queen Mother died in May 1699, the position of 'Alī al-Ṣughayyir became increasingly anomalous. The king was spending his spare time in target practice.[70]

A major problem confronting the court of Sinnār in 1700 was unrest in the northern provinces. The initial settlement of the Northern Funj in Dongola had caused considerable resentment, and as the strength of the colony waned, it became more vulnerable to the attacks of its neighbours. *Makk* Aḥmad of Dongola,[71] for example, would hardly have appreciated the proximity of the Funj *mānjil* Qandīl, his equal in wealth and dignity,[72] nor the periodic visitations of the Sinnār cavalry under the *arbāb* Ibrāhīm. Even an outsider such as Brevedent could not escape the conclusion that the government of Sinnār 'wants to diminish' the kingdom of Dongola,[73] and at the first sign of revolt, numbers of expatriate Danāgla would return from Dār Fūr to support their king.[74] East of the Funj settlement the Shāīqīya country was in open revolt, being occupied by 'rebels against Sinnār who plunder the caravans'.[75] A whispering campaign was organized to brand the Funj as 'pagans from the White Nile'.[76] In response, the authorities in Sinnār sent a letter for public proclamation in Dongola, announcing that the *mānjil* Qandīl and his folk were descended from Arabs, and indeed from Umayyads. 'And so you have seen the facts', the letter concluded; 'the tongues are silent, and the slave 'Azīz may see the virtue of the use of discretion in regard to injurious speech!'[77] But the tongues were not to be so easily silenced, and the crisis deepened.

Not all of Bādī's problems lay in the north. He inherited strained relations with Ethiopia from his predecessor Ūnsā II, whose campaigns in the southern borderlands had culminated in the annexation of Fāzūghlī. The *arbāb* Ya'qūb, a Funj border prince whose lands lay 'near Sawākīn' went into revolt; it was probably no coincidence that he had close family connexions with the Ethiopian emperor.[78] Funj and ʻAbdallāb forces succeeded in suppressing Yaʻqūb, and several of the European missionaries assisted in smoothing relations between Ethiopia and Sinnār.[79] It seems that Bādī sent his new corps of royal musketeers against Yaʻqūb, for he enlisted the services of a European 'to teach his people how to shoot'.[80] It may well be that this successful campaign, in which guns imported by the sultan's privileged caravans figured prominently, inspired the leaders of the older, conventionally-armed forces to conspire against Bādī.

The leader of the conspiracy was the *amīn* Irdāb, who drew support from among 'his people, the Funj' and from military units at Sinnār, Alays and Qarrī.[81] The ʻAbdallāb *mānjil* Ḥammad al-Simayḥ supported the conspiracy,[82] as did also, it would seem, the kings of Dongola and Alays, and the '*wazīr*' ʻAlī. The conspirators located a brother of Bādī named Awkāl who had escaped the usual fate of brotherly rivals to the sultan, having fled the sword of the *sīd al-qūm* and taken refuge in Dār Fūr.[83] Awkāl was to become the new sultan after the success of the coup. But it was difficult to keep such a large project secret. Suddenly, early in 1705 Bādī had ʻAlī executed, a fair indication that his role in the plot had been discovered. The other conspirators abandoned secrecy, justifying their revolt as a response to the execution of ʻAlī.[84] In about April Awkāl returned from Dār Fūr accompanied by numbers of Danāgla supporters, and was invested as anti-sultan.

According to the *Ṭabaqāt*, the insurgents scored initial victories, and Bādī was forced to seek refuge with the Queen Sister Kāmīr. She appealed on his behalf to the *faqīh* Khalīl b. al-Rūmī;[85] with the blessing of the holy man, Bādī routed Irdāb's forces and killed the rebel *amīn*. The missionaries were given an account of the battle:

> When the rebels arrived at Sinnār they gave battle to the king and went out with a mighty thrust, but the king, an

> invincible man without fear, met them with bravery. The ominous threat of the missionaries, who told him [Irdāb] that he would be the first to die came true. As he advanced through the thick of the battle to the king himself, he [Bādī] encountered him and ran him through from side to side . . . [Irdāb] was thrown to the ground and killed with thousands of spears as he had the temerity to rise against his sovereign. The king, too, was slightly wounded on the arm. After the death of their chief, the rebel army shamefully fled and the king remained the sole victor against his enemies, who withdrew.[86]

The missionaries also heard of Bādī's celebration after the death of Irdāb.

The revolt continued in the north; even as Bādī celebrated, Ḥammad al-Simayḥ was no farther away than Qarrī,[87] and in Dongola, the insurgents held out for 'that rebel, Ardab', until the spring of 1706.[88] Sometime after April 1706, Bādī moved against Ḥammad al-Simayh, and sent after him 'Umar Abū Zinter, a former *makk* of Taqalī whose ferocity as king had cost him his throne and driven him into exile at the sultan's court.[89] Some Shilluk soldiers seem also to have participated in this campaign.[90] Driven from Qarrī, the *mānjil* Ḥammad established his capital at Merawī in the Shāīqīya country.[91] He fought a savage rearguard action at Shandī, sacking the city and killing the king of the Jamū'īya who had been sent to defend it.[92] By the next spring the tumult had subsided, and the missionary Bayard emerged from hiding to greet the man appointed to be the new king of the 'Abdallāb, a placid, superannuated grandson of 'Ajīb the Great.[93] The Shāīqīya country remained in rebel hands.

VI · Sinnār in decline

The Christian missionaries who visited Sinnār during the first decade of the eighteenth century found it a prosperous kingdom, whose essential integrity did not seem to be imperilled by the occasional disputes among the nobility. The atmosphere in the Funj capital was tolerant and cosmopolitan. About a century later a small merchant caravan accompanied by the explorer Burckhardt worked its way gingerly through the devastated provinces of northern Sinnār, avoiding as best it could the banditti, Mamlūk adventurers, robber barons and feuding princes, whose wars and intrigues had plunged the region into chaos. Burckhardt travelled in disguise, and feared for his life should his true identity as a non-Muslim foreigner be revealed. Clearly the same century that witnessed the dismemberment of Sinnār also produced a revolution in the earlier Sudanese attitude towards foreign influences. The new xenophobia was in a sense justified, for the state of the kingdom was largely the result of the impact upon Sudanese society of cultural innovations borrowed during the earlier age of cosmopolitan confidence. The decline of Sinnār in the eighteenth century may be broadly attributed to the erosion of traditional Funj institutions and values under the combined pressure of commerce and Islam.

The rise of the merchant class

Trade served to strengthen the Funj government only as long as the sultan initiated and controlled it, and during the eighteenth century both initiative and control passed out of royal hands. Merchants of foreign origin, so conspicuous in Sinnār in the time of Bādī III, could as outsiders be controlled with relative ease. As the foreigners became established, however, they gave birth – literally and by example – to an indigenous, independent Sudanese merchant class, outside of and below the traditional ruling elite. The new merchants were far less inclined to associate their own interests with those of the king.

The core of the new merchant community was composed of Sudanese traders in lowly commodities, who were eager to collaborate with the foreigners and expand their commerce to items previously monopolized by the king. Many of these traders were from nomadic groups, and among them the Beja were predominant by virtue of their strategic location between the Nile and the Red Sea and their long tradition of commercial expertise. Beja merchants established residences on the Nile, swelling the population of the new trading centres such as Berber and Shandī, as well as the older town of Arbajī. A Beja dynasty came to dominate Arbajī about 1725, and received quasi-recognition as provincial lords of Sinnār.[1] The people of Arbajī, and indeed all Sudanese traders who were not Funj, were known to their neighbours in Sinnār as '*ḥuḍūr*' (singular, Ḥaḍarī), which would seem to be a variant form of 'Ḥaḍāriba';[2] obviously the new merchants were associated in the popular mind with the Ḥaḍāriba and similar folk. As the private traders assumed an ever-increasing importance in Sinnār, the port of Sawākīn received a corresponding proportion of the trade of the Funj kingdom at the expense of Egypt; the pre-Funj trading system of the Ḥaḍāriba reasserted itself.[3]

Not all the new merchants were Beja. Wealthy citizens of Sinnār itself, notably the lesser provincial nobility, were also anxious to profit from trade. The provincial lords of Sinnār often allied with Beja merchants to usurp the trading prerogatives of the sultan; in some cases they began to tax passing caravans,[4] while in others they embarked upon trading ventures of their own.[5] Those excluded from access to legitimate commerce might take up a career of banditry.[6] Probably commercial rivalries exacerbated the feuds among the eighteenth century provincial kings. One may also infer that the acquisition of commercial interests by the provincial lords made any return to centralized government on the old pattern very difficult; the sultan was unable to enforce his trading privileges, and his vassals were unwilling to relinquish their newly-won source of wealth.

By the end of the century the role of the sultan in the economy of Sinnār had been much reduced. The Spanish dollar, imported by the private merchants, was the accepted currency of the whole kingdom except in the remote southern provinces and Berber, where a conservative *makk* kept the notion of the gold ounce alive. Gold smuggling and the prominence of the Ḥaḍāriba as gold traders noted by Burckhardt would suggest a substantial dilution of the royal monopoly over this branch of commerce.[8] Within its reduced sphere of influence the central government clung to its right to sponsor caravans; Burckhardt could still speak of the merchants of the city of Sinnār as being 'chiefly agents of the King of Sennaar and his vizier, who are the principal merchants of that place'.[9] Yet in most cases the last sultans of Sinnār were forced to sacrifice the profits of long-distance trade; though occasional caravans still embarked for Egypt, the sultan no longer had any share in them, and slaves captured by the *salaṭīya* were sold on the spot to the private merchants who trailed behind the army.[10]

The life-style of the new middle class was most evident in trading centres such as Shandī and Arbajī. Rectangular courtyard houses replaced *tukuls*; dwellings of the more prosperous had rooftop terraces, and occasionally a second storey or private bathing pool.[11] Many aspects of traditional culture were abandoned. The funeral dance, for example, was frowned upon as un-Islamic,[12] while the conical straw hat or *keskesega* and local dialects fell into disfavour. Men cut their hair short in modern fashion, while women began to wear garments that covered the upper torso. Lejean described the ordinary Shandī merchant:

> One is sure to see them everywhere, clad in white and bearing on the back a great straight sword in the form of a cross,[13] driving before them a donkey, robust and well-nourished. . . . Their profits are very small, but their sobriety is proverbial and their overhead nil. . . . Thus they achieve an honest well-to-do status, very rarely wealth.[14]

The merchants' bourgeois values of thrift and sobriety were quite in contrast to the looser mores of the hard-drinking peasantry and the excesses of court life. The ideological justification for the new middle-class style of life was provided by orthodox Islam. Mosques were built in the towns, and prayers performed communally in public.[15] Schools were founded in the towns, and literacy in Arabic became common among men of the middle class. Individuals with training in Islamic law could be found in every town. Some sought more advanced training at the major centres of Islamic learning abroad, and returned to the Sudan with collections of books. The aura of Muslim respectability of the new middle class was reinforced by the adoption of a new self-identity – they proclaimed themselves to be Arabs. In support of these claims there arose first a trickle, then a flood of putative genealogies, tracing family descent from son to father carefully back to various distinguished Arabs of the early days of Islam.[16]

Essential to the new bourgeois household was the possession of slaves. The role of slaves in facilitating the rise of a tradesman or farmer to middle-class status was illustrated by Cailliaud:

> Some men make cloth of their cotton, and work themselves in the fields. Those who enjoy a measure of wealth (*aissance*) employ slaves of both sexes for the latter work, and devote themselves entirely to commerce.[17]

Even the most modest trader owned field hands to cultivate the family landholdings and girls to carry water and grind grain, while the leading merchants had large slave establishments. The major slaveholders often set their female slaves to work as prostitutes in towns along the trade routes; the girls were given quarters, but paid a fixed monthly fee from their earnings to the master.[18] This form of prostitution accompanied the spread of the money economy and the new bourgeoisie, though sometimes noblemen, faced with competition from the merchants, also adopted the system.[19] Such prostitution was unknown in the more traditional and commercially isolated southern provinces.[20]

The peasants

The explorer Hartmann paused in a village along the Blue Nile to observe a court case. A wealthy merchant and landlord was suing one of her tenant farmers before the local prince for the recovery of some grain that she, the trader, had lent to the farmer. As the debtor offered excuses instead of repayment, the prince ordered his soldiers to seize the defendant's crops, and to burn down his homestead if a sufficient quantity could not be found. This case is illustrative of an exploitative relationship, called *sheil*, that developed between the peasantry and the new eighteenth-century bourgeoisie.[21] It was not uncommon for a peasant family to run short of food during the weeks immediately preceding the major harvest each year. At that time the farmer might borrow a certain amount of grain valued at a set monetary amount from the storehouse of a private merchant. After the harvest the farmer would ordinarily be able to repay his debt, but since the price of grain plummeted at harvest time when the market was flooded, he would have to return to the merchant a considerably larger quantity of grain than he had originally borrowed in order to discharge the debt. Peasants who objected to the sharp practices became known as troublemakers and might be denied credit altogether, while the fact that the merchant was literate and the peasant was not opened the door to further abuse, even if the trader did agree, as the saying went, to 'write him the bread-money'.[22]

The peasants, understandably enough, came to detest the merchants as a group. Such was the burden of a folk-tale current during the latter years of Sinnār, that found its way into one version of the *Funj Chronicle*. The story was set in the time of the legendary famine of Umm Laḥm, and recounted the policies of three merchants who received the insight that they would soon die. All had been hoarding grain for sale at inflated prices during the height of the famine. The first and senior merchant advised his juniors to cease hoarding and to begin selling at whatever price the market would bear. One of the junior merchants found this inadequate, gave away all the grain that he had been hoarding, died, and went to Paradise. The second junior merchant refused to sell freely, and continued to haggle at great length in order to wring every possible profit out of each handful of grain. He died also, according to the story, and though the precise fate awaiting him remained unexpressed – undoubtedly unpleasant – it was at least certain that he would not be alone, for immediately after his death he passed through the great market town of Arbajī and found profiteering rampant.[23]

The role of the prince in the case observed by Hartmann was typical. The lord might be just, or even sympathetic to the debtor, but he was under great pressure to support the claims of the merchant. Of course not all kings were honest, and it was not unknown for a ruler to engage in grain profiteering on his own account.[24]

The peasantry could not expect assistance or relief from the ruling elite, and were forced back upon their own resources. One method of escape from the burden of the *sheil* system was for the peasant to become a merchant himself, and undoubtedly many such individuals found a respectable niche for themselves in the trading systems of eighteenth-century Sinnār. The greatest opportunities for a newcomer with little capital and no powerful patron lay in the frontier region of Kordofan. Petty traders from the northern Funj provinces flocked to the area and founded the first towns there, Bāra and al-Ubayyiḍ.[25] Most peasants, however, were unable to attain middle-class status by becoming successful merchants. Their discontent found another outlet.

In 1814 Burckhardt visited the community of al-Dāmir near Shandī, a neat and well-governed community ruled by the head of the Majdhūb family. Though small, al-Dāmir was prosperous, and a centre of peace and learning in troubled times.[26] Strictly speaking it was not a part of the Funj kingdom at all, but an autonomous community of holy men or *fuqarā'*. Al-Dāmir was the best documented of a great number of similar religious communities, large and small, that dotted the Nile banks from Dongola to the capital itself. Each community was organized as a Sufi *ṭarīqa*, and often received a charter from the Funj government freeing it from all obligations to the state; it paid no taxes, nor were royal officials even permitted to enter it without permission.[27] The community was a haven for debtors, who could seek asylum, repudiate old obligations and start a new life there. The community kept its own stores of grain, and manipulated food prices to the benefit of the peasants.[28]

Religious communities were founded through the grant of land and privileges by the ruler to individual holy men. The political influence of the *fuqarā'*, however, was derived from their role as spokesmen for the masses; it was they, observed Brocchi, 'who direct public opinion'.[29] Those among the *fuqarā'* who asserted themselves against the powers-that-be were to become the great folk heroes of eighteenth-century Sinnār.[30] The religious status of the communities was ambiguous. Some of the *fuqarā'* were highly educated in the Islamic sciences, and the royal charters were given as alms in the Islamic sense. Yet the popularity of the holy man among his supporters was not primarily based upon respect for his orthodoxy, but upon his possession of *baraka* or supernatural power. Perhaps it would be most accurate to say that the *fuqarā'* reorganized and gave legitimacy to the pre-Islamic practices of the Sudanese countryside in vaguely Muslim terms. This conservative orientation was clearly visible in the political sphere, for the *fuqarā'* did not hesitate to adopt the insignia, rights and obligations of traditional Funj provincial kings.[31]

The royal dilemma

The rise of the merchants and the spread of religious communities in the countryside challenged the authority of the Funj royalty simultaneously from two opposing directions. The merchants, as their wealth and power grew, were willing to tolerate the king only if he observed an orthodoxy that crippled the Funj system of government and gave free play to their own economic interests. Royal concessions to the merchants, however, were certain to further alienate the peasantry. These pressures were most acute in the central provinces of Sinnār, which were the most heavily exposed to foreign influences.

One of the points at which traditional royal rights and orthodox Islam clashed most sharply was in regard to the administration of justice. Traditionally the responsibility of the kings, Islamic political theory assigned it to the *'ulamā'*, the most competent experts in religious law of each generation. In the context of the Funj kingdom that meant those of the educated middle class who had received advanced legal training. The influence of the merchants and the *'ulamā'* was strongest in the major trading towns, of which Berber may serve as an example. By the end of the eighteenth century the king of Berber had lost both political and economic dominance; the government of the province had passed into the hands of several powerful trading families.[32] Justice in Berber was administered by a court of middle-class *'ulamā'*, and the king had been reduced to the role of process-server and chief of police.[33] The case of Berber is illustrative of a series of local coups in the towns of eighteenth-century Sinnār, through which the local king lost some or most of his authority to secretive clubs of the leading merchants. The merchants would then choose a leader from their own ranks; according to Turkish records, by the fall of Sinnār most of the larger towns had such an official, entitled *sirr al-tujjār*.[34]

As kings sought to defend themselves against charges of heterodoxy, there resulted a general disestablishment of divine kingship in much of northern and central Sinnār. Kings no longer wore the veil; they cut their hair short, and tried to set an example of piety by renouncing alcoholic beverages, performing Muslim prayers in public and abandoning the use of blasphemous praise-titles.[35] Muslim holy men were exempted from the traditional form of obeisance, and could no longer be obligated to appear at court to account for their activities.[36] Many kings abolished such un-Islamic practices as the yearly carnival and public reconfirmation of the royal right to rule, and the ceremonial ploughing by the king. They sought to retain their judicial prerogatives by studying Islamic law and becoming *'ulamā'* in their own right. They joined the orthodox merchant families in promulgating claims to Arab origin; even the sultanic Ūnsāb clan suddenly discovered a fact hitherto unknown – they were Umayyads![37]

Royal accommodation to Islam, however, failed to contain the ambitions of the middle class, and it had a disastrous impact upon the political institutions of Sinnār. Kings who claimed to be descended through the father's line from noble Arabs of Islamic antiquity proved unable to believe indefinitely that the status of nobility in Sinnār should be reckoned from mother to son. The core of the royal investiture ceremony, from the political viewpoint, was the marriage of a new ruler to a woman of his overlord's clan, but as the belief in the efficacy of women as bearers of noble status waned, the rite was perverted in one of several ways. In some cases, any suitable woman might become the new king's wife;[38] in others, a slave woman was chosen to take part in the ceremony, by which she became merely a royal concubine rather than a legitimate wife,[39] and in yet other instances the woman's role was reduced to a purely ceremonial presence, and was performed by a little girl.[40] Similarly, the new code of belief denied the necessity of the mother's return to her family for the birth of her children; 'Abdallāb traditions from as early as *c.* 1706 indicate that the king raised his sons in his own household.[41] In short, the acceptance of Islam by the ruling elite gradually destroyed the system of marriage alliances and princely hostages upon which the coherence of the Funj state depended. In its place there arose a series of local patrilineal dynasties upon whose loyalties the sultan exercised only a sentimental claim. As the sword of the *sīd al-qūm* fell into disuse princes proliferated, and so did petty dynastic feuds.

The new Muslim piety of the kings had important repercussions among the common people. To the degree that a ruler succeeded at projecting the image of orthodoxy, he not only lost the aura of sanctity surrounding traditional monarchs but also became associated in the popular mind with the cult of the merchants. It became increasingly difficult for peasants to believe that a lord who could not even enforce a just market price for food held the power 'to make live or make die'. When a peasant debtor joined a religious community he was in effect seceding from the Funj kingdom, transferring his hopes both for just government on earth and for access to Paradise to the leader of the community. The kings, for their part, had no real defence against a leader such as Muḥammad Ṣughayyirūn; he had studied at al-Azhar and was undoubtedly their superior in terms of orthodox Islamic education and the authority it gave, yet could still deliver potent and paralysing spells. The rulers often sought to placate powerful holy men by establishing them as secular rulers of their own autonomous communities. The example of Ṣughayyirūn is illustrative; 'beyond a site of unoccupied land and a watering-place for the holy men and a place for burial', he said, 'I want nothing'. 'Give him all the land he wants,' growled the king, 'and mark the boundaries for him.'[42]

In summary, the kings of eighteenth-century Sinnār progressively lost influence to merchant groups centred in the towns and to peasant communities in the countryside. The political history of the last century of Sinnār reflected this two-sided crisis of allegiance. To an ever-increasing degree the quarrels of various factions among the ruling group were divorced from the interests of either peasants or merchants; both were content to go quietly about their business, enjoy their wealth and tax-exempt status, and observe the military spectacle of the suicide of the old order.

The coup of 1718

At the dawn of the eighteenth century the disruptive forces within Sinnār were contained by the inherited authority of the traditional structure of government and the weight of customary usages throughout society. From about 1715, however, this brittle *ancien régime* was to be tested and ultimately fractured by an accelerating sequence of political crises. The first casualty of the time of troubles was to be the Ūnsāb dynasty itself.

In 1718 Sultan Ūnsā was deposed and replaced by Nūl, a pious Muslim and a capable leader, but a man ineligible for the royal title according to the constitutional practices of Sinnār.[43] Information about the coup is largely confined to the *Funj Chronicle.* The chronicler charged that Ūnsā had become dissolute in his private life; upon learning of the scandal 'his people, the Funj' resolved to depose him. They were 'the *junūd* of Lū'lū', who depose and appoint kings . . . but they depose without killing'. The *junūd* called Ūnsā to account, then marched against him out of the south, investing Nūl as anti-sultan. They then informed Ūnsā that if he killed one of his ministers named Ḍiyāb, he might retain the throne. After some hesitation Ūnsā executed Ḍiyāb, but the insurgents nevertheless forced through his deposition, though sparing his life.[44]

The *junūd* may be identified as the high court officials of the Funj – the *jundī* and his people – who had the right to appoint and depose kings, and who might well have been associated with Lū'lū' or 'Lūl', the ancestral home of the royal clan. Their demand for the fall of Ḍiyāb suggests that perhaps the Funj nobility were resentful of authority delegated to slave or commoner *wazīrs*. The chronicler's charge of loose morals against Ūnsā should be matched with his praise of Nūl's orthodoxy; perhaps the fall of Ūnsā was also a concession by the court to the pro-Islamic and politically restive north. In essence, though the method of the revolt of 1718 was traditional and its intended goals probably conservative, the result was nevertheless a significant precedent for those who argued that Islamic orthodoxy rather than traditional right gave legitimacy to a king.

The reign of Bādī IV

The peaceful and uneventful reign of Nūl came to an end after four years, and his son assumed the throne as Bādī IV (8 July 1724 to 27 March 1762). 'He was young during the early part of his reign', noted the *Funj Chronicle*, 'and was guided by his *wazīr* Dūka, a man both wise and just'.[45] The young king's advisers sought to perpetuate the aura of Islamic orthodoxy that had given legitimacy to the accession of Nūl; it is significant in this regard that numbers of Arabic charters authorizing grants of land to Muslim holy men have survived from the early years of Bādī's reign. It would seem that the use of written documents in Arabic was an innovation; court patronage of Muslim notables was not new, but was certainly characteristic of Dūka's policies.

Islamic principles were also finding acceptance among the rulers of the 'Abdallāb. 'Ajīb III, chosen to replace the deposed *mānjil* Ḥammad al-Simayḥ, was very old when invested, but he made important changes in the dynastic system of Qarrī that corresponded in significance to the election of Sultan Nūl. He initiated the practice of isolating his own sons, and an 'Abdallāb folk historian could boast with reasonable accuracy that 'his descendants succeeded him without break, until the conquest of the Sudan'.[46] Taken together, these traditions seem to imply the collapse of the old dynastic relationship between Qarrī and Sinnār, and suggest that 'Ajīb replaced it with a patrilineal dynasty, still subject to the sultan, but without the hostages and controls that had bound the early Funj state together.

Early in the reign of Bādī IV there arrived in Sinnār a noble refugee from Dār Fūr named Khamīs b. Janqal.[47] Khamīs was a son of the previous sultan of the Musabba'āt in western Kordofan, and he also had a more distant claim to the throne of Dār Fūr itself. He easily dominated the circle of foreign dignitaries-in-exile at the court of Sinnār, for he came attended by a small army. The Fur-speaking immigrants were given estates in the Funj heartland,[48] and began to plan an active role in the internal politics of Sinnār. Slow to assimilate, they remained a discrete ethnic group and military faction for several generations.[49]

In 1743 the Ethiopian emperor Iyāsū II began massing his forces along the frontier for an invasion of Sinnār, and made some preliminary raids near Qallabat along the major road from Gondar to the Funj kingdom. When the campaign season opened in the spring of 1744, Iyāsū's army – estimated at 30,000 by the Sudanese – crossed into Funj territory and marched against the capital.[50] Ethiopian and Sudanese sources reveal little of the background to the conflict, but portray vividly the religious and emotional fervour that accompanied the war. The *Funj Chronicle* told of Bādī's appeal to all the Muslim holy men of the kingdom for prayers of victory, while ordinary citizens in the capital made pious vows to be fulfilled if God spared them. Iyāsū's chronicler listed the Christian relics carried into battle by the king, and described the fasting and prayer-vigil of Iyāsū's mother and grandmother while he was away at war.[51]

Iyāsū seems to have planned a two-pronged attack against the city of Sinnār; one party, led by the Rās Walda Le'ul, probably crossed the upper Blue Nile and advanced down the west bank, while the king himself descended the Dinder with the main body of the army.[52] Bādī did not have enough time to summon forces from the outlying provinces. He quickly mustered an army in the capital, and the *amīn* Bishr walad Yūnus took command.[53] The army crossed the Blue Nile and joined with Khamīs and his followers on the east bank. Their combined forces rode against Iyāsū.

The armies met in pitched battle on 7 April 1744 on the bank of the Dinder.[54] The Sudanese carried the day, capturing Iyāsū's royal kettledrum, holy relics, and a number of firearms and cannon. Khamīs and the Musabba'āt seem to have made the greatest impression on the Ethiopians; Iyāsū's chronicler mentioned the presence of Khamīs, described as the 'Degazmac of the king of Sinnār', and later Ethiopian stories about the battle as recorded by Bruce directly attributed the victory to him.[55] Meanwhile the Ethiopian left under Rās Walda Le'ul also fell back after inconclusive fighting; a large cannon abandoned by the Ethiopians and too heavy for the Sudanese to move marked the farthest advance of this force.[56]

There need be little doubt that the Funj capital rang with celebration for seven days after the victory, though the congratulatory messages from India and Istanbul mentioned by the *Funj Chronicle* were probably imaginary. 'Such are the fortunes of war,' concluded Iyāsū's chronicler philosophically, 'sometimes to conquer, and sometimes to be conquered.'[57] Relations between Ethiopia and Sinnār remained strained for many years, but the respective provincial governors of both countries around Qallabat worked out an unofficial *modus vivendi* that served to keep the trade routes open and the nomads of the border region in check.[58] 'We understand one another as good neighbours ought to do,' the Sudanese general 'Adlān told Bruce with a twist of irony, 'and what else is peace?'[59]

Following his victory over the Ethiopians, Bādī undertook a settling of accounts within the government of Sinnār. The *Funj Chronicle*, which did not regard Bādī highly, gave the following version of the events:

> When Dūka died he [Bādī] took over the kingdom. He killed the remainder of the Ūnsāb, and took from the people of noble lineage their ancestral estates. He took the side of the Nuba, and gave them the estates of the old nobility. For example, he made shaykhs of Fūr people such as Khamīs walad Janqal and took their side against the Funj and the family of the former kings.[60]

The basic elements of Bādī's policy may be discerned in spite of the chronicler's bias. The death of the powerful *wazīr* Dūka and the need to reward Khamīs and other non-Funj defenders of Sinnār during the Ethiopian war combined to give the young king an opportunity to assert his personal authority over the other court officials – who like Dūka were probably men of Nūl's generation – and also over the clan of the former sultans, the Ūnsāb. The latter, as heirs to the previous dynasty, would have been Bādī's hereditary enemies. The precise extent of the confiscations and bureaucratic reshuffling may not be determined from the sources, but it is certain that Bādī's measures were insufficient to render powerless his opposition.

Bādī's internal reforms were interrupted by the outbreak of a crisis in Kordofan. Funj rule in eastern and central Kordofan was at that time exercised largely through the Ghudiyāt, a group culturally akin to the Funj themselves, who lived between the site of the modern al-Ubayyiḍ and the Nuba mountains.[61] Since the riverain kings regarded Kordofan as primarily nomadic territory, however, it fell under the overlordship of the 'Abdallāb *mānjil*.

At the accession of the Fur sultan 'Umar Lel in about 1746/1747, several brothers of the previous ruler sought refuge with the Musabba'āt of northwestern Kordofan, and then their combined forces invaded Funj territory. Bādī dispatched an army under the command of the *muqaddam al-khayl* 'Alī walad Tūma,[62] but at the decisive battle of Qiḥayf (see Map 1) in 1747 the Fūr were victorious and killed both the *muqaddam* and the *mānjil* 'Abdallāh III. In a second battle the *mānjil's* brother Shammām and the latter's son were killed; the victors then settled near the modern al-Ubayyiḍ. Further dynastic intrigues among the Fūr, however, soon led to the evacuation of Funj territory, and five years after Qiḥayf Kordofan had been reincorporated into Sinnār.[63] It was elevated to provincial status under the Ghudiyāt shaykh, 'Alī Karrār b. 'Umar.[64] Private merchants from Dongola and the Shāīqīya country settled in Kordofan, founded the towns of Bara and al-Ubayyiḍ, and began to prosper in the gold and slave trades.

The wars in Kordofan set the stage for the rise to power of a young cavalry officer named Muḥammad Abū Likaylik, who was destined to dominate the political life of Sinnār for two decades.[65] After the defeat at Qiḥayf, according to the *Funj Chronicle*, it was he and 'Adlān walad Ṣubāḥī, the shaykh of Khasm al-Baḥr, who rallied the Funj army.[66] Following the second defeat they again gathered the remnants of the shattered force, and late in 1747 Bādī placed Abū Likaylik in command in the place of the late 'Alī walad Tūma, elevating him to the rank of shaykh.[67] With the restoration of peace in Kordofan following the withdrawal of the Musabba'āt, Abū Likaylik sank into temporary obscurity, but retained his command over the Funj forces in the west.

Meanwhile the opposition to Bādī was gradually mounting, and he in turn increased the severity of his repressive measures. 'Everyone who angered him', wrote the chronicler, 'he sent to Ḥillat al'Akūra to dig a reservoir for him with the slaves'.[68] A conspicuous atrocity was Bādī's execution of 'Abd al-Laṭīf, the *khaṭīb* of the Sinnār mosque, and his adult sons, while 'ruined people rose against him on every side'.[69] But it was the old court officials and nobility who probably suffered most from Bādī's measures, and it was they who succeeded in bringing about his downfall. Numbers of them were in Kordofan, and after considerable discussion they prevailed upon Abū Likaylik to march on Sinnār and depose Bādī. When the army reached Alays (during 1760–61) a council was held in which Bādī was formally set aside and replaced by his son Nāṣir, who came to join the insurgents. The whole force descended upon the capital, and Bādī stepped down quietly and fled to Ethiopia.[70]

The coup of Muḥammad Abū Likaylik was a decisive turning point in the history of Sinnār. Bādī IV, noted the chronicler, 'was the last of the kings with power, and with him ended the real monarchy. After him the power of binding and loosing passed to the Hamaj.'[71] The Hamaj were one of the 'Red' peoples of the Blue Nile valley above the capital and the Ethiopian borderlands;[72] Bruce, who passed through Sinnār in the time of Abū Likaylik, noted the predominance at court of men from Fāzūghlī and other southeastern provinces.[73] In short, the 'Reds' had replaced the 'Blues' as the dominant ethnic group of the kingdom. The Hamaj, like other Prenilotic peoples, were patrilineal, and disinclined to renew the faltering Nubian dynastic marriage system inherited from the Funj. This was pleasing to the petty 'Arab' dynasties of the north, but in spite of the great personal abilities of Abū Likaylik and several of his successors, offered no viable solution to the festering constitutional crisis of Sinnār. The Hamaj king-makers were commonly addressed simply as 'shaykh', and signed official documents with the title of *wazīr*.[74] Their true position was without precedent in the history of Sinnār, however, and it has become a useful convention among writers in English to refer to them as 'regents'.

At the level of practical politics the establishment of the regency was a dramatic failure. The first to be disillusioned were the old Funj nobles who had incited Abū Likaylik to revolt, for one of his first acts after assuming power was to complete Bādī's programme of reducing them to impotence.[75] Having thus tamed the parties both of Bādī and of his opponents, Abū Likaylik undoubtedly hoped to bring an end to the factional strife. His victory was complete; his army was the only effective authority in the capital city. But the army was soon needed in Kordofan. Its departure opened a Pandora's box of civil strife, for the balance of power between the central government and the provinces had been overturned.

The basic issue of the wars to follow was the existence of the regency; puppet sultans conspired with ambitious provincial kings to oust the Hamaj, while local political and commercial rivalries among the vassals assured many allies for the regents. The process of decline was irreversible. The possibility of effective military rule was precluded by involvement of the army in the long and unsuccessful war in Kordofan, while the advance of private commerce and Islam, and the reduction of the sultans, made a return to the old monarchy impossible. The class rivalry between merchants and peasants, feuds among the territorial princes, and residual respect for the old system closed the door to the establishment of a new order. The prophecy of Idrīs wad al-Arbāb was being fulfilled; 'in the end they will be divided and fight among themselves and their rule will disappear and the Turks will conquer the country'.[76]

The civil wars

Sultan Nāṣir reigned for eight years (1762–69); in the end he chafed at the role of figurehead and conspired against Abū Likaylik, who deposed him and sent him into exile. There he continued to plot. The regent dispatched his nephew Bādī walad Rajab and Aḥmad walad Maḥmūd the *muqaddam al-qawwārīya* with soldiers. After a fight with the sultan's supporters the *muqaddam*, who held a personal grudge against Nāṣir, killed him. 'He knew how to write', lamented the chronicler, 'and, by God, his script was fair!'[77] The war between the supporters and opponents of Abū Likaylik was under way.

Opposition to the Hamaj regency was to find its strongest partisan in the 'Abdallāb *mānjil* Muḥammad al-Amīn (*c.* 1750 to 1790).[78] Though soft spoken and unexceptional in physique,[79] his appearance was deceiving; events proved him to be ferocious in battle, tenacious in defeat, and tireless in intrigue. An initial supporter of Abū Likaylik, his reversal of loyalties was probably not based upon principle, but rather resulted from the pressure of feuds among his vassals and their intrigues with the regents.[80]

The Shāīqīya country, following the abortive revolt of 1705–1706, was occupied by the heirs of Ḥammad al-Simayḥ. They challenged the legitimacy of all subsequent eighteenth-century 'Abdallāb *mānjils*, and Muḥammad al-Amīn was forced to concede that in effect his power did not extend any farther north or west than the Ja'aliyīn country.[81] Traders from the northern provinces were prominent in Kordofan and the kings in the Shāīqīya country probably sought the favour of Abū Likaylik on their behalf even before the fall of Bādī IV; there are also hints that they offered the regent military support in controlling the nomads of northern Kordofan.[82] These factors tended to bring the northern kings and the Hamaj into alliance against Muḥammad al-Amīn.

A second dispute involved the kings of the Ja'aliyīn country who, with the general collapse of traditional Funj dynastic practices during the eighteenth century, had established their own ruling patrilineage. The fourth king of this line, 'Abd al-Salām, was 'killed by the Funj of Sinnār' – presumably before the Hamaj coup of mid-century – and was succeeded by his son al-Faḥl.[83] Al-Faḥl married a sister of Muḥammad al-Amīn, who bore him a son Idrīs.[84] There followed a feud among the sons of 'Abd al-Salām; al-Faḥl was killed, but his wife with the assistance of the *mānjil* her brother held the Ja'alī capital of Shandī on behalf of the young Idrīs.[85] The rival faction settled in al-Matamma opposite Shandī, and controlled the Ja'aliyīn country on the west bank of the Nile. They made common cause with the northern kings in the Shāīqīya country and by 1772, if not before, they had received the official endorsement of the regents.[86]

It is reasonably certain that Muḥammad al-Amīn took part in Nāṣir's conspiracy to regain power, for following the sultan's execution Abū Likaylik launched the Jamū'īya, neighbours, tributaries and now rivals of the 'Abdallāb, against Muḥammad al-Amīn.[87] The regent invested a new and docile *mānjil*, while Muḥammad al-Amīn went into temporary exile.[88] Abū Likaylik replaced the rebellious sultan with Ismā'īl, but was soon called to Kordofan (1771–2) by the invasion of Hāshim, sultan of the Musabba'āt, Hāshim was victorious; the ageing Abū Likaylik was obliged to abandon the province, leaving Sa'd, *makk* of the Ja'aliyīn of al-Matamma (known from his reign as the Sa'dāb) to guard the west bank of the White Nile and the approaches to Alays.[89]

In 1775–6 Abū Likaylik died, and was succeeded as regent by his nephew Bādī walad Rajab. Since Abū Likaylik had numerous sons, this choice laid the groundwork for a schism within the regent's clan. The passing of Abū Likaylik also stimulated a new conspiratory to oust the Hamaj, but after two months of warfare the regent Bādī suppressed the rebels, exiled the sultan Ismāʿīl, the central figure of the plot, to Sawākīn, and appointed ʿAdlān sultan in his place.[90] The weakness of the central government was demonstrated by defeats on every hand; Kordofan was lost to the Musabbaʿāt, the Dinka overran Funj positions on the east bank of the White Nile south of Alays,[91] the Baqqāra closed in on Taqalī,[92] and the large nomadic tribes of southern Sinnār, notably the Shukrīya, Halānqa and Rufāʿa, asserted their independence.[93]

Bādī was a man of great personal courage and resolve, but even his limited initial success soon foundered on the hostility of his cousins, the sons of Abū Likaylik. Claiming that one brother, Nāṣir, had become ill after having been beaten at the order of Bādī, and needed medical care available only in the capital, they gathered at Sinnār and conspired against the regent. The plotters also included the sultan ʿAdlān, Muḥammad al-Amīn, and the shaykh of Khasm al-Baḥr. They seem to have been ill-prepared militarily, for they began their revolt by raiding the nomads of the southern Gezira for horses and seizing the arms of a patrol that Bādī had sent there in an attempt to collect taxes. Nevertheless the conspiracy was successful; Bādī was defeated and killed – according to tradition, in single combat with Muḥammad al-Amīn. The year was 1780.[94]

The conspirators then came to cross purposes. The sons of Abū Likaylik were content to see one of their number, Rajab, installed as regent, while the sultan remained unsatisfied. Muḥammad al-Amīn was reinstated as the ʿAbdallāb *mānjil*.[95] Rajab, the *Funj Chronicle* noted wryly, then 'went to Kordofan, as had his fathers before him, and busied himself with blockading the mountains'.[96] He then advanced against Hāshim in al-Ubayyiḍ. The Musabbaʿāt leader felt resistance to be futile and retreated towards his stronghold in the northwest; some of his followers chose to fight and were crushed by Rajab.[97]

While Rajab was in Kordofan, Muḥammad al-Amīn in some

way aroused his suspicions; Rajab dispatched his brother Nāṣir to dispose of the *mānjil* and appoint another. In a sharp engagement along the Blue Nile Muḥammad al-Amīn repulsed the superior force of Nāṣir and escaped; Nāṣir then invested Bādī b. Mismār as *mānjil* in the place of his brother. Bādī lay low in Wad Madanī while Muḥammad al-Amīn rallied support among the nomads; in 1783–4 he turned savagely on the town of Arbajī, whose leaders had supported the candidacy of his brother Bādī, and razed it to the ground.[98]

The revolt took a more serious turn the following year, when the sultan ʻAdlān summoned Muḥammad al-Amīn, the rulers of Shandī and other opponents of the Hamaj, and with their assistance imprisoned, enslaved and executed many of the regent's faction at Sinnār. One who survived the purge was the distinguished poet al-Nāʻisān, who fled from the scene of the atrocities to warn Rajab. By the time he reached Kordofan he had set his account of the woeful events into moving verse, and Rajab at once marched east, abandoning Kordofan to Hāshim. Rajab ordered *makk* Saʻd to leave his old position on the western marches and to accompany him, along with al-Ḥājj Maḥmūd al-Majdhūb of the ruling family of al-Dāmir. Clearly Rajab hoped to sow discord in the ʻAbdallāb kingdom while Muḥammad al-Amīn was involved in Sinnār.[99]

Meanwhile ʻAdlān was preparing his forces against Rajab's return. The two armies clashed at al-Taras; Rajab and al-Ḥājj Maḥmūd were killed and the partisans of the sultan emerged victorious. Probably because of illness, ʻAdlān failed to press his victory. The defeated Hamaj were rallied by the *faqīh* Ḥijāzī Abū Zayd, appointed Rajab's brother Nāṣir as regent, and spent the years from 1786–7 to 1788–9 rebuilding their strength. Thereupon ʻAdlān recovered sufficiently to send an army against Nāṣir. Muḥammad al-Amīn was not present, possibly because of the rising pressure of the northern kings in the Shāīqīya country, and the core of ʻAdlān's army seems to have been provided by the Sinnār Musabbaʻāt under Muḥammad Abū Rayda b. Khamīs. The resurgent party of the regent won a major battle at Inṭaraḥna and besieged their opponents in the capital city, forcing them at length to fight or starve. In the battle that followed Nāṣir emerged victorious; he entered Sinnār, appointed a new puppet sultan ('Adlān had not survived the news of the defeat at Inṭaraḥna), and proceeded to root out all opposition. Abū Rayda escaped to join Muḥammad al-Amīn in the north.[100]

The *mānjil* and the Musabba'āt general were now the last important opponents to the Hamaj, and they appointed one Rubāṭ as anti-sultan to the regent's puppet, Tabl. Shortly after his victory at Sinnār Nāṣir gathered his army and rode down the Nile in pursuit of Abū Rayda. Not far from Shandī Muḥammad al-Amīn and Abū Rayda turned and fought, defeating Nāṣir and killing Ṭabl. They hounded Nāṣir back up the river and drove him from the 'Abdallāb capital; in this battle both the anti-sultan Rubāṭ and the new Hamaj puppet died. The following year (1790), however, the two opponents of the regent fell out, and Muḥammad al-Amīn was assassinated by the Musabba'āt. Abū Rayda withdrew to his estates in the south, leaving the battered factions to seek their own destiny.

The northern kings

Following the death of Muḥammad al-Amīn the civil wars continued on a local level throughout Sinnār, but no individual or faction was strong enough or possessed of sufficient legitimatizing charisma to re-establish a central authority. The provinces north of the fourth cataract were geographically removed from the troubles in the south. Local politics produced their own tensions, to be sure, and the southern factions found partisans north of the Bayūḍa. Nevertheless the towns and palaces of the north were spared the ceaseless parade of plundering horsemen that passed through southern centres between 1760 and the fall of the sultanate. Through a policy of Islamic orthodoxy, aggressive political and commercial expansion, and the extensive emigration of potentially disaffected elements, the northern kings were able to maintain and even strengthen their positions in an age of general decline.

The northernmost province of Dongola, governed by a ruling house known as the Awlād Zubayr,[101] was loyal to Sinnār but militarily weak and cut off from potential allies by the heirs of Ḥammad al-Simayḥ in the Shāīqīya country. On the left bank of the Nile between al-Dabba and al-Qurayr lay the territory of the northern Funj; by 1780, however, the functions of government had largely passed into the hands of several religious orders. In the Shāīqīya country a dynastic dispute, possibly in about 1780, led to the establishment of two rival royal lineages, the Ḥānnikāb and the ʿAdlānāb.[102]

The people of the northern Funj district had on occasion looked to Muḥammad al-Amīn for protection, confirmation of their rights and adjudication of their disputes. One such individual was the *faqīh* Muḥammad of the Awlād Dūlīb, who received a charter to which the *mānjil* appended a special warning to ʿal-Shūshī' (probably the ʿAdlānāb king Shawīsh, also called Shūsh, Jawīsh, etc.) not to disturb the lands of the *faqīh* Muḥammad.[103] One may infer that very soon after their rise to power, the ʿAdlānāb began to display an acquisitive interest in their downstream neighbours. By about 1782, Hoskins was told, the resistance to the ʿAdlānāb had been broken in the northern Funj district;[104] armies from the Shāīqīya country struck north and west across the desert, devastating parts of Dongola. With the death of the leading men of the Funj and the court of Dongola, the 'chiefs of Dongola' were forced to come to terms by their war-weary people.[105]

A new puppet king was chosen for Dongola from among the old royal family, and marriages were arranged to link his fortunes to those of the ʿAdlānāb.[106] His position as *makk* of Dongola was complicated, however, by the outbreak of war between Shawīsh of the ʿAdlānāb and Bashīr of the Ḥānnikāb.

Manṣūr, a son of Bashīr, seized the capital of Dongola, but then came to terms with Shawīsh; Bashīr and his successor Zubayr held a central region from Kajabī in the Shāīqīya country to central Dongola, while Shawīsh retained control of northern Dongola and the Shāīqīya country from Kajabī to the fourth cataract. The newly-appointed king of Dongola, compromised by his 'Adlānāb connexions, left the capital city and withdrew to Arqū island in the extreme north. There he took the local dynastic title Tombol[107] and the honorific, 'king of the Isles'.[108] He promulgated a genealogy linking himself to one Ḥākim al-Ja'alī, allegedly a brother of the famous family of holy men, the Awlād Jābir, who had many followers in northern Dongola.[109] The result of his attempt to build an independent political position was a punitive campaign by Shawīsh that drove him into exile in Egypt. Shawīsh placed a garrison at Arqū,[110] and his men raided far north into Egyptian Nubia.[111]

Having resolved their internal differences and consolidated their control over Dongola, the heirs of Ḥammad al-Simayḥ turned their attention to the south, and attempted to assert their claim to the whole 'Abdallāb territory. Shawīsh secured his left flank by occupying the fourth cataract and placing a garrison in one of the castles at al-Kāb.[112] Crossing the Bayūḍa, his raiders established villages on the west bank of the Nile to facilitate extended campaigns; from these forward bases Shawīsh himself would often lead his troops personally.[113] The raids of Shawīsh fell most heavily upon the 'Abdallāb capital, whose main settlement, Ḥalfāyat al-Mulūk, was reduced in population by one half to about three or four thousand souls.[114] The 'Adlānāb campaigns at the Nile confluence isolated the provinces of Berber and Shandī. Shawīsh defeated the *makk* of Berber and replaced him with a dynastic rival – 'and he paid tribute'.[115] The Sa'dāb of al-Matamma became junior partners of Shawīsh, but the *makk* of Shandī offered vigorous resistance; though his kingdom suffered greatly it did not fall.[116] In about

1809 Shawīsh's attempt to reunify northern Sinnār ended in failure; the invasion of Mamlūks fleeing the wrath of Muḥammad 'Alī in Egypt demanded the presence of his troops on the northern frontier.

The political and military accomplishments of the last northern kings were facilitated by a unique set of economic and social circumstances. The kings adopted without equivocation the role of champions of orthodox Islam. They followed an Islamic course of education as far as the opportunities of the Sudan permitted, and occasionally one would study in Egypt. They set an example of pious living. This policy tended to give them a legitimate right – which their military might enforced – to administer Islamic justice personally without the intervention of middle-class '*ulamā*'. In commercial matters the middle class were given a free hand. There is no evidence of royal control; Shāīqīya merchants of the early 1800s enjoyed the greatest geographical range of any in Sinnār, and were among the most prosperous.[117] The kings sought an alternative to profiting from the trade of their own merchants in the systematic plundering of others, and to maintain their economic predominance over their subjects through the seizure of booty abroad as the kingdom expanded. They frequently adjusted their political policy to ensure good relations with each passing government of Kordofan, because that province was the source of much of their subjects' wealth.

Lower-class discontent among the Shāīqīya and Danāgla was dissipated through emigration; thousands sought their fortunes as petty traders abroad, particularly in Kordofan. The kings replaced the agricultural labour sacrificed through emigration with slaves. Some of these were probably imported from Kordofan; others were captured on raids into Egyptian Nubia,[118] and a substantial portion were simple folk from Dongola.[119] Most were settled in the Shāīqīya country in agricultural communities.

One may conclude that the system of the northern kings was

unstable. The predominance of royalty over the middle class depended upon a continual flow of booty from military expansion, and the successful resistance of Shandī may indicate that this had reached its natural limits. Emigration offered upward mobility to the old peasantry, but the agricultural slaves imported to replace them formed an explosive element. It was they and not the Turks who burned castles in the Shāīqīya country in 1821,[120] and they might well have found occasion to do so without foreign intervention.

PART TWO
DĀR FŪR

VII · The prehistory of Dār Fūr

Sinnār, it has been suggested, was the heir to an ancient tradition of state formation in the Nile valley. In the vast region between the Nile and modern Chad, states are apparently a more recent phenomenon, but the evidence is so scanty that our perspective may simply be foreshortened. Within this area, much of it a paradise for nomads but inhospitable to more settled ways of life, only central Dār Fūr, in and around the Jabal Marra mountains, appears to have offered a nuclear area favourable to state-forming activity. And even here the external impetus of trade seems to have been a crucial factor in the expansion of the state beyond its original tribal homeland.

Our knowledge of early Dār Fūr, indeed until the beginning of the eighteenth century, is confined to a series of very confusing quasi-historical traditions, with many variants, and a handful of external contemporary references. The traditions are vaguely related to the many ruins, none of which has yet been excavated, which are to be found in the central zone of Dār Fūr. Unlike Sinnār, these traditions cannot be controlled by contemporary accounts; the first visitor to Dār Fūr to leave us a written record, Browne, arrived at least two hundred years after the establishment of the Keira or Fur state. The few external references we have give some chronological markers but are difficult to marry to the traditions. Therefore an account of early Dār Fūr and of the rise of the Keira dynasty must be a speculative attempt to interpret these traditions.

Although traditions concerning the history of Dār Fūr have been recorded at intervals over a period of nearly two hundred years, the early travellers, Browne and al-Tūnisī, give only fragments. The only comprehensive attempt to collect and collate the historical traditions current in Dār Fūr before the fall of the first Keira Sultanate in 1874, was that made by Gustav Nachtigal in that year. Despite later research, Nachtigal's collection, made before the chaotic period of Turco-Egyptian and Mahdist rule in the province (1874–98), must still be our starting point.

The traditions collected by Nachtigal, and these are not substantially at variance with later versions, assert that three dynasties ruled successively in Dār Fūr, the Daju, Tunjur and Keira.[1] They further suggest that the Daju had their main centre of power in southern and eastern Jabal Marra, the Tunjur somewhere to the north of the mountain zone and that the Keira expanded outwards from the same mountains. With each dynasty particular places and rulers are remembered; Kosbur and 'Umar Kassifuroge, 'Eater of the Fur', with the Daju, the mysterious Show Dorshid with his palace at Uri with the Tunjur, and the sacred places around Turra in Jabal Marra with the early Keira rulers. But the point of greatest confusion in the traditions is the supersession of the Tunjur by the Keira and the role in the change-over played by Aḥmad al-Ma'qūr, Ahmad 'the hamstringed', described as an Arab of exalted lineage whose coming to Dār Fūr leads, directly in the later versions of the traditions and indirectly in the earlier, to the establishment of the Keira dynasty.

The Daju

The traditions about the Daju can be briefly summarized; a long time ago the Daju rulers, who appear to have come to Dār Fūr from the east, lived in the southern Jabal Marra region, but their sway was limited since the chiefs of the Fur and other tribes simply paid them tribute. Their first king, Gitar or Kosbur, was a pagan and so probably were his successors; another of their kings was 'Umar Kassifuroge, whose nickname implies that he warred against the Fur. The Daju were superseded by the Tunjur,

> The intellectual superiority of the immigrant Tunjur, and their more refined customs (their hospitality was especially celebrated), wrested power from the Daju without any fighting, or violence.[2]

The last Daju king, called in some versions Aḥmad al-Daj, was so oppressive a tyrant that his subjects persuaded him to mount a *teital* antelope which galloped away with him to Dār Sīla in Chad, where a Daju state which survived until recent times was established.[3]

It is difficult to say much about these traditions; peoples speaking languages of the Daju language group are to be found widely spread in the eastern and central Sudanic belt, from Kordofan to Chad. There is also a group, called Ngulgule, in the Baḥr al-Ghazāl, in the southern Sudan.[4] Groups or clans claiming to be Daju by descent are also to be found interspersed among many of the peoples of Dār Fūr.

A variety of theories has been proposed on the origin of the Daju, or at least of their ruling clan, although there is little evidence that such a distinction is valid. Browne was told that the Daju came from the region of Tunis in North Africa, although from other remarks of his, he may have confused them with the Tunjur.[5] Of more recent writers, MacMichael supports an eastern origin connecting them with the Funj, while Arkell suggests that they are possibly to be identified with the Tājūwa or Tājūwiyīn, mentioned in several medieval Arab geographers, writing between 1152 and 1278, as a branch of the Zaghāwa and vaguely located in the Sahara between Kanem and Nubia.[6]

The traditions of the Daju peoples have not been systematically collected. Until they are, and until the sites associated by the traditions with the Daju kings are examined, the Daju phase of Dār Fūr's history must remain largely a matter of legend. The slight linguistic evidence we have may support the tradition of an eastern migration, if only from Kordofan.[7] If Arkell's identification of the Daju with the Tājūwa is accepted, their period of rule may belong to the twelfth to thirteenth centuries.

Aḥmad al-Ma'qūr and the Tunjur

The traditions claim that the Daju were peacefully replaced by the Tunjur, but the latter are an even greater mystery than their predecessors.

Today people calling themselves Tunjur are to be found scattered from Northern Nigeria to Dār Fūr, speaking either Arabic or Kanuri, and with half-forgotten memories of their imperial past.[8] From an analysis of the traditions about the Tunjur collected by the travellers and later colonial officials, some general points can be derived, at least in so far as they concern Dār Fūr. They appear not to be Arab in origin, although they are often so classified today, and may have migrated from the east, although the theme of migration from the east is a common one in the Sudanic belt. Their imperial career appears to have been short but grandiose, since by the sixteenth century a Tunjur empire apparently covered Dār Fūr and Wadai with its capital in northern Dār Fūr, where the sites of Uri and 'Ayn Farāḥ are particularly associated with them. They appear to have had a subsidiary or later capital at Kadama in Wadai. This empire disappeared in the seventeenth century and was replaced by the Keira in Dār Fūr and by a Maba dynasty in Wadai. The traditions of the downfall of the Tunjur in Wadai seem relatively straightforward; the story is more complicated in Dār Fūr since the traditions suggest a link, expressed in dynastic terms, between the Tunjur and Keira through the person of a 'Wise Stranger', Aḥmad al-Ma'qūr.[9]

We are told more about the end of Tunjur rule than its

beginning. The Wadai traditions describe how one Ṣāliḥ or 'Abd al-Karīm, the grandson of Woda, a Ja'alī immigrant from Shandī on the Nile, was governor of a province under the Tunjur king, Dā'ūd. Some time in the early seventeenth century, 'Abd al-Karīm, inspired by Islam, led a revolt against the Tunjur, who were expelled towards Kanem, and established a new dynasty which derived its support from the Maba peoples of Wadai.[10]

Barth dates the revolt of 'Abd al-Karīm to 1611 and Nachtigal to 1635; both imply that Tunjur rule in Dār Fūr had already been overthrown by the Keira. The geographical compendium of Lorenzo d'Anania, *L'Universale Fabrica*, published in Venice in 1582, provides what may be a reference to a Tunjur state in northern Dār Fūr about 1580, although they are not actually named,

> Uri, a very important city, whose prince is called Nina, or emperor, and who is obeyed by neighbouring countries, namely the kingdom of Aule, Zurla (which we have mentioned above), Sagava (or Sagaua), Memmi, Musulat, Morga, Saccae and Dagio. This prince, who is allied to the Turks, is very powerful and is supplied with arms by merchants from Cairo.[11]

D'Anania continues by saying that the great attraction in the region for the Cairo merchants was gold. Uri, described below, is firmly associated with the Tunjur, and of the subordinate peoples mentioned, the Zaghāwa (Sagava or Sagaua), Mīma (Memmi), Masālīt (Musulat) and Daju (Dagio) can be identified with some certainty; all are peoples to be found in Dār Fūr today. The gold trade is more problematical, since Dār Fūr appears to have none, but it may have come from the alluvial deposits in southern Kordofan, or possibly from farther west.

The picture of a powerful state in contact politically with Ottoman Egypt and trading for arms does not disagree with the traditional memory of the Tunjur as arbitrary rulers lording it over their subjects from their hill-top palaces. Unfortunately the traditional accounts are not explicit on how the Tunjur lost their power; instead they present a confused picture in which the change-over from Tunjur to Keira rule is associated with the figure of Aḥmad al-Maʿqūr.

Aḥmad 'the hamstringed' was an Arab from North Africa and is usually described as an Hilālī by tribe and linked to Abū Zayd al-Hilālī, the great folk hero of the storytellers of Egypt and North Africa.[12] In the desert to the north of Dār Fūr, Aḥmad quarrelled with his brother over a woman, was hamstringed and deserted.[13] However, he was rescued and taken to the court of Show Dorshid, the Tunjur king. Now Show was a tyrant, who forced his subjects to level the tops of mountains, where he built his palaces. Aḥmad soon became a favourite of the tyrant, perhaps because he introduced Islam, but more probably because he introduced new and more civilized ways – for example, of eating. Or, at least, so runs the simplified version of the story current today.[14]

A hundred years ago the story appears to have been more complex. Thus Nachtigal: Aḥmad came to the court of a Fur chief called Kurooma. Kurooma had married a daughter of the Keira chief and his wife, Fora, bore him a son, Show Dorshid. Later he divorced Fora, and when Aḥmad became his favourite at court, Kurooma gave her to the Arab; from this marriage came Daali or Dalīl Baḥr. Another version has it that first Rufāʿa, the son of Aḥmad al-Maʿqūr, married the Keira chief's daughter and from this marriage Show and Daali were born. Nachtigal noted the confusion of the traditions at this point,

> But the two men (Show and Daali) cannot have had both parents the same; in all the lists of rulers Shau concludes the Tunjur rulers, and in popular tradition also he is generally known as the last king of the Tunjur, while his half-brother Dali, whose proper name is Delil Bahar, is always recorded as the founder of the Kera dynasty.[15]

The Tunjur: Interpretations

In interpreting the Tunjur traditions we appear to be confronted with three problems; the identity of the Tunjur and the duration and extent of their empire, the role of Aḥmad al-Maʻqūr, and the Tunjur connexion with the Keira. For the present, none of these can be answered satisfactorily.

In seeking to understand these traditions, Arkell first suggested that the Tunjur dynasty was probably to be linked with the Tumagera, a clan or tribe of the Tibesti massif in northern Chad, but who are also found in Kanem; this lies behind the Hilālī claim of Aḥmad al-Maʻqūr. The Tunjur, migrating from the north-west, became rulers of a vast empire, based on trade, that appears to have dominated Wadai as well as Dār Fūr and even for a time Kanem, east of Lake Chad. Associated with the Tunjur are such hill-top palaces as Uri and ʻAyn Farāḥ in northern Dār Fūr and Jabals Māsa and Ḥurayz, in the east and south respectively. Uri is perhaps the most striking of these sites,

> a 1000 ft. peak ringed at foot and middle by solid Tora walls (strong stone walling, without mortar, generally about one metre wide but often two or three, with well faced sides enclosing a packing of smaller stones), its whole face covered with Tora houses including two remarkable 'palaces' with impressive platforms-of-audience with stepped approaches and rather unexpectedly a fine stone mosque. Up the final sheer 300 yards zigzags a stone-paved road.[16]

To account for the collapse of this Tunjur empire, Arkell posited a period of Bornu rule in Dār Fūr. This he placed in the reign of the great Bornu king, Muḥammad Idrīs b. Katakarmabe (1524–45), and saw in Daali, the reputed founder of the Keira state, a memory of a governor of Kanem on behalf of Bornu who also ruled in Dār Fūr, a Hausa slave called Dala Afuno (Afuno is the Kanuri for Hausa). The name, Dala, may also be preserved in the title of the great slave official of Keira times, the *āb shaykh* or *abbo shaykh daali*. The red brick buildings at 'Ayn Farāḥ recall Bornu building techniques and thus it may have been the seat of Bornu rule.[17]

When some fragments of pottery of Christian Nubian type from 'Ayn Farāḥ were brought to his attention, Arkell modified his views radically,[18]

> Ain Farah is now recognised to have been a monastery with two churches, all built in red brick, which probably flourished before A.D. 1240, when the Moslem kingdom of Kanem established control over the trade route between Kanem and Egypt via Sai Island (between Dongola and the second cataract). Judging by a glass window pane found there, this could have been as early as A.D. 700.[19]

This discovery led Arkell to consider that the Tunjur were probably an offshoot of the Christian Nubian kingdom of Makuria, whose rule in Dār Fūr was brought to an end in the thirteenth century by Kanem rather than in the sixteenth by Bornu.[20] Other fragments of Nubian type pottery of the Christian period have since been found in the Chad Baḥr al-Ghazāl, so that it is becoming very likely that there was some Nubian activity, possibly trade, during the Christian period in the Dār Fūr/Chad region, but the evidence is still very slim.[21]

In the absence of archaeological investigation in Dār Fūr, especially at 'Ayn Farāḥ, it is difficult to go much further than Arkell has taken us. But it may be possible to take an analysis of the traditions a little further.

Central to all versions is Aḥmad al-Ma'qūr, who as the 'Wise Stranger' appears to serve as a device legitimizing the take-over by the Keira from the Tunjur. The theme of the 'Wise Stranger' is widespread in the Sudanic belt; he comes to a remote and barbarous land, introduces new customs, often associated with eating, and marries the chief's daughter and their descendants rule but in a different style and under another dynastic name.[22] But because of later preoccupations, the traditions usually emphasize the Muslim aspect of the 'Wise Stranger' and describe his distinctive innovation as the introduction of Islam, but one may ask if he does not, in his religious guise, conceal another innovation of greater importance for state formation, namely the beginnings of long distance trade. Thus it may be that we have subsumed in the traditions concerning Aḥmad 'the hamstringed' the memory of a series of events, which probably took place over a considerable period of time; the immigration of a Muslim person or group, although Islam need not be emphasized, their marriage alliance with a local chief to exploit trade possibilities, and the beginnings of political expansion and of contacts with the outside world.

Is there a Nubian substratum behind the Aḥmad al-Maʿqūr legend? By the eighteenth century most of the traders in the Dār Fūr/Kordofan region and as far west as Wadai were Arabized Nubian Muslims from the Nile, mainly Jaʿaliyīn and Danāqla, and there is, as we have seen, some archaeological evidence that Nubians had been active in the region many centuries before then. It may be in the movements of Nubians as traders away from the Nile, prompted by political insecurity and pressure on the land in the river valley, that the origin of the 'Wise Stranger' should be sought.[23]

Al-Zubayr, the conqueror of Dār Fūr in 1874, and Rābiḥ Faḍlallāh, who had an even more grandiose career of conquest in West Africa, were probably only the latest in a line of riverain Sudanese traders who turned state-builders in alliance with local rulers. In the traditions on the origins of Wadai there is a clear memory of Nubian involvement; Ṣāliḥ or ʿAbd al-Karīm is described as the grandson of a Jaʿalī. The small state of Dār Qimr, between Dār Fūr and Wadai, is also said to have been founded by a Jaʿalī, Qimr b. Ḥasaballāh, from al-Matamma on the Nile.[24]

There are also in Dār Fūr two peoples, the Meidob and Birged, who speak or spoke in recent times, languages of the Nubian group and who have traditions of migration from the

Nile. Neither, however, claim any connexion with the Tunjur or Aḥmad al-Ma'qūr.[25]

But there is, as yet, no evidence to link the Tunjur empire with a Nubian diaspora, despite the archaeological indications, beyond the vague traditions that the Tunjur came from the east, nor to suggest that they, at least in Dār Fūr, have ever spoken any language other than Arabic.[26] In the absence of any certain evidence we can only speculate that the scale of the remains associated with the Tunjur dynasty may reflect a trading empire in the Dār Fur and Wadai region built through Nubian initiative.

If, however, this Tunjur state is to be associated with the Christian Nubian pottery from 'Ayn Farāḥ, at a period well before the thirteenth century, as Arkell suggests, it becomes difficult to explain the collapse, following the traditions, of a Tunjur empire at the beginning of the seventeenth.[27] Such a long-lived state would surely have attracted some notice by the Arab geographers. But if the traditions and the D'Anania reference are accepted, one may suggest that following the break-up of a Tunjur state, presumably after about 1580, local groups in Wadai and Dār Fūr began to link up with the traders to create their own imperial and commercial networks. In Wadai this change is linked with the Islamic propaganda of 'Abd al-Karīm, although one of his companions was called *al-jallābī*, 'the merchant'.[28] In Dār Fūr the events surrounding the change of dynasty were more complex.

VIII · The rise of the Keira

The Keira sultan, Ibrāhīm b. Muḥammad al-Ḥusayn, who was killed unsuccessfully defending his state in 1874, was only seven generations removed from Sulaymān, the first historical Keira sultan, who, as is argued below, probably ruled about the middle of the seventeenth century. Concerning the Keira kings between Sulaymān and Daali, 'the father of the Fur', *jadd al-Fūr*, the traditions are very confused, but taking an average of the regnal lists we have, the period between them would appear to be about eight generations.[1] This may suggest, although it cannot be proved, that a Fur or Keira kingdom existed in Jabal Marra as early as the fifteenth century and therefore was contemporary with the Tunjur empire in northern Dār Fūr.

If this supposition is correct, then the traditions concerning the origins of the Keira state may be interpreted in the following manner. The Keira clan, who came from the Kunjara section of the Fur people, ruled a kingdom in Jabal Marra which formed part of the Tunjur empire, to whose ruling dynasty they may have been connected by dynastic marriage. Sometime after about 1580 (d'Anania's reference) but before 1660 when the name Fur first appears in contemporary records, the Tunjur state collapsed and the Keira expanded rapidly to fill the vacuum.

The ambiguity of Aḥmad al-Maʻqūr's relationship to the Tunjur and Keira thus may conceal the fact that the two dynasties were related. It may not be too fanciful to note that the names Tunjur and Kunjara could form a singular/plural pair in Fur.[2] Their Tunjur connexions were naturally soon forgotten by the Keira, particularly if they also arrogated to themselves traditions concerning immigrants from the Nile – the other aspect of the Aḥmad al-Maʿqūr cycle – which had originally belonged to the Tunjur. But the Tunjur connexion was not forgotten in Wadai, since the latter continued to pay to the Keira the tribute formerly paid to the Tunjur.[3]

This interpretation of the traditions, although admittedly speculative, would help to explain the shadowy nature of the pre-Sulaymānic Fur traditions, belonging as they do to a Fur tribal chiefdom, about which in the time of later imperial and Islamic splendour it was convenient to forget. It would also explain the apparently very rapid spread of Keira power under Sulaymān and his immediate successors in the latter part of the seventeenth century. Heirs to an imperial tradition, they were expanding to take control of a Tunjur trading network and empire that had existed in the recent past.

The Jabal Marra kingdom

In the northern part of Jabal Marra around Turra, there are a series of ruins associated by local tradition with a line of Keira rulers, Daali, Kuuruu, Tunsam, Sulaymān, his son Mūsā, and Mūsā's son, Ahmad Bukr.[4] Turra was the cradle of the Keira state, where most of the later sultans were buried.[5] It never lost its sanctity in Keira eyes; when in 1200/1785–6 the great sultan Muḥammad Tayrāb died on campaign in Kordofan, over 400 miles to the east, his body was carefully embalmed and brought back to Turra for burial.[6] Even the consciously Islamizing sultans of the nineteenth century continued to venerate Turra; before the annual 'Covering of the kettledrums' festival, officials were customarily sent to offer sacrifices at the tombs of both the pagan and early Muslim Keira rulers.[7]

Daali, in one of Nachtigal's versions, is described as the son of Aḥmad al-Maʿqūr and the first ruler of the Keira line, who established some of the most fundamental Keira institutions. From the sacred tree, *numaŋ fadda*, at Turra, he divided the state into the provinces of *dār daali* (east), *dār aba uuma* (south-east), *dār aba diima* (south-west), *dār al-gharb* (west) and *dār al-takanyāwī* (north). From its Arabic name, *dār al-gharb* sounds like a later innovation; possibly it was established following Aḥmad Bukr's campaigns in the west. If this is so, and *dār al-gharb* never had much administrative reality, the four remaining provinces recall the quadrant provincial organization of Kanem/Bornu, as Arkell has pointed out,[8] but they may simply be an inheritance from the Tunjur. These provinces remained the essential territorial units of Keira administration until they were overshadowed but not superseded by the maqdūmate system in the nineteenth century.

Daali is also credited with the codification of the laws and customs of the Keira kingdom in the so-called 'book of Daali', *kitāb dālī.* According to Nachtigal, these laws were in no way based upon the Sharī'a, 'but rather on an effort to secure power and an income for the ruler and his officials, and to bind the two more closely together'.[9] Punishment was solely by fine, either of cattle or rolls of cloth, called *takkīya* (pl. *takākī*), the latter being in many parts of Dār Fūr the main unit of payment throughout the history of the sultanate. Arkell saw several manuscripts that purported to be the *kitāb dālī* and concluded that Daali's code was an attempt to reconcile Fur custom with the Sharī'a according to the Mālikī school, which was the form adopted in Dār Fūr.[10]

Among the complex of ruins at Turra, *toŋ daali* ('Daali's house or palace') at Jabal Foga is a large, roughly circular compound, containing blocks of circular stone-built rooms. Nearby is *toŋ kuuri*, the palace of Kuuruu, a successor of Daali who is usually described as the father of Sulaymān, a large compound, over a hundred yards in diameter, with particularly massive walls. At Jabal Naami, the most conspicuous peak at Turra, is another, seemingly more complex, compound associated with Sulaymān and his son Mūsā. Arkell, who alone has described the Turra ruins, discerned a decline in the quality of building from the well-constructed *toŋ daali* to the more massive but clumsier *toŋ kuuri* and *toŋ kiilo* (the palace of Sulaymān). This, he suggested, can be explained by supposing *toŋ daali* to be the work of foreigners and to civil war and upheaval in the time of Kuuruu and Sulaymān.[11]

This interpretation is supported in part by the traditions recorded by Nachtigal. After Daali there was a long period of confusion and conflict; ten kings are said to have followed Daali in rapid succession. Nachtigal interpreted the accounts he was given to mean that Kuuruu did not actually reign at Turra, but whether he did or not, it was in his time that a major split occurred in the Keira clan. Kuuruu is said to have quarrelled with his brother, Tunsam (a name later Arabicized to Tumsāḥ, 'crocodile') over some land in Dār Fia, west of the mountains, and was forced to flee with his young son, Sulaymān, to Dār Masālit in the west. There Sulaymān grew up among his mother's people, the Serbung section of the Masālīt, until he was strong enough to wrest back Jabal Marra from his uncle. Tunsam and his followers fled the Jabal Marra region and migrated to the east, probably to the border country between Dār Fūr and Kordofan, becoming known as the Musabba'āt, according to popular etymology, 'the people of the east' (from *ṣabāḥ*, 'morning, east'). The Musabba'āt did not forget their claims and were, over the next century, to seize whatever opportunities they could to try to oust the Keira.[12]

Sulaymān's predecessors, Dali, Kuuruu and the others whose names appear in the regnal lists, and indeed Sulaymān himself, remain shadowy figures, who were only remembered in traditions first written down 200 years later. Nor can we safely disentangle the traditions concerning them from those concerning the Tunjur; indeed the civil war among the Keira that led to the migration of the Musabba'āt may be connected with the collapse of the Tunjur empire. Until the palaces at Turra are excavated, we can only note that the traditions credit

Daali with the establishment of the Keira state and are unanimous in regarding Sulaymān, several generations later, as the second founder of that state.

Sulaymān and Mūsā

Sulaymān Sɔlɔ̄ŋduŋɔ 'the Arab' or 'of reddish complexion', so called either because of his complexion[13] or because of his alleged descent from Aḥmad al-Maʿqūr, reigned probably between 1660 and 1680.[14] Although Fur tradition remembers little about Sulaymān's deeds beyond vague generalities, it is clear that he and his grandson, Aḥmad Bukr, were responsible for the transformation of their Fur tribal kingdom into a multi-ethnic empire in succession to the Tunjur.

A few contemporary records appear to confirm this rapid emergence of the Fur and to suggest the cause or motive, the maintenance of the long-distance caravan trade with Egypt and the riverain Sudan across the desert that had probably been initiated by the Tunjur. By the end of the seventeenth century this trade was well established.

In 1663 the Dominican traveller in Egypt, Vansleb (or Wansleben), reported that,

> To the west of Cairo lies the land of Fur (Fohr), to which caravans repair frequently in order to purchase slaves. Its Sultan resides in Ogra. The present sultan is called Uriz-mellis. When the *kafīla* (caravan, goes there from Cairo, it comes by way of Kab, Dago and Issueine to Fur in one and a half months. From that country it brings as goods, ostrich feathers, tamarind, elephant tusks, pitch-black male and female slaves, and even little children.[15]

Vansleb describes also the sale of slaves, who were tattooed, in Cairo; to entice would-be buyers, the women were put up for sale naked, although for the Europeans it was a case of 'noli me tangere'. 'The one and a half months' fits the later name for the desert route from Upper Egypt to Dār Fūr, the *darb al-arbaʿīn*, 'the forty days road'.[16] However neither Ogra nor a sultan called Urizmellis can be identified, although *ari*, an archaic form of the Fur title for their king, *aba kuuri*, may possibly be detected in the name. That the trade route was in regular use by the end of the seventeenth century seems confirmed by the account of some Franciscan missionaries on their way to Sinnār; in September 1689 they were at the Kharja oasis, the first main stage on the desert route from Egypt, where they saw merchants, some of whom were preparing to go to Dongola, Sinnār and Ethiopia, while others were preparing to set off to the kingdom of Fur (regno di Fur).[17]

Contacts, both commercial and political, between Dār Fūr and the Nile valley begin to appear in the records from the mid-seventeenth century on. Krump reported trade between Sinnār and Dār Fūr, while slaves belonging to the *faqīh* Ḥasan b. Ḥasūna (died 1075/1664–5) are said to have traded for him in Dār Fūr.[18] In the Dongola revolt of 1705–6 the rebel leaders appear to have been supported by Danāqla merchants based in Dār Fūr.[19]

Sulaymān is remembered in the traditions as a warrior and conqueror; in one version he is said to have led thirty-three campaigns, conquering the Masālīt, Oro and Marārīt to the west, the Zaghāwa to the north and the Birged, Beigo and Tunjur to the south and east. The frontiers of his kingdom are said to have stretched as far north as the deserts where the Bideyāt nomads lived and as far east as the Atbara river.[20] This is too sweeping to be likely and has no support from the Nile valley records. But the Fur seem to have been raiding into Kordofan; a raiding party was captured by the Banī Jarrār Arabs and taken to the *faqīh* Ḥammad b. Umm Maryūm (1055–1142/1646–1729/30), who lived near the confluence of the two Niles. They were converted to Islam and sent back to their country, 'probably to act as missionaries'.[21]

The motive for Sulaymān's conquests or raids was probably to increase his catchment area for the trade items, pre-eminently slaves, he could barter with the merchants from Egypt and the riverain Sudan for arms and armour, horses from Dongola and fine cloth, with which to reward, arm and encourage his followers and chiefs.

The Keira kings of Jabal Marra were essentially divine kings on the common African model, as were the rulers of Sinnār and probably of Nubia before them. What is not known is whether the Keira chiefs took over any of the ritual and customs of 'divine' kingship from the Tunjur or whether those customs, described in a later chapter, were part of their Fur inheritance. Divine kingship can be learnt very quickly; the Feroge of the western Baḥr al-Ghazāl, below Dār Fūr, created in the nineteenth century a Keira-like state in imitation of the slave raiders from the north.[22] Unlike Sinnār, the Keira sultans never lost their divine aura, although it became transformed under the impact of Islam.

The traditions credit Sulaymān with the introduction of Islam as the state cult, with building mosques for his subjects and encouraging Islamic practices.[23] The traditional accounts are ambiguous on the religious affiliations of the Tunjur and the early Keira kings – they may have been pagan – and some versions stress Sulaymān's religious innovations.

> He preached Islam in Jabal Marra and after several conversions, also converted *malik* Dukkume, chief of the Tomourki (a Fur section), whom he circumcised with a razor that he had brought from Cairo and which had to do for several thousand people.[24]

But the Islamization of the Keira state was a slow process; pre-Islamic beliefs co-existed at the court with Islam and continued to be expressed in the state rituals throughout the history of the state, although some were to be discontinued as the influence of Islam grew and the old religious beliefs came to be frowned upon. As in the riverain Sudan, the slow spread of Islam may be attributed to the itinerant holy men. The relationship between the holy men and the secular power was to be enshrined later in legal formulas, the granting of lands, rights and tax immunities, and the building of mosques, but in the earlier period it was probably more informal.

Several Dār Fūr holy families have traditions that their ancestors settled in the sultanate in the time of Sulaymān. One such was the Jawāmi'a *fuqarā'* family of Azagarfa, north of al-Fāshir, whose ancestor, Ḥāmid b. 'Abdallāh, came from the east and was invited to settle in Dār Fūr by Sulaymān. Later they moved to Azagarfa where Sultan Muḥammad al-Fadl (1215–45/1801–38) built them a mosque that still stands.[25] Near to Azagarfa at Arāri is another Jawāmi'a family who trace themselves back through twelve generations to one Aḥmad, who, it is said, was given land at Arāri by Show Dorshid, the grant later being confirmed by Sulaymān.[26] Another Jawāmi'a family whose ancestor came either in Sulaymān's time or that of his son, Mūsā, were the *imāms* of Turra. Their ancestor, Idrīs, who came from Kordofan, was granted land at Turra as *imām* of the mosque there with responsibility for the royal tombs, and the position and land has been in the family ever since.[27] In the examples given here, Jawāmi'a probably does not have an ethnic connotation, but simply means 'people of the Mosque' (Ar. *jāmi'*, 'mosque').

Sulaymān's position as the 'founding father' of the Keira state is stressed not only in the oral traditions but on the seals of the later sultans, who invariably trace their pedigree back to Sulaymān and no further; on one he is called 'the pious and bountiful lord' (*ṣāḥib al-birr wa'l-aḥsān*).[28] His son and successor, Mūsā, is a more shadowy figure. The confusion of the regnal lists at this point probably reflects a confused reign, while the paucity of traditions about Mūsā suggests a short one. Nachtigal records Mūsā fighting the Qimr of western Dār Fūr with little success and the Musabba'āt with greater success, the latter being defeated in two battles at Ṭinna and Kolge near Jabal Marra. Like his father, Mūsā was buried at Turra.[29]

IX · The imperial age

About 1700 the Keira chiefs ruled as sacred kings over a Fur state, but one which was rapidly embracing many other ethnic groups. The Fur were apparently ruled through a hierarchy of Fur office-holders and, although some non-Fur groups, seemingly of slave status, were physically moved into the Fur area and largely acculturated, in the main the other ethnic groups were ruled through their own chiefs.[1]

Islam probably did not loom very large at their court, even if nominal allegiance was given to it. However, by the end of the eighteenth century, the *aba kuuri*, 'the lord of obeisance', had also become 'Sultan of Dār Fūr, model of the Muslim princes, successor of the Prophet of God, the example of justice and piety, guardian of the two holy places (i.e. Mecca and Medina).[2] The Keira chiefs were to become, in the course of the century, Muslim rulers, albeit on the fringes of the Islamic world, ruling in part through the Sharīʿa and legitimizing their position, when under threat from the outside world, by reference to Islamic principles.[3]

Given the paucity of our information on the eighteenth century – even the chronology of the sultans is uncertain – the process whereby the Keira sultan's position was enlarged and changed is imperfectly known. Nor can the underlying social and economic patterns be documented, since, for the period 1660 to 1790, we have no contemporary accounts to balance the central court traditions. Thus, until the oral traditions of the other ethnic groups within the state and of the religious families are collected, our account must be largely a chronicle of the Keira sultans and their activities.

The expansion of the state

Whatever the range of Sulaymān's raids or conquests, expansion beyond the immediate area of Jabal Marra is associated with Aḥmad Bukr. Bukr is described as the youngest son of Mūsā who replaced the eldest son, Giggeri, because the latter was an epileptic and therefore ineligible for the throne; he ruled probably in the early years of the eighteenth century.[4] Although the chronology of his conquests is difficult to determine, their direction is easier to reconstruct. The natural direction in which to advance from the mountains was westwards, where the gentle and well-watered foothills lead onto a plain that extends to Wadai. Thus Bukr moved west and then north; this progress is reflected in the location of his *fāshirs* or royal encampments. These were successively at Gurri in Dār Kerne, immediately to the west of Jabal Marra, at Murra in Dār Fia, farther to the north, and perhaps as an inaccessible refuge in the time of the Wadai war, Jabal Abū ʿAsal near Turra, where there is a small rectangular building of red brick associated with Bukr.[5]

Nachtigal records that Bukr in a series of campaigns conquered the small but strategically located state of Dār Qimr, north of Dār Masālīt and east of Dār Tāma.[6] The Qimr rulers, the Miggi, seem to have extended their power widely over the Zaghāwa nomads to the north and east, and to the south around Jabal Mūn.[7] Some of the Miggi clan seem later to have sought refuge in Sinnār.[8]

The conquest of Dār Qimr may have been part of a wider Keira penetration into Zaghāwa country. We do not know when the earliest contacts between the Keira and Zaghāwa were, but we can speculate on the former's motive in wishing to control the latter. The Zaghāwa lands lay across the southern end of the caravan route from Upper Egypt and because of the harshness and poverty of their country they were, as they still are, constantly forced south and interacting, not always peacefully, with the settled peoples.[9] Their chiefdoms lay in an arc across the north of Wadai and Dār Fūr, with Zaghāwa Kobe in the centre. Kobe marked the frontier and area of conflict between the two sultanates; east of Kobe, the Keira became paramount, in Kobe their hold was more tenuous.[10]

Keira penetration into Dār Zaghāwa was characterized by marriage alliances and by support for one chiefly faction against another; thus it was probably Aḥmad Bukr who first gave the more prestigious *naḥās* or copper kettledrum to the Kobe chief, Tā b. Kwōre, to replace the wooden *diŋer*. He also married into Tā's clan, the *aŋu*, since his son sultan Muḥammad Tayrāb was nephew to Kharūt, a later Kobe sultan. Each year after the rains, a caravan left Kobe for the Keira court taking as tribute horses, cattle and sheep; in return, the Keira sultan sent gifts of horses – presumably imported war horses – and clothes.[11]

East of Kobe, Keira penetration was probably related to the rise of the title-holder, the *takanyāwī*. The title's origin is obscure. Similar-sounding titles were used by different peoples in Dār Fūr; among the Daju the *togonye* was a ritual expert associated with rainmaking, among the Fur a similar figure was called *tɔgɔn* and in Kobe *takanyon* (or *taganyaw*) was the title given by ʿAbdallāh Bōrū, founder of the *aŋu* royal clan to the *mira* clan chief whom he had dispossessed. The *takanyon* was second-in-command to the Kobe sultan, living and eating with him.[12] Because of the title's links with the north, it probably had its roots in Tunjur times; the *Konyuŋa* clan who held the title claimed to be Tunjur in origin.[13]

A late tradition says that Bukr quarrelled with his *takanyāwī*, described as a sort of chamberlain to the sultan, as in Kobe, and had him executed. He then appointed one of the dead man's sons as governor of the north with the same title. If the *takanyāwī* was originally a ritual expert, the tradition may conceal a crisis within the state with religious implications and the appointment a banishment from court.[14] The *takanyāwī*'s capital was at Tandalti, east of Jabal Marra on the Wādī al-Kū‘, where al-Fāshir was later established; they ruled in northern Dār Fūr until the mid-nineteenth century when the title faded away in the face of a new title-holding family, the *maqdūms* of *dār al-rīḥ*.

Some Zaghāwa resisted; Muḥammad Fa'it of the Agaba, the ruling clan of the Tuer Zaghāwa, rebelled against Bukr. He was eventually killed by Bukr's successor, Muḥammad Dawra, who permanently weakened the Agaba by cutting off Dār Beiri and the Anka wells from their land and giving them to the *Kaitiŋa*, a branch of the *takanyāwī*'s clan. Another Zaghāwa chief, ‘Ubayd of the Awlād Dawra, chose flight and led his people to Kajmar in northern Kordofan, where their descendants still live.[15]

The Keira conquests under Bukr may have provoked the invasion by Wadai that came towards the end of his reign. Both states sought to control the borderlands between them, but Dār Fūr, which appears to have emerged first from the debris of the Tunjur empire, was regarded as the senior state, and Wadai continued to pay the tribute formerly paid to the Tunjur. Wadai under a line of vigorous rulers appears to have grown rapidly, and Sultan Ya‘qūb renounced the tribute and invaded Dār Fūr. He reached as far as Kabkābīya, on the way to the Kawra pass through Jabal Marra. Meanwhile Bukr, who had retreated to Abū ‘Asal, brought in firearms and weapons from Egypt and made an alliance with Baqirmi to attack Wadai in the rear. After two years of preparations he swept down from the mountains and drove the Wadai army out of Kabkābīya, whose name *kebi kebia* ‘they threw their shields down’ commemorates his victory, and out of Dār Fūr.[16] But this was only the first round in a series of wars between the two states.

Bukr is said to have died on campaign against the Musabba‘āt in Kordofan, although another tradition has it that the cause of his campaign was some abusive remarks made about him by

Sultan Bādī of Sinnār. But while on the march, the noted *faqīh* Khujalī b. ʻAbd al-Raḥmān appeared to the sultan in a vision. As a result of the vision or curse, Bukr died shortly after.[17]

By the time of Bukr's death about 1730, the Keira sultanate had begun to reach very approximately the boundaries of the present province of Dār Fūr – an area of about 140,000 square miles. But Keira control east of the mountains was probably still tenuous and to the south among the Baqqāra non-existent. The use of cavalry and Fur levies, the security provided by the Jabal Marra base and control over the most fertile and populated part of Dār Fūr and perhaps an imperial heritage from the Tunjur all contributed to this rapid expansion. But the traditional accounts tell us little of the details of the Keira conquests or how their new subjects were incorporated into the Keira state.

The sons of Aḥmad Bukr[18]

The political history of Dār Fūr from the death of Bukr to the accession of the last of his sons to rule, ʻAbd al-Raḥmān (from *c.* 1730 to 1204/1789–90) was dominated by a struggle within the ruling dynasty between those Keira who sought to strengthen the position of the clan as a whole and those who, as sultans, sought to centralize power in their hands. To ensure the continuity of the central authority, the sultans attempted to establish *pre-mortem* lineal succession, through the institution of the *khalīfa* or nominated successor; the rest of the Keira fought against this development, in effect for a more diffuse system of power. But our information is insufficient for us to analyse the significance of these conflicts or to determine how the various contenders mobilized support or what was the nature of that support, except in the case of the Musabbaʻāt, or indeed why one contender was successful and another not.

A tradition from al-Tūnisī says that the formal cause of

these conflicts was that Bukr, on his deathbed, made the assembled notables of the state swear an oath that they would ensure that the sultanate pass to each of his sons in turn, beginning with Muḥammad Dawra.[19] Upon succeeding as sultan, Dawra ruthlessly set about eliminating as many of his brothers as possible, either killing them or imprisoning them in Jabal Marra. Eventually his son, Mūsā ʻAnqarīb, led a revolt against his father. It seems that Dawra had originally nominated Mūsā as *khalīfa*, but then began to favour another son, ʻUmar Lel (Fur, ʻdonkey'). Mūsā and his partisans were successful in battle and so his father asked some *fuqarā'* to intervene, including one from Katsina and ʻAlī b. Yūsuf al-Fūtūwi, the founder of a line of noted Fulani holy men. But this first recorded intervention of the *fuqarā'* in Keira politics ended inauspiciously; they made the sultan swear on the Qur'ān not to harm his son, but at a meeting Dawra tricked and murdered Mūsā.[20]

ʻUmar Lel, who succeeded his father after the latter's death from leprosy, faced such hostility from his uncles, the sons of, or Awlād Bukr, that he appears to have contemplated abdication. The account of this episode, given in Shuqayr, says that ʻUmar was a just and pious man, who after three days as sultan told his council that he wished to abdicate in favour of one of his uncles, since the burden of the sultanate was greater than he could bear. He was prevailed upon to stay on the throne and executed a few corrupt officials at the gates of his *fāshir* as a warning to the rest. Apart from the hostility of his uncles, ʻUmar as a devout Muslim may have had scruples about ruling what was still a largely pagan state.[21]

But the hostility between nephew and uncles remained, a hostility that perhaps had its roots in the very success of the Keira. As the state grew, so the clan and territorial chiefs such as the *abbo konyuŋa*, whose clan had acquired great power in the north, the *aba diimaŋ*, who ruled *dār aba diima*, and the *aba uumaŋ* of *dār aba uuma* and others had grown more powerful, and the stakes for which they contended were much greater than before as land, women and booty came into their hands. The basis of their power and the military strength of the state appears to have been the Fur levies they could mobilize, the *jureŋa* or young men called out in each locality under a war leader, *ɔrnaŋ*, for military service.[22] Armed with the *sambal* or iron throwing knife, the *jureŋa* must have been an effective force in the area around the mountains.[23]

In the course of expansion, the interests of the sultans began insensibly to diverge from those of their Fur supporters and chiefs. On the plains small bodies of horsemen equipped with imported arms and armour were more useful than the *jureŋa*, and to reap the profits of empire, particularly from trade, the sultans needed to concentrate more and more power in their hands, a process that could not fail to bring clashes with the title-holders. This development intensified conflicts within the Keira clan; ʻUmar Lel imprisoned his uncle, Abu'l-Qāsim, because he was 'the most dangerous of the other claimants to the throne, who had a large popular following because of his liberality and chivalrous disposition'.[24]

The conflict widened; two of ʻUmar's uncles, Pelpelle and Sulaymān al-Abyad, escaped to Kordofan, where they took refuge with the Musabbaʻāt sultan, ʻĪsāwī b. Janqal, whose father had unsuccessfully fought Mūsā.

The Musabbaʻāt, unable to maintain themselves in Dār Fūr, except for some who made their peace with the Keira, had infiltrated into the Dār Fūr/Kordofan borderlands, the area roughly between Umm Kiddāda and al-Nuhūd. Some from their ruling clan, the Basna, under Khamīs b. Janqal, moved farther east and took service with Sinnār, but others gathered around them adherents from both Kordofan and Dār Fūr and began to play a part in the politics of the area.[25]

ʻĪsāwī and Sulaymān al-Abyaḍ joined forces to invade that part of Kordofan held by the Funj; at the battle of Qiḥayf the Sinnār forces were decisively defeated.[26] ʻĪsāwī appears to have received Sulaymān's support in exchange for help in ousting 'Umar from Dār Fūr. To provoke the Keira sultan, the Musabba'āt leader wrote to him demanding, since he was about to bestow his father's wives and concubines on the leading Dār Fūr notables, that 'Īsāwī be given 'Umar's mother, a demand outrageous both politically and morally. The enraged sultan promptly invaded Kordofan, causing the Musabba'āt sultan to flee to Sinnār, but giving Sulaymān the chance to slip into Dār Fūr.[27]

Sulaymān is said to have sought the aid of the Rizayqāt; if so, this was the first appearance of this most warlike and independent of the cattle-keeping tribes in Keira affairs. Sulaymān defeated a force under the slave official, the *āb shaykh* Baraka, but was finally brought to battle by the sultan, who had hurriedly returned from Kordofan, at Kalamboa in Dār Birged and there defeated and killed.[28]

Apparently Sulaymān had been promised military support by Wadai, which, however, did not come in time. In retaliation 'Umar Lel, probably in 1166/1752–3, invaded Wadai, but before leaving on campaign he released Abu'l-Qāsim from confinement. The traditions imply that 'Umar was so sickened by the precariousness of his position that he deliberately sought a soldier's death in Wadai.[29]

'Umar sent two armies ahead into Wadai, one under the *aba diimaŋ* and *aba uumaŋ*, the other under the *abbo konyuŋa*. Although one of the Dār Fūr armies was successful, the other was defeated. Thereupon the two sultans joined their forces and in a final battle 'Umar found himself deserted by his army and was captured. He spent his captivity at Abū Kundi in Wadai, 'where he spent his days in reading the Quran and now lies buried there'.[30]

The defeat and capture of 'Umar led to a confused period in Dār Fūr, in which Abu'l-Qāsim was able to seize power. In the confusion 'Īsāwī and the Musabba'āt tried once more to intervene, although whether on his own behalf or for a Keira claimant is not recorded. He advanced into eastern Dār Fūr, but was beaten by Abu'l-Qāsim at Rīl, northeast of the modern Nyala, and driven back to Kordofan.

The conflict continued into Abu'l-Qāsim's reign, although he was a stronger man than his nephew. Although one of the Awlād Bukr, he soon turned against his brothers and tried to strengthen his position by recruiting slave troops instead of the Fur levies and outsiders instead of the title-holders; 'he completely alienated himself from the free men of the country, preferring slaves and heaping upon them riches and places of honour'.[31] He appointed as his *wazīr* a Zaghāwa man called Baḥr; this appointment angered the Fur title-holders rather as Bādī IV's reliance on Khamīs b. Janqal, at about the same time, angered the Funj nobility.

Against this background of discontent, Abu'l-Qāsim planned to invade Wadai to revenge 'Umar Lel's defeat. But even his preparations caused trouble, since he levied an additional tax of a cow from each household throughout the state to support the war. The sultan invaded Wadai, but at the crucial battle further insulted the Fur title-holders, whom he had very good reason to mistrust, by putting them in the second rank behind his slave troops and the *wazīr* Baḥr's men. The Fur promptly deserted the sultan, crying out, it is said, 'Children of Fur, take to flight, for only flight can save us. Desert Abu'l-Qāsim, let the cows he has taken from us and the Zaghāwī, Baḥr, fight for him.'[32] The sultan was wounded and left for dead on the battlefield, the Fur joining the fight only to rescue the sacred drum, *al-manṣūra*, 'the victorious', which was in danger of being carried off by the Wadaians.

After the battle, the title-holders nominated as sultan Muḥammad Tayrāb b. Aḥmad Bukr. But Abu'l-Qāsim was not dead; he had been found and nursed back to health by a member of the Maḥāmīd tribe who as nomads wandered between Dār Fūr and Wadai. When the former sultan reappeared in Dār Fūr his brother wanted to abdicate, but the title-holders opposed this and Abu'l-Qāsim was put to death. Nachtigal's account of the secret strangling of the former sultan and of his sister, Zamzam Sendi Suttera, by a man from Dār Tāma called Wīr has ritual overtones.[33] Wīr was rewarded with the title, *abbo daadiŋa*, with responsibility for the markets and for executions ordered by the sultan. The *abbo daadiŋas* who succeeded Wīr were notable soldiers and commanded the *daadiŋa* regiment of the sultan's slave troops.[34]

The desertion and killing of Abu'l-Qāsim was the high point of the resistance of the title-holders to the sultans' attempts to centralize power. Thereafter their position relative to the sultan declined as he and the new forces gathered around his court grew stronger, and Tayrāb, a man of powerful personality, decisively shifted the balance in his favour.

Tayrāb and the conquest of Kordofan

The defeat of Abu'l-Qasim led to a species of peace between Dār Fūr and Wadai which lasted nearly a hundred years, despite border raids and intrigues. Tayrāb is said to have made a formal treaty with his Wadai counterpart, and the border was delimited by a demilitarized zone marked, in part, by stone cairns and walls, known as the *tirja*, 'the barrier'.[35] Wadai had proved too strong, and if the Keira were to continue to expand, and the internal tensions provided the goad to further conquest, it would have to be in the east. The change of direction, which is discernible in the latter part of the eighteenth century, was probably not a simple consequence of military stalemate in the west, but part of a wider opening of the sultanate to contacts and influences from the Nile valley. The coming of holy men and adventurers from the Nile and increasing trade links with Egypt coincided with military expansion eastwards leading to the conquest of Kordofan, and to the further strengthening of the sultan's position *vis-à-vis* the traditional elements within the state.

The growth in the sultan's power is difficult to document, but the main factor was the transformation, through conquest, of the state from a Fur tribal concern into a multi-ethnic sultanate open to new influences from the outside, in which the Fur were no longer so prominent. Geographically this change is reflected in the shift of the *fāshirs*, first down onto the plains west of Jabal Marra, then to the east of the mountains, culminating in the establishment of al-Fāshir by Tayrāb's successor, 'Abd al-Raḥmān. Since most of the Fur lived west or south of the mountains, this move served to weaken or modify their ties with the sultan, and it is from Tayrāb's reign that we hear less of the Fur title-holders who had apparently dominated the state so far.

The title-holders miscalculated when they nominated Tayrāb. They had objected to Abu'l-Qāsim because, among other aggravations, he had employed a Zaghāwī as his *wazīr*; Tayrāb's mother was from the Kobe royal clan, whom he now began to bring into the title-holders' ranks. He confirmed his maternal uncle, Kharūt b. Hilān, as the Kobe sultan and gave court titles to two of Kharūt's sons; 'Umar was made *ɔrreŋ duluŋ* (Fur, 'doorposts'), responsible for the security of the *fāshir* and the main intermediary between the sultan and his subjects, and Ḥasīb *abbo irliŋo*, whose honorary task was to place the turban on the sultan during the accession rituals, but who also ruled the Tunjur and Mīma. The Zaghāwa connexion continued into the next generation since the mother of Tayrāb's son and *khalīfa*, Isḥāq, was from the Tuer Zaghāwa.[36]

In the early years of his reign, Tayrāb had his *fāshir* at Shōba near Kabkābīya, where he built a palace and mosque of red brick and where he settled various Fur groups.[37] But probably about 1770 he moved across the mountains to Rīl in the southeast, leaving Isḥāq to govern western Dār Fūr from Shōba.[38] The sultans never moved back permanently across the mountains.

From Rīl, Tayrāb consolidated Keira rule in eastern Dār Fūr, although the area, ethnically diverse, never achieved the same administrative stability as the west. The consolidation either caused or resulted from sporadic rebellions against Keira rule. The Birged, a loose conglomeration of petty chieftancies in the plain between al-Fāshir and the Baqqāra to the south, are said to have rebelled because they thought Tayrāb was selling to the slave merchants the girls they sent to his court as concubines or servants.[39] They probably did not object to sending some of their daughters as such, since one could well become the mother of the next sultan, as in the case of Tayrāb and Kobe. Tayrāb began to suppress the petty Birged chiefdoms, Musku, Adawa, Doleaba and Muḥajirīya in favour of larger units under his own nominees. Thus he gave large tracts of Birged country to a Kinānī Arab from the Blue Nile, Sulaymān b. Aḥmad Jaffāl, who had pleased the sultan by his skill in the treatment of horses. Later when Tayrāb was preparing to invade Kordofan, he gave further parts of Dār Birged to Sulaymān. By the reign of ʻAbd al-Raḥmān, Sulaymān ruled as *sharṭay* or chief over most of the Birged in the area now called Dār Kajjar.[40]

It was from Rīl that Tayrāb set out to bring the Rizayqāt to heel in a series of expeditions, but as the Keira army moved south the nomads simply withdrew farther south to the Baḥr al-ʻArab and beyond.[41] Military expansion and a joint interest in slave raiding the pagans of the south brought the Keira into contact with the cattle-nomads, but the sultans were never able to deal with them satisfactorily.[42] Their failure was to have disastrous consequences in the next century.

Al-Tūnisī implies that Tayrāb invaded Kordofan to remove from Dār Fūr those of the Awlād Bukr opposed to him and the succession of his son, Isḥāq.[43] But with the weakening of the Funj, central Kordofan was an attractive prize; the gum trade and the alluvial gold and slaves from the south all passed through the commercial centres of Bāra and al-Ubayyiḍ, established in the eighteenth century by immigrants from the Nile. A threat also to the Keira lay in the attempts of the

Musabba'at under their remarkable leader, Hāshim b. 'Īsāwī, to create an empire in central Kordofan.[44] Although Tayrāb had earlier in 1772 supported Hāshim's seizure of central Kordofan from the Funj,[45] ten years later Hāshim seems to have reverted to the older Musabba'āt strategy of attempting to overturn the Keira. The Musabba'āt leader is said to have raised a force of 10,000 mercenaries from the Danāqla, Shāīqīya, Kabābīsh and Rizayqāt and raided into eastern Dār Fūr, threatening on one occasion Rīl itself.[46]

After a half-hearted attempt to reach a peaceful settlement with Hāshim, Tayrāb collected a great host and marched on Kordofan.[47]

Tayrāb's expedition was completely successful; Hāshim fled to his Shāīqīya allies, where he continued to scheme for a Musabba'āt empire in Kordofan. The Dār Fūr host is said to have reached the Nile near Omdurman, where they successfully fought the 'Abdallāb, but Tayrāb was soon faced with a disgruntled army – they were over 500 miles away from home – and conspiracies from the Awlād Bukr, and was forced to turn back.[48] The campaign was no mere raid, however, since it marked the beginning of nearly forty years of Keira rule in Kordofan.

The succession crisis at Bara, 1200/1786–7[49]

Tayrāb retraced his steps to Bāra, but he was a dying man and so the army encamped there. The sultan wrote to Isḥaq telling him to come immediately to Kordofan, leaving his own son, Khalīl, in charge of Dār Fūr.

The news that Tayrāb was dying began to be known in the camp and factions were starting to form. As the crisis deepened one of the court eunuchs, Muḥammad Kurra, began to negotiate with the *iiya kuuri* (the sultan's premier wife) Kināna in the *ḥarīm*; Kināna wanted her son, Ḥabīb b. Tayrāb, as sultan and sought Kurra's help. Kurra pointed to the claims of the

Awlād Bukr and implied that one of them, 'Abd al-Raḥmān, was a more likely candidate. The eunuch therefore suggested a compact whereby they both worked for 'Abd al-Raḥmān who, successfully installed as sultan, could marry Kināna. She could thus continue as *iiyakuuri*, and since the proposed sultan was childless, Ḥabīb could be nominated as his successor or *khalīfa*.[50]

The subject of this intrigue, 'Abd al-Raḥmān, had been living as a *faqīh* at Kerio in eastern Dār Fūr, the home of the descendants of the Fulani *faqīh*, 'Alī al-Fūtūwī, but had come to Bāra. Nicknamed *al-yatīm*, 'the orphan', he was a poor and unimportant member of the Awlād Bukr, although there had been portents of his future greatness.[51] His lack of sons was an advantage;[52] the earlier succession conflicts had, in part, centred on the reigning sultan's attempt to transmit his position to his son and the determination of his brothers to stop him. Only Dawra had been followed by his son.

Kurra thus approached 'Abd al-Raḥmān with the plan. In return for the support of the eunuch and the *iiya kuuri*, the prospective sultan promised to make Kurra *āb shaykh*, the senior slave official.

Meanwhile Tayrāb, who was slowly sinking, called together his *amīns*, that is his leading title-holders at court. To each he gave a specific task; to 'Alī b. Jāmi', Kurra's former master, to take the army back to Dār Fūr and hand it over to Isḥāq, to another charge of the camels and other animals, to a third charge of the royal women and to a fourth charge of the weapons and clothes.[53] The assembled *amīns* swore to obey Tayrāb's last commands and wept to see him dying. The scene was the more poignant in that most of them were sons-in-law of the sultan. Then Tayrāb, perhaps the greatest of the Keira sultans, died.

When Tayrāb was dead, Kināna gave Kurra the dead sultan's rosary, handkerchief, seal and amulet to take to ,Abd al-Raḥmān as proof of his death. The sultan's body was then embalmed to be taken back to Turra for burial. But 'Abd al-Raḥmān seems to have been unsure of his position, since he took Tayrāb's possessions to his elder brother, Rīz.[54]

Now that the decisive moment had passed, the *amīns* appear to have doubted that they could carry out Tayrāb's commands in the face of opposition from the Awlād Bukr. But 'Alī b. Jāmi' decided to try and ordered Kurra to go to his son, Muḥammad b. 'Alī, and tell him to collect the army in front of the dead sultan's encampment.[55] Kurra now played his own game, since he told the son that his father wished him to assemble the soldiers outside the encampment of the Awlād Bukr. Kurra then returned to the father and told him that his son had drawn up the troops outside the Awlād Bukr camp. To 'Alī it must have seemed like betrayal by his own son and he is said to have committed suicide.[56] The other *amīns* lost heart and left Tayrāb's camp to rejoin the contingents they commanded; the attempt to carry out Tayrāb's wishes had failed.

There were now, at the very least, three factions in the camp at Bāra; first the soldiers who were agitating for an end to the crisis and a speedy return to Dār Fūr, and to their number probably belonged the title-holders and court officials whose positions were in some sense in abeyance until a new sultan emerged. And among the Keira candidates there were at least two factions, the Awlād Bukr and their nephews, the other *awlād al-salāṭīn*, namely the sons of Tayrāb, 'Umar Lel, Dawra and Abu'l-Qāsim. While in Dār Fūr there was the *khalīfa* Isḥāq, who for reasons not recorded did not come to Bāra. He appears to have had powerful support among the Zaghāwa through his mother.

The *fuqarā'* were now brought in; apparently some of the officials, to break the deadlock, requested some of the *fuqarā'* to go to the Awlād Bukr and ask them to choose one of their number as the next sultan.[57] The Awlād Bukr nominated Rīz, the eldest, but for reasons not given by al-Tūnisī the other Keira and the army rejected him.

Following the rejection of Rīz, Ṭāhir was proposed but he too was rejected because he had too many children, he was a threat to the Keira's future prospects.[58] Finally 'Abd al-Raḥmān was proposed and he proved to be acceptable.

The new sultan hurried back to Dār Fūr, pausing only to leave a governor at al-Ubayyiḍ for Kordofan and to collect recruits from the Nuba mountains by slave raiding and from the Misīrīya Baqqāra by promises of booty.[59] These recruits were needed since it took a bitter civil war of three years, fought in part between Fur and Zaghāwa, to defeat and kill Isḥāq. From the war 'Abd al-Raḥmān emerged, somewhat shakily, as master in Dār Fūr. Kurra received the position as *āb shaykh* he had been promised, but Kināna was executed following a conspiracy against the new sultan.[60]

X · Keira institutions

'Abd al-Raḥmān's victory over Isḥāq was a turning point in the history of the sultanate. The new sultan/*faqīh* ruled over a state in which the centralizing forces and the Islamizing influences were being rapidly consolidated and where Keira dominance was strengthened by the growth of a permanent capital at al-Fāshir from about 1206/1791–2.[1]

We know far more about Keira institutions than those of Sinnār, and the following description is necessarily selective. There is, however, a danger of presenting both too static a picture and one that is too Islamically biased. The first because our earliest contemporary information comes at the end of the century from Browne (1793–6) and al-Tūnisī (1803–11), the second because what they observed they saw through Muslim eyes and were not aware or able to record much of the Fur dimension of the state. Unlike Sinnār, the Keira state had a firmly-based ethnic identity, although it was not simply a Fur state; unfortunately contemporary observers, with the exception of Nachtigal, saw Fur customs as quaint or barbaric deviations from the Islamic norm and many aspects of the Fur dimension are now beyond recovery.

The sultan

Central to these institutions was the *aba kuuri* (Fur, 'lord of obeisance') or sultan. Although some divine kingship customs were abolished as concessions to Islamic sentiment and although the later sultans adopted some of the attributes and style of the *fuqarā'*, the *aba kuuri* was not 'disestablished' as in Sinnār,[2] and he kept a quasi-divine aura until the end. Rather, by the use of magniloquent Islamic titles, the divine kingship image was projected anew into an Islamic context. The pious Muḥammad al-Ḥusayn did not blush to call himself *khalīfa sayyid al-mursalīn*, 'Successor to the lord of the prophets' (i.e. Muḥammad), and *amīr al-mu'minīn*, 'Commander of the Faithful' was regularly used.[3]

Succession to the sultanate was essentially a political decision. Rights to succession were not elaborately defined and whatever the practice in pre-Islamic times, in historical times succession followed the basically Islamic patrilineal pattern; all the Keira sultans from Sulaymān onwards, except the last,[4] were the sons of sultans – *awlād al-salāṭīn* – who formed a distinct element in the political set-up.[5]

But in the warlike eighteenth century, men of proven ability were needed as rulers, not children. Thus succession was largely brother-to-brother, despite attempts by fathers to pass their position directly to their sons, through the institution of the nominated heir or *khalīfa*.[6] The candidate who succeeded was the one who commanded the most military and political support.

Father-to-son succession became the rule in the very different circumstances of the nineteenth century, when in the political arena provided by al-Fāshir, powerful slaves found it expedient to ensure the accession of young sons against the ambitions of uncles and elder brothers. After the invasion of the sultanate in 1874, brother-to-brother succession reappeared when the Keira, fighting for survival around the mountains of Jabal Marra, needed mature leaders.

Succession may have been a matter of political and military power but, once chosen, the sultan elect entered upon a life bound by ritual, which served both to demonstrate the ruler's sanctity and his importance to the welfare of the state. While the slow beating of the copper kettledrums announced the death of a sultan, a faster beat proclaimed the beginning of the accession rituals for the new sultan.[7]

The sultan elect was first secluded for seven days, during which he gave no orders nor transacted any business.[8] At the end of the seven days, the *ḥabbūbāt* (Fur, *abɔŋa*, 'grandmothers') or old women who were ritual experts came to him led by the *malikat al-ḥabbūbāt*. Each carried throwing knives which they clashed together, while one carried a brush made from date palm leaves, with which she sprinkled the sultan from a jar of anointing fluid, whose composition was a closely-guarded secret.

The old women took the sultan in procession to the *bayt al-naḥās* or drum-house, within the *fāshir*, where they ranged themselves around the great drum, *al-manṣūra*, the most sacred of the ten drums kept in the drum-house.[9] Here they continued to clash their throwing knives. From the drum-house the sultan was taken to a nearby place, where the throne or *kukur* had been set up.[10] This was the only occasion when the sultan ever sat on the *kukur*, which had a bar between the two front legs on which the sultan could rest his feet, so that they would not touch the ground. Then one of the office-holders, the *abbo irliŋo*, placed the sultan's *taqīya* (cap) on his head, another title-holder his *'imma* (a long piece of cloth wound around the *taqīya*), another his shawl. until he was fully clothed. It was then announced that the sultan had ascended the throne. The *kukur* was returned to its lodging in the *bayt al-naḥās*.[11]

The sacred character of the sultan was emphasized throughout his reign by the taboos that surrounded him, by the ritual objects and insignia associated with his office and by the great national festival of the 'covering of the kettledrums'. The taboos surrounding the sultan's person differed little from those found in other African divine kingship states and may be compared with those in Sinnār. The sultan wore a veil, greeted his courtiers and spoke only through intermediaries, and ate alone. When he spat, his spittle was covered, when he sneezed, all around him made a clicking noise.[12] His person was inviolable; a taboo that included all members of the royal family.[13]

The most important of the insignia associated with the sultan were the drums (Fur, *gildany* or *gaŋgaŋ*), a potent and widespread symbol of royal authority in the Sudan, kept in the drum-house and tended by the 'king of the drums', *malik al-naḥās*, a powerful title-holder from the Fur *konyuŋa* clan. One of these drums was the previously-mentioned *al-manṣūra*, 'the victorious', another was called *ginsi* and dated from Sulaymān's time.[14] Lodged with the drums were seven sacred spears (Fur, *kɔr*), of which one was regarded as male and the rest as female. Also kept in the drum-house were the sultan's ostrich-feathers (Ar. *rīsh*), umbrella (Ar. *dallāl*), Qur'ān and carpet (Ar. *firsha*).[15] Relics marking episodes in the Keira rise to greatness were also kept, among others was the beard of a Birged chief subdued by Tayrāb.[16] All these relics had their appropriately titled officials.

The importance of the drums to the concept of royalty was demonstrated each year, when in spring about February or March, the great national festival, the *jalūd al-naḥās*, was held during which the drums were re-covered.[17] The ceremonies and rituals performed during this festival were long and complex and can only be briefly described here; as elsewhere Fur and Islamic practices were confusingly intermingled.

The festival in al-Fāshir was preceded by sacrifices and readings of the Qur'ān, for the good of their souls, at the graves of the past sultans at Turra in Jabal Marra. Similar sacrifices were made at the tombs of the pagan kings nearby, although in this case the Qur'ān was not read. At the festival in the capital all members of the royal family and the title-holders had to be present. In the drum-house within the *fāshir*, during a ceremony accompanied by much ritual, the old covers were removed and the new ones, made from the skins of bulls who had been chosen previously by the sultan, were put on. The chief figures in this ceremony were the *ḥabbubāt* and other Fur ritual experts.

Then followed the *kundaŋa* feast, a grim test of loyalty to the sultan. Putrefied meat, seasoned with pepper, from the animals whose skins had served to cover the drums was offered to the members of the royal family and the title-holders. Anyone who could not eat or who coughed during the meal was taken to be either generally disloyal or plotting treason and instantly executed by slaves set to watch over them. Some accounts suggest that in the pre-Islamic past the flesh of a boy and girl was included in the meal, but it seems that this particular relic of the Fur pagan past was discontinued in Islamic times.[18]

The *kundaŋa* feast was followed by a series of military parades (Ar. *'arḍa*), during which the sultan greeted his notables, who included his sister, the *iiya baasi*, riding in public like a man, reviewed their following of soldiers and received their presents (Ar. *salām*, 'greeting').[19] The presents had to be commensurate in value with the rank of the giver; Browne noted that the head of the foreign merchant community, the *malik al-jallāba*, gave presents, 'worth sixty head of slaves'.[20] It was at the time of the festival that the provincial officials brought into the capital the animal taxes and other revenues due to the sultan as well as criminals for trial.[21]

The *jalūd al-naḥās* festival was the highpoint in the ritual year, but there were other festivals. Browne describes the inauguration of the agricultural year by the sultan,

> At the beginning of the *harif*, or wet season, which is also the moment for sowing the corn, the king goes out with his *meleks* and the rest of his train; and while the people are employed in turning up the ground and sowing the seed, he also makes several holes with his own hands.[22]

Little is known of the funerary rites which followed the death of a sultan. The body was apparently taken by stages in procession to Turra, where all the sultans were buried, except for 'Umar Lel who died in Wadai and Ibrāhīm who was buried in the Bornu mosque at Manawāshī.[23]

The fāshir

Given the position of the sultan, it followed naturally that the physical centre of the Keira sultanate was the *fāshir* or sultan's residence, whose lay-out illustrated succinctly the political and spiritual order within the state. Its physical dimensions, the distance and location of the various groups within and outside the *fāshir* graphically portrayed the political and administrative hierarchy of the state. In the reigns of 'Abd al-Raḥmān and his son and successor, Muḥammad al-Faḍl (1215/1801–1254/1838), the *fāshir* was still basically structured as the residence of a divine king, to some degree modified by the needs of the new Islamic order.

From the plans of the eighteenth-century *fāshirs* of western Dār Fūr,[24] a continuity of form appears to run from the stone-built compounds of the Jabal Marra kingdom through the magnificent red brick palace of Tayrāb at Shōba to the elaborate but more ephemeral structures of the Tandalti/al-Fāshir region.[25] All these structures preserve the basic 'African palace' form of a large outer or girdle-wall, enclosing a series of inner courts at the heart of which lay the sultan's own huts and those of his women.

The cosmic significance of the original divine king's palace is still apparent in the later *fāshirs*. Al-Tūnisī gives us a schematic representation of Muḥammad al-Faḍl's *fāshir*, which consisted of a series of enclosures approached through a number of gates (see diagram).[26] The alignment of the *fāshir* was north/south and at the northern end lay an open area to which, strictly speaking, the word *fāshir* alone applied, and where the market was held and the military reviews and public festivals celebrated. The huge enclosure of the palace, surrounded by a thorn-bush fence (Ar. *zarība*), had two entrances, one facing north and the other south; these were the 'men's gate' (Fur, *ɔrrɛ de*) and the 'women's gate' (Fur, *ɔrre baya*) respectively. The northern half of the *fāshir* was thus regarded as the male

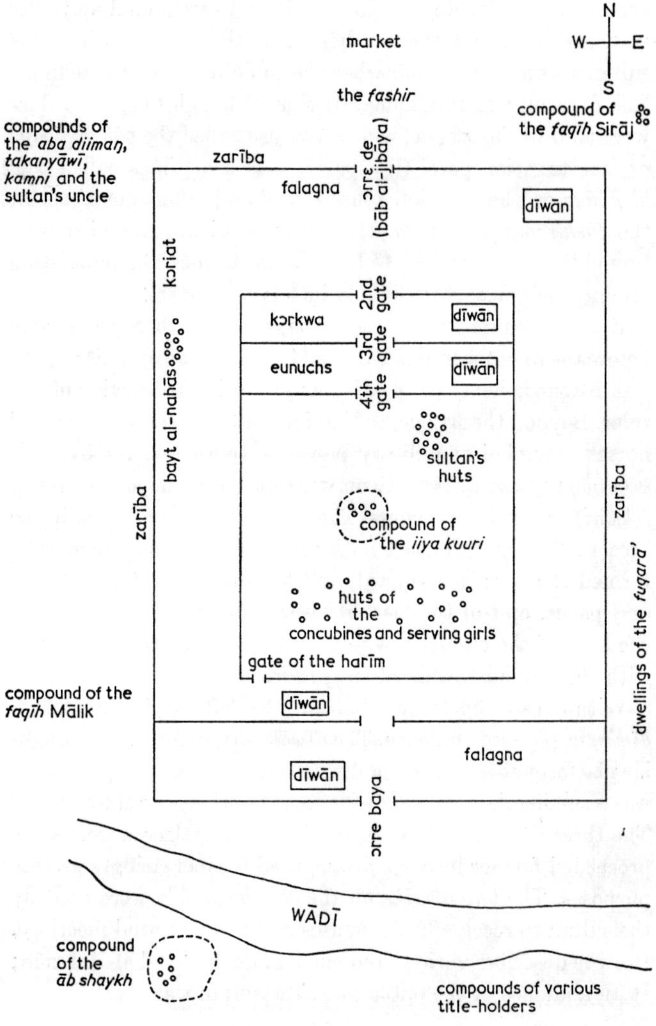

Muḥammad al-Faḍl's *fāshir*

area and was devoted to the public and ceremonial activities of the sultan, and the southern half the female, where the sultan's women lived and where he could live his private life.[27] The division was fundamental; thus although taxes and dues were paid to the *ɔrrɛ de*, which was also called the *bāb al-jibāya* or 'the taxation gate' (the palace was sometimes called *bayt al-jibāya* or 'the taxation house'), food and other provisions for the *fāshir* supplied from the sultan's private domains were brought to the *ɔrre baya*.[28] In a similar fashion the population around the palace was divided into two quarters.

Each enclosure within the *zarība*, of which there were three before the innermost area reserved for the sultan and his women was reached, housed a particular group in the service of the ruler. Beyond the *ɔrrɛ de*, to the right of the entrance, the royal horses – symbol of military power – were cared for by their grooms, the *kɔriat*. With them were stationed the *falagna* (sing. *folgoni*) or royal messengers. The second enclosure, again in the area to the right, housed both the *kɔrkwa* or spearmen, who formed the royal bodyguard, and the *somiŋ dogala*, or cadets and pages, and in the last enclosure before the sultan's were the huts of the eunuchs, who were most intimately connected with the administration of the *fāshir*.

Within each enclosure, but on the left-hand side, was a *dīwān* or place of audience. The *dīwān* was, in form, a rectangular platform of earth, covered with fine white sand, upon which was a smaller dais, covered with carpets, where the sultan sat.[29] The three *dīwāns* on the *ɔrrɛ de* side of the palace were, as one proceeded farther into the *fāshir*, used for increasingly private purposes. The two *dīwāns* on the *ɔrrɛ baya* side were used by the sultan to receive his intimates and for nocturnal meetings. Browne describes various audiences given by 'Abd al-Raḥmān; at an audience in the outer court the sultan was,

> mounted on a white mule, clothed with a scarlet benish (outer garment), and had on his head a white turban; which,

> however, together with part of his face, was covered with a thick muslin.[30]

Later the traveller saw the sultan listening to a case in the Fur language on one of the inner *dīwāns*,

> He was seated on a kind of chair (kursi) which was covered with a Turkey carpet, and wore a red silk turban; his face was then uncovered: the imperial sword was placed across his knees, and his hands were engaged with a chaplet of red coral.[30]

The interior court or *ḥarīm*, served only by the eunuchs and slave-girls, contained in the centre the huts of the *iiya kuuri* or premier wife of the sultan, and at the back the huts of the concubines and slave-girls who ground the grain and prepared the food. In the northeastern part of the court were the sultan's huts and as a protection against the common hazard of fire, store-houses built of earth, in which the sultan's clothes and valuables were kept.

The Keira clan

The *aba kuuri* was head not only of the state but also of the Keira clan. The origin of the Keira, and indeed of the name, is, as we have seen, obscure, but they apparently belonged to the Kunjara section of the Fur people, who had their home in eastern Jabal Marra.[31] Those Keira most closely related to the reigning sultan were called *baasiŋa* (*baasi* means approximately 'royal' in Fur), the remoter branches, *teliŋa*.[32]

The male members of the royal family, the *baasiŋa* or *awlād al-salāṭīn*, were an irresponsible element within the political life of the state. They were rarely given direct administrative authority and appear to have spent most of their time on their estates or at the capital, theoretically under the authority of two *baasiŋa* who arranged their marriages and were responsible for discipline among them.[33] They were a constant political danger to the sultans; it is said that one of

Tayrāb's motives in invading Kordofan was to remove from Dār Fūr not only the Awlād Bukr but all the *awlād al-salāṭīn*, who were a threat to his own son, the *khalīfa* Isḥāq, and who were causing discontent by their arrogant behaviour.[34]

The royal women had a more clearly-defined role. The elderly female relatives of the sultan were often ritual experts or *ḥabbūbāt*, while the sultan's mother, the *ḥabbūba*, had a respected position, but little power. Nor did the *iiya kuuri* ('mother (of) power') which was the title given to the sultan's premier or favourite wife. However, her position as 'the administrator of the domestic royal household'[35] could, in times of crisis, lead to political influence, as we have seen with Kināna at Bāra.

More powerful was the *iiya baasi* ('royal mother'), the title bestowed by the sultan upon his favourite sister.

> She was to be considered as an actual official, had her own military force, appeared in public processions on horseback, was available for anyone to speak to, and, as people said, was often only too accessible; many a high dignitary used her as a go-between with the sultan, for naturally no one else had such easy access to, or such frequent relations with, him.[36]

The *iiya baasi* Zamzam, sister to Sultan Muḥammad al-Husayn, virtually ruled Dār Fūr after her brother went blind in 1856, using her position to seize whatever estates she fancied.[37] But they could pay a price for their power; another Zamzam was executed along with her brother, Abu'l-Qāsim, after his disastrous invasion of Wadai.[38]

Al-Tūnisī was astonished at the freedom allowed the royal women, particularly the *mayārim* (sing., *mayram*, a word of apparently Kanuri origin) or princesses. Beer was drunk in the *ḥarīm* of even the pious 'Abd al-Raḥmān, and Umm Būṣa, his *iiya kuuri* and mother of sultan Muḥammad al-Faḍl, scandalized the capital with her liberated style of life.[39] The *mayārim* were given their own estates and as a consequence of their economic independence their husbands had little control over them.[40] But here, in fact, we have a survival, in the midst of an increasingly Islamized society, from the more purely Fur days: even today Fur women have markedly more social and economic independence than their counterparts in the modern northern Sudan.

The offices of state and the slaves

The Keira sultans were surrounded by a complex hierarchy of title-holders, both slave and freeman, to the number of several hundred. It is impossible to describe them all here and to categorize them too neatly would be misleading. Offices were made by men, and the sultanate was a competitive political arena in which men and families fought for power and place; offices and titles rose and fell with their holders. Thus the travellers often give a deceptive picture of the strength of a particular office; the ā*b shaykh*, the head of the slave hierarchy, was never so powerful after the rebellion and death of Muḥammad Kurra.

At the heart of the hierarchy were a group of title-holders, whose offices and titles were rooted in the Jabal Marra kingdom. Some were apparently territorial in origin, such as the *aba uumaŋ*; others became so, although they may have originally been ritual offices, such as the *takanyāwī*, an office that probably goes back beyond Keira times. More difficult to describe satisfactorily are titles that seemingly originated as Fur clan chieftainships, the *abbo duguŋa*, the *abbo konyuŋa*, i.e. the heads of the *duguŋa* or *konyuŋa* clans. These latter were never very prominent, although the *konyuŋa* family chiefly became very powerful, accumulating such titles as *malik al-naḥās* and *takanyāwī*. Their most famous member, Ibrāhīm b. Ramād, was something of an elder statesman for much of the reign of ʿAbd al-Raḥmān and his son.

Al-Tūnisī and Nachtigal have both left descriptions of the court title-holders and of the elaborate rules of precedence and ceremonial that governed their public lives. The former's account suggests that at the beginning of the nineteenth century these were still offices of political and military significance; seventy years later new titles had arisen and some of the old ones were only of ceremonial importance.

Al-Tūnisī describes the chief title-holders metaphorically as parts of the sultan's body.[41] Thus 'the face of the sultan' was the *ɔrreŋ duluŋ*, who commanded the advance guard of the army, ruled over part of the Birged people and was, as his title implies, *majordomo* of the *fashir*.[42] His troops were followed by those of the *kamni* or *aba forɛ*, 'the neck of the sultan', a 'shadow' sultan who at one time was killed when the sultan died; like the sultan he wore a veil.[43] There followed three of the provincial governors, the *aba uumaŋ*, 'the sultan's backbone' who commanded the rear guard, the *aba diimaŋ*, 'the right arm' who commanded the right flank but who was allowed only wooden drums instead of copper ones, and the governor of the north, the *takanyāwī*, 'the left arm'. The fourth provincial governor was more important as the *āb shaykh* or head of the slave hierarchy; he was likened to the sultan's 'backside'.

Below these great office-holders were the *kōrāyāt* or grooms of the royal horses, the *malik somiŋ dogala* (Fur, 'king of the children of the house') or overseer of the young cadets of the royal household, the chiefs of the royal bodyguards, the *kɔrkwa* (Fur, 'spearmen'), the *malik jodɛ*, a eunuch in charge of the *ḥarīm*, and many more. In al-Tūnisī's account, few of the titles owed anything to Islamic precedent; *wazīr* was used possibly as the equivalent of the Fur title, *abbo kotiŋo*,[44] and *amīn* seems to have been an honorific given to close confidants of the sultan.

Nachtigal describes the system in even greater detail. The offices of state, as he calls the titles given by al-Tūnisī, still existed and he further details the elaborate hierarchy of officials specifically attached to the *fāshir* – ritual experts, masters of protocol and guardians of the royal heirlooms. But his minute description conceals the fact that power now lay elsewhere, in the hands of the slaves and of new title-holders, such as the *maqdūms*.

The sultans made extensive use of slaves and in a variety of ways, as soldiers, as agricultural labourers on the royal domain, as gifts to the powerful and holy, and as bureaucrats.[45] Within the *fāshir*, adolescent slaves and boys from the subject tribes were trained to serve the sultan in a school, called *som*, under the supervision of the *malik somiŋ dogala* and his officials.[46] The free cadets could be sent back to serve as rulers of their tribes: an important line of Zaghāwa chiefs, the Kiliba of Dār Galla, owed their rise to 'Abd al-Karīm, who as an orphan was brought up in the *fāshir* of sultan Muḥammad al-Faḍl. He won the sultan's notice fighting the 'Irayqāt Arabs and was rewarded with a command in Dār Galla.[47] From the boys of the *som* were also recruited the *falagna* or *toŋ kuurikwa*, the sultan's messengers or heralds.[48]

As in Sinnār, various regiments or bands of slave troops were stationed in and around the capital. The *kɔrkwa*, the sultan's life-guards, were armed pages who guarded him during public audiences and processions.[49] They were commanded by six *malik al-kɔrkwa*, of whom one, as *abbo kɔrkwa* had precedence and could be either a slave or a freeman.[50] The names of other military groups have been preserved; the *saariŋa* (Fur, 'swordsmen') under a *malik saariŋa*; the *kotiŋo* who appear to have been subordinate to the *wazīr* or *abbo kotiŋo*, the *andaŋa* or scouts and the *daadiŋa*, stationed just outside al-Fāshir, who were divided into two regiments, *kebi dikɔ* 'black shields' and *kebi fuka* 'red shields' under the command of the *abbo daadiŋa*.[51]

One group of slaves whose intimate position within the *fāshir* gave them access to great executive power were the eunuchs, imported mainly from Dār Runga on the southern

Dār Fūr/Wadai border. They were lodged by the *ɔrre baya* gate and were organized in an elaborate hierarchy under the *abbo jodɛ*.[52] From their ranks came the most powerful of the slave bureaucrats, the *āb shaykh*, 'the father shaykh', *ex-officio* governor of the eastern province, *dār daali*, and controller of the sultan's household of which he took charge during the interregnum between one sultan and another.[53]

Provincial administration

The sultans ruled their Fur subjects through an administrative hierarchy that led directly to themselves. Their non-Fur subjects, sedentary and nomad, Arab and non-Arab, and accounting for perhaps two-thirds of the sultanate's population, they ruled more arbitrarily. Thus their major instrument of administration were bands of horsemen, and administration itself oscillated between coercion and conciliation, depending on the relative strength of the parties concerned. Naturally, the farther from the centre the weaker was the Keira hold.

The underlying system of administration appears to go back to the Jabal Marra kingdom and is associated in Fur tradition with Sultan Daali. The Fur areas particularly have exhibited a remarkable continuity in their administrative structure until the present day.

The basis of administration was the quadrant division into provinces. Although Nachtigal refers to five provinces, only four had governors, and the fifth, *dār al-gharb*, was never much more than a geographical term.[53] New provinces were not created, rather as the empire grew the old provinces were extended; when Kordofan was conquered, the northern and eastern provinces were simply extended eastwards to embrace it.

The Fur were to be found mainly in two provinces, *dār aba diima*, southwest of Jabal Marra, and *dār aba uuma*, to the southeast, ruled by their respective title-holders. *Dār aba diima*, roughly the present Zalingei District, was a particularly stable administrative unit, reflecting the fertility of its soil and the homogeneity of its population. Administratively it was divided into twelve *sharṭāyas*, of varying size, each administered by a *sharṭay* (Ar. pl. *sharāṭī*) or *kiiso*,[54] an office hereditary in a local clan.[55] The *aba diimaŋ* ruled his own district, *rɔ diima*, directly, as well as governing the whole province. Each *sharṭāya* was divided into several *dimlijīyas*, administered by a *dimlij* (Fur, *dilmoŋ*); each *dimlij* was responsible for several villages under their village heads, *ɛliŋ wakīl*, who was, at least in Islamic times, usually assisted by the local *faqīh*.[56]

Dār aba uuma was divided in a similar manner.

A *sharṭay*'s powers were considerable and he had his own messengers or *falagna* and administrative officials, *sambɛ* (Fur, 'barbed spear') or *kursī* (Ar. 'chair') to assist him. He was responsible for the collection of taxes, for minor offences such as cursing and adultery — more serious cases were dealt with either by the *aba diimaŋ* or the sultan – and for supervising the local warriors.[57]

The Fur of Jabal Marra, the *fugokwa* ('mountain people'), and those to the west of the mountains lay outside the provincial system. The *fugokwa* were divided into several small *sharṭāyas* directly responsible to the sultan. Jabal Marra, with its sacred places and state prisons, where recalcitrant Keira and dangerous commoners were kept, was considered to be royal domain and was known as *rɔ kuuriŋ* (Ar. *ḥākūrat al-sulṭān*) 'the sultan's farm or estate'. Taxes of grain and other foodstuffs were sent directly to al-Fāshir.[58]

West of the mountains, *dār al-gharb*, into which the Fur appear to have spread in historical times, was divided into large *sharṭāyas*, Fia, Made, Kerne and Konyir, 'the sherati of which had in accordance with the size of their territory a higher rank and a more independent status; they reported directly to the king.'[59]

The northern province, *dār al-rīḥ* (Ar. 'the land of the wind') or *dār al-takanyāwī*, which embraced the Zaghawa, Berti, Tunjur and Zayādīya among other groups as well as the Arab camel nomads when they could be subdued, was likewise divided into twelve *sharṭāya*s. But these were not so stable as in *dār aba diima* and their *sharṭay*s appear to have been changed more frequently. All were subordinate to the *takanyāwī*, who lived originally in the Tandalti region, but moved north to Kutum when al-Fāshir was established in the former area.[60]

The eastern province, *dār daali* or *dār al-ṣabāḥ*, lacked the administrative coherence of the other provinces, being a patchwork of tribal chiefdoms, Birged, Daju, Mima and others, with ill-defined boundaries, particularly to the south and east. The chiefs were loosely controlled by the *āb shaykh*, who unlike the other governors resided at court. Eastern Dār Fūr, especially those districts close to the capital, appears early on to have become a victim of the *ḥākūra* system, described below, which further weakened its administrative structure.

On the margins of the provincial heartlands, the bonds between ruler and subject gave way to those between suzerain and tributary state; these defy generalization. In the west along the border with Wadai the situation was particularly complex; of the small states there, Dār Qimr was firmly in the Keira orbit, while Dār Tāma fluctuated according to the power struggle between the two empires.[61] Farther south, the pagan tribes, known collectively to the Fur as Fartīt, were sometimes described as tributary states instead as simply the objects of slave raiding.[62]

The administrative framework described above had its roots in the many peoples, with their own internal political systems but owing allegiance to the Keira ruler, who had been incorporated into the state over a period of time. Two institutions began – when is not certain – to cut across this traditional pattern, the *ḥākūra* system and the *maqdūm*ate. Both owed their rise to the breakdown of the territorially-based tribal leadership and its replacement by a class of title-holders, recruited both from slaves and freemen, who derived their position from the sultan, lord and owner of the land.

An *ḥākūra* (pl. *ḥawākīr*; Fur, *rɔ*, pl., *rɔta*) may be defined as an estate, comprising usually a number of villages, less often a group of nomads, granted by the sultan to a member of his family, a title-holder or a *faqīh*.[63] Although the granting of *ḥākūra*s and associated rights came, in the land-charters, to be expressed in the terminology used in the Islamic heartlands of a concession by a ruler of ownership (*iqṭāʿ al-tamlīk*) or of usufructary rights (*iqṭāʿ al-istighlāl*), such grants appear to be an indigenous Sudanic practice. The *ḥākūra* may thus be compared with the territorial fief in Bornu.[64]

Al-Tūnisī describes how the title-holders were granted, in lieu of salary, estates, out of whose revenues they maintained their soldiers and followers. The revenues included the many customary dues and charges elsewhere paid to the local administrative officials; items such as a proportion of the blood-money paid in cases of homicide, fines on adultery, cursing, injury, fire-raising, the proceeds from the sale of stray animals and slaves and lost property. It is uncertain but probable that military service and labour formed part of the obligations owed by his tenants to the *ḥākūra*-holder.[65] Local officials, *sharṭay*s and others, were forbidden to enter an *ḥākūra*, and the land and people granted as such thus passed out of local jurisdiction.

Until more land-charters have been collected and published, it would be premature to describe too confidently the complex of relationships involved. But from ʿAbd al-Raḥmān's reign onwards, *ḥākūra*s were apparently granted more frequently and in greater numbers than before. The fertile region of western Dār Fūr and the land around the capital were rapidly carved up into estates; in *dār aba diima*, for example, the *sharṭāya* of Dār Nyoma was divided into seven *ḥākūra*s, Dār Kobara into six and so on.[66] The *ḥākūra*-holders lived in the capital and their estates were administered by a steward; a procedure obviously open to abuse. Although *ḥākūra*s were apparently not originally intended to be hereditary, they became so; in 1317/1899–1900 'Alī Dīnār issued a charter restoring to the *maqdūm* of the north his ancestral *ḥākūra*s to the number of seven.[67] They also became the object of bitter dispute between the title-holders; a land-charter of 1223/1809 records a judge ment of the *āb shaykh* Yūsuf on a dispute over an estate by members of the same family.[68]

The *ḥākūra* system, which became essential to the maintenance of a privileged class of title-holders in al-Fāshir, hastened the breakdown of the traditional patterns of rule and built a barrier between the ruler and his subjects. The local system was further overridden by the *maqdūm*s, who were commissioners appointed directly by the sultan. When the first *maqdūm*s were appointed is not known,[69] but Nachtigal describes their functions,

> The king from time to time sent commissioners into the provinces, who, in some measure representing the king in person, took charge of the supervision of affairs there. During their period of office, these commissioners, *maqdūm*, were furnished with the external marks of royal dignity and exercised supreme authority. The appointment of a *maqdūm* was usually for two to three years, and only in the northern province had there for a long time been any permanent *maqdūm*. Any officials, whether slaves or free men, could be appointed to this office, and after completing their mission they returned to their former positions.[70]

The economic basis of the sultanate

The elaborate festivals, the cavalry, bodyguards and staff of the *fāshir*, indeed the whole ostentatious style of life appropriate to a Sudanic ruler, had to be maintained out of the revenues of the state. Generally, the revenues raised internally provided the food and clothes for the sultan's staff and the title-holders, who were also maintained by their *ḥākūras*. But specialized needs, essential to a Sudanic ruler, such as war horses and saddlery, fine clothes, weapons and jewellery had to be satisfied by foreign trade and the taxes upon it. It may be added that in the nineteenth century slave raiding increasingly provided the manpower with which the state was run.

The collection was not centralized; part was kept back to maintain the *sharṭay*s, *dimlij*s and other local chiefs. Animal taxes from the nomads, when they could be forced or induced to pay them, were sent directly to al-Fāshir,[71] but only part of the canonical taxes, *zakāt* and *fiṭr*, paid in grain, was stored in different localities for the use of the sultan, to whom accounts were forwarded.[72] The collection of these taxes and of the fines, paid usually in cloth and which appear to have been an important item in the sultan's revenue, was the responsibility of the *sharṭay*s through his *dimlijs* or the tribal chiefs. But the collection was supervised by a class of officials, the *jabbayīn* (Fur, *jubaŋa*) under the *abu'l-jabbayīn*, who travelled through the state.[73]

Provisions for the *fāshir* came directly from the crown domains in Jabal Marra and Dār Fongoro, in *dār aba diima.*

From the abundance of material given us by the travellers, it would be possible to give here a very detailed account of the sultanate's foreign trade and of the groups involved in it. But it is doubtful whether, beyond the sultan and the title-holders, this commercial activity was of such importance, and the merchants certainly never attained the position they had in Sinnār; the Keira sultanate was, overall, a stronger institution in relation to external forces in the eighteenth and nineteenth centuries than its riverain counterpart had been in the centuries before.

Dār Fūr's main link with the outside world was the *darb al-arba'īn*, the desert route to Upper Egypt, difficult to traverse but for that reason immune to nomad raids or ransom.[74] But the trade along it fluctuated, reaching its apogee between 1800 and 1850 and thereafter declining as the trade in the two main items sent along the route, slaves and ivory, was captured by the Khartoum traders to the south of the sultanate. A second trading axis through the sultanate ran from west to east, part of the great pilgrimage route from the Western Sudanic belt to the holy cities of Arabia; the pilgrims engaged in petty trade to sustain their journey. The pilgrimage route deposited not only well-known holy men in the sultanate but also humbler folk; people from Kotoko, Bagirmi and Hausaland all settled in Dār Fūr.[75] Trade routes also crossed the desert from Dār Fur northwestwards to Tunis and Tripoli; North African merchants settled in Dār Fūr and slaves from the sultanate were sold in Tunis.[76]

The commercial centres in the north, Kobbei and Suwayni, were kept separate from the capital, as with Sinnār and Arbajī. In them settled traders from Upper Egypt, from Asyūṭ particularly, Muslims and some Copts, and Jaʿaliyīn and Danāqla as well as local merchants.[77] The trade appears to have been controlled by a small number of large-scale merchants. The organization of a caravan for the *darb al-arbaʿīn* was a great affair; 5,000 camels were commonly needed and Browne estimated the value of the goods carried by the caravan with which he returned to Egypt in 1796 at about £115,000.[78] This scale must have ensured that the trade was largely a monopoly operated by the sultan and a few large traders, which had little impact on the daily lives of most of the state's inhabitants.

> The king is chief merchant in the country, and not only dispatches with every caravan to Egypt a great quantity of his own merchandise, but also employs his slaves and dependents to trade with the goods of Egypt, on his own account, in the countries adjacent to Soudan.[79]

The sultan profited from the trade not only by participating and using his position to enforce a monopoly when needful but through customs dues, paid at the rate of five per cent on slaves and ten per cent on other goods, and from presents given him by the merchants.[80] The title-holders' share came from slave raiding.

The travellers give lists of items exported from Dār Fūr; a French list of about 1800 includes ivory, rhinoceros horn, ostrich feathers, gum arabic, tamarind and natron.[81] But slaves were the staple export.

The slaves were taken from the pagan peoples south of the sultanate, known to the Fur as Fartīt, through a formalized system of raiding, known as *ghazwa* or *salaṭīya*. These raids were organized and led by the title-holders, who first sought permission from the sultan and then led a band of volunteers south in search of slaves. The slaving bands under their *sulṭān al-ghazwa* were often away for many months – al-Tūnisī spent three months with one – and appear to have penetrated very far south, probably as far as the present-day Central African Republic.

The mechanics of the *ghazwa* were complex and have been described elsewhere.[82] The slaves thus captured or given as tribute were used as manpower for the state or as exports. How many were exported is difficult to determine; probably between 2,000 and 3,000 annually were sent to Egypt, at least in the period 1750 to 1830, although the trade goes back to the sixteenth century, as has been described in Chapter VII.[83]

It was argued earlier that long-distance trade was a powerful factor in the rise of the Keira state. It would appear that in the mid-nineteenth century, under Sultan Muḥammad al-Ḥusayn, there further developed a community of interest between the court and the traders, reinforced by Islam, to the detriment of older ties; a change perhaps symbolized by the marriage of a leading merchant, the *khabīr* ('caravan leader') Muḥammad to the sultan's daughter. The Keira were beginning to move towards that alienation between ruler and subject noted in Sinnār.

XI · The Dār Fūr sultanate

'Abd al-Raḥmān ruled until his death about 1801,[1] and was succeeded by his adolescent son, Muḥammad al-Faḍl, who ruled until 1254/1838. The sultanate had now reached middle age; the fierce internal struggles, the wars with Wadai, the warrior sultans ceaselessly moving around their kingdom, gave way to palace intrigues, to sultans as immersed in Islamic studies as the *fuqarā'* around them and to increasing contacts with the outside world.

The external contacts were varied. 'Abd al-Raḥmān is said to have sent a gift of ivory to the Ottoman sultan, who replied awarding him the honorific, *al-rashīd*, 'the just', which duly appeared on the Keira sultan's seals.[2] The English traveller, Browne, spent, very unwillingly, nearly three years (1793–6) in Dār Fūr and has left a valuable if uneven account. But Dār Fūr was never a highway for European explorers, and Browne had no significant successor until Nachtigal. The increasing commercial contacts with Egypt even led to a hare-brained scheme by a Christian Greek turned Muslim Mamluk to take over Dār Fūr; Aḥmad *Agha* had been sent to Dār Fūr to make cannon for the Sultan as part of a commercial venture sponsored by the Mamluk rulers of Egypt, but became involved in a plot to overthrow the sultan. The plot was discovered and he was executed.[3] The originator of the scheme whereby Aḥmad Agha was sent to Dār Fūr, Rosetti, the Venetian Consul in Alexandria, tried to interest the French in Dār Fūr after Bonaparte occupied Egypt in 1798. The French general did, in fact, correspond with 'Abd al-Raḥmān asking him to send able-bodied slaves to be used as soldiers in Napoleon's eastern schemes.[4]

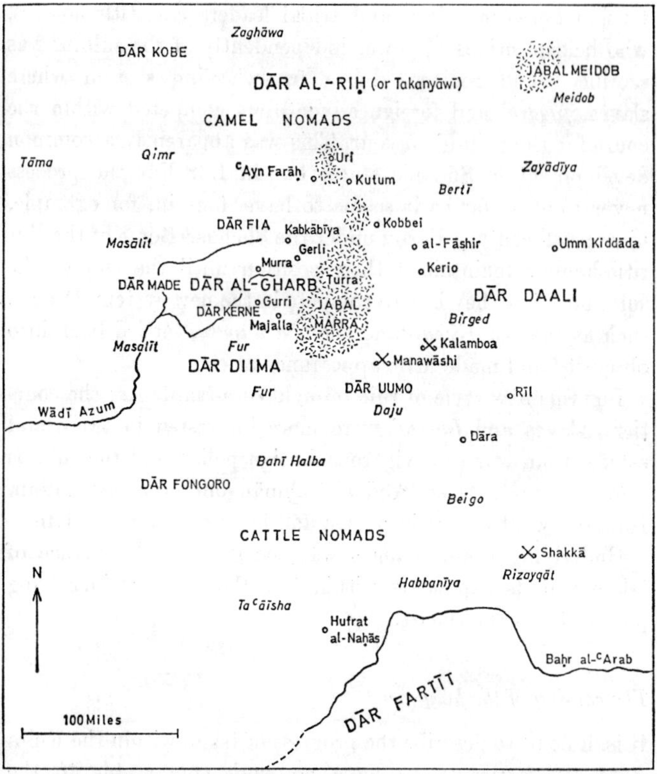

The Dār Fūr Sultanate

The centralization of the state seems to have been achieved at the cost of a loss of vigour at the centre. The balance and tension between sultan and tribal leaders and title-holders, who held positions of power independently of the sultan, was sacrificed and replaced by a free-wheeling system where slaves, *fuqarā'* and foreign adventurers competed within the court for the sultan's favour. This was apparently a common development in Sudanic states but in Dār Fūr the process never went so far as it seems to have done in, for example, nineteenth-century Bornu under the Shehus.[5] Some of the Fur title-holders maintained their position until the end of the sultanate, but they had to compete in the new system. Others, such as the *aba diimaŋ* and the *aba uumaŋ*, settled back into obscurity and made little appearance at court.

But this new style of rule brought disadvantages; the courtiers, slaves and *fuqarā'* were more interested in trade and estates than war or a vigorous foreign policy and the sultans were as timid. After 'Abd al-Raḥmān only the last sultan, Ibrāhīm, went to war in person and by then it was too late.

Underlying these changes was the growing dominance of Islam and its exponents within Dār Fūr and the increasing power of slaves at court.

The coming of the holy men

It is difficult to describe the progress of Islam within the Keira state satisfactorily; we have no work comparable to the *ṭabaqāt* of Wad Ḍayfallāh from Dār Fūr nor has there been much investigation of the particular characteristics of Islam in Dār Fūr.[6] The few references in the *ṭabaqāt* to Dār Fūr suggest that to the *fuqarā'* of the Nile valley it was a remote and barbarous, if increasingly powerful, land effectively beyond their ken. The very size and ethnic diversity of Dār Fūr make generalizations dangerous; it is clear that the reception of Islam by the Fur was very different from its impact on the peoples east of the mountains, the Birged, Mīma, Berti and others, but the differences have yet to be charted. The mountains today appear to mark a rough frontier for Arabization and Arabicization; thus the Birged and Berti languages have almost been supplanted by Arabic,[7] west of the mountains Fur, and the other languages have as yet been little affected. Whether this difference is due to Islamization, contacts with the Arab nomads to the north and south, the influence of al-Fāshir or later developments under the Mahdīya or Condominium, or a combination of these factors, cannot yet be determined.

The adoption of Islam by the Keira was probably of little significance to the mass of the Fur people and did not affect their attitude to their rulers. The Islamization of the institutions of the state was a slow and piecemeal process, only rarely being marked by some public act, such as the abolition of a pre-Islamic ritual. The degree to which the Keira state was itself an agent for the spread of Islam and Islamic institutions is not certain. If by Islamization is meant the acculturation of the peoples of Dār Fūr to the Islamic/Arabic culture of the Muslim heartlands, this is perhaps only now beginning in the province, but if the increasing acceptance of Islam and adaptation of elements from Islamic culture is meant, then the eighteenth century seems to have seen the speeding-up of earlier trends. By the end of the century Islam had won out at court, and in the surrounding areas its influence seemingly weaker the farther from the capital. By the reign of ʻAbd al-Raḥmān a second stage becomes evident; the beginnings of the rejection of the syncretist patterns of the earlier period in favour of greater orthodoxy. Both of the Muslim visitors who came to Dār Fūr at the beginning of the nineteenth century, al-Tūnisī and Zayn al-ʻAbidīn, regarded Dār Fūr as a Muslim country, but a very backward one and in need of reform.

The carriers of Islam to Dār Fūr and its protagonists within the state, the Muslim holy men, were a heterogeneous group of diverse and varied attainments, ranging from highly-educated *'ulamā'* from al-Azhar and other centres of Islamic learning to local *fuqarā'*, barely literate, running a village mosque, often a patch of ground marked out by stones, and a school (Sudanese Ar. *khalwa*; Fur, *som*) under a shady tree. The predominant pattern of Islamization in eastern Dār Fūr at least appears to be the settling of an immigrant holy man in a district, intermarriage with local people, proliferation of the family now in the possession of the *baraka* of its founder and in some cases a split within the family into secular and religious branches. This was essentially a localized phenomenon since, unlike the riverain Sudan, the religious brotherhoods, the *ṭarīqa*s, never obtained much hold in Dār Fūr.

Dār Fūr's geographical position is reflected in the coming of holy men from both the older Muslim areas of West Africa and from the Nile valley. Although some families came in the seventeenth century, the main influx came in the following century. Their origins were diverse; from the Nile valley came Abū Zayd b. al-shaykh 'Abd al-Qādir, a pupil of al-Zayn b. al-shaykh Ṣughayrūn (died 1086/1675–6), who travelled in Dār Fūr and Wadai.[8] From farther east and somewhat later, came Muḥammad b. Ṣāliḥ al-Kinānī from the Ḥijāz, who became *imām* of a mosque built at Terjil, northwest of Nyala, by Sultan Dawra.[9] Others came from Kordofan; a Ja'alī immigrant was Ḥasan al-Aḥmar, who settled at Ḥufrat al-Naḥās in southern Dār Fūr on the fringes of pagan territory, and was 'famed for his knowledge of Muhammadan law'.[10] Thirty years later Ḥasan's clan was forced to leave Dār Fūr and settle in Kordofan. The *ṭarīq sūdān* or 'Sudan Road', the famous pilgrim route from West Africa to the holy cities, was increasingly used from the seventeenth century onwards because of the security that Wadai and Dār Fūr could provide.[11] Some of the pilgrims, on their return from Mecca, settled in Dār Fūr; a Bornu holy man is said to have founded the *aba diimaŋ*'s clan, the *morgiŋa*, and another holy family who achieved political prominence were descended from a Fulani from Bagirmi, 'Alī b. Yūsuf al-Fūtūwī.

The sultans were not passive spectators of this religious immigration, but actively encouraged it for their own purposes, just as they encouraged peoples with useful skills to settle in the sultanate.[12] As an inducement to settle, the sultans could offer the holy man land through the *ḥākūra* system or tax exemptions known as *jāh* (an Arabic term that in this context appears to mean something like tax-free 'status') for himself and his descendants. Our knowledge of these transactions comes from the land-charters and tax exemptions that have been collected and is, as yet, too fragmentary to chart the development of the system fully. The charters we have, whereby a sultan would confirm a grant made by one of his predecessors, come exclusively from the nineteenth century, although in some cases they provide information on the eighteenth.

The holy men were thus early on integrated into the pre-existing system, described above, whereby the sultans granted lands or rights to members of the royal family and title-holders. Sultan Dawra 'gave to the *faqīh* Muḥammad 'Izz al-Dīn and his descendants to the end of time the land of Qiray-wud al-Zarāf', near al-Fāshir.[13] The grantee was usually exempted by the sultan from both the canonical taxes (*zakāt* and *fiṭr*) and the various customary dues (*al-subul al-'ādīya*), which he instead collected.[14] The recipient and his descendants took care to have their grants confirmed by later sultans.[15] In some cases the grants appear to have developed into a form of *waqf* or religious endowment for the maintenance of a mosque and its attached holy family.

Jāh, or exemption from both the canonical and customary taxes, was also granted to holy men and their kin.[16] *Jāh* would thus appear to be similar in purpose to the *maḥram* in Bornu; in *maḥram* charters the holy men and descendants were stated to be '*ḥarīm*, "set apart" or "privileged", that is exempted from taxes, military service, hospitality charges and the like'.[17] In the Dār Fūr charters the holy men are described as 'cripples' in the eyes of the state; thus from a charter of sultan Muḥammad al-Ḥusayn,

> Thereafter: the *faqīh* Aḥmad al-Zākī presented to us a letter which I looked upon and which explained clearly the *jāh* (granted) to the *faqīh* Aḥmad al-Zākī . . . (and others). They have become as cripples to the *dīwān*, and there is not to be taken from them either a twist of thread or a cow. They are freely remitted all the customary dues.[18]

These immunities could apparently be transferred from one state to another; some *fuqarā'* from the Nile presented a charter of exemption to Sultan 'Abd al-Raḥmān from one of the 'Ajīb shaykhs, asking that it be confirmed for Dār Fūr, which was duly done.[19]

By these means and by the building of mosques particularly around al-Fāshir, the sultans actively encouraged the spread of Islam.[20] Coming at a time when the state was growing, and encouraged to come by that fact, the holy men helped to transform the state, but in the process were integrated as a part of the new bureaucracy. The holy men were attracted by the spiritual and material rewards to be gained, while the sultan profited from their expertise in writing and their diplomatic skills. Religion was not the sole motive for granting estates and immunities to them; *fuqarā'*, newly established by the sultan's favour, could provide a new focus of loyalty, breaking down the old clan and tribal particularisms.

During the wars and disputes of the eighteenth century the role of the holy men had been ambiguous; their religious prestige and political neutrality tempted some of them into a mediatory role. The intervention of 'Alī al-Fūtūwī and another *faqīh* in the dispute between Sultan Dawra and his son was hardly a success and although the intervention at Bāra seems to have been crucial, ʻAbd al-Raḥmān rejected any attempt by his friend, Mālik b. ʻAlī, to mediate between himself and the *khalīfa* Isḥāq.[21]

Not all the *fuqarā'* joined the establishment. Al-Tūnisī tells of the *faqīh* Ḥasan al-Kaw. Once in Tayrāb's reign, the *āb shaykh* Ūr Dikɔ̄ summoned a levy of men for war and made them stand in the sun until they were very hot and thirsty. Suddenly the *faqīh*, who was among them, cried out and so frightened Ūr Dikɔ̄ that he fled. Ḥasan then caused rain to come.[22]

The transformation of the holy men from rainmakers and thaumaturges into bureaucrats can be illustrated in the history of ʻAlī al-Fūtūwī's descendants. ʻAlī met Sultan Bukr on his return from Mecca and was persuaded by an *ḥākūra* to settle in the sultanate. Of ʻAlī's many sons, Mālik settled as a teacher at Kerio, just south of al-Fāshir, where he befriended ʻAbd al-Raḥmān. Upon the latter's accession Mālik was given Kerio as an *ḥākūra*, but the local people, many of them Kotoko immigrants from south of Lake Chad, went to al-Fāshir to complain. They were met by Mālik who won them over, 'You are free to keep and work your own lands, but you will be my followers and pay me the customary dues.'[23] He became the guardian of the nomad (Bororoje) Fulani in the sultanate and defended their interests at court.[24]

Mālik's sons profited from their father's favoured position at court and several received their own estates; Jalāl al-Dīn traded for slaves in the south, *al-ḥājj* Sanūsī became *imām* of the Kerio mosque, and another son went to al-Azhar. It was Muḥammad Salāma who succeeded to his father's position at court, where he became responsible for land affairs with the title of *wazīr* and played a crucial part in the accession of Muḥammad al-Ḥusayn in 1254/1838.[25]

Mālik was the most influential *faqīh* at ʻAbd al-Raḥmān's court at the time of ʻUmar al-Tūnisī's visit. Muḥammad al-Tūnisī vividly describes how his father obtained the sultan's favour. When 'Umar first reached Dār Fūr, after an unprofitable visit to Sinnār, he stayed at the commercial centre of Kobbei with the *faqīh* Ḥasan b. 'Awwūda. There, at the invitation of the *fuqarā'*, he taught part of the Mālikī lawbook, the *Mukhtaṣar* of Khalīl. Soon his reputation for learning reached Mālik, who spoke of him to the sultan. 'Umar was sent for and well received by the sultan, who gave him concubines and assigned him a home with the *faqīh* Nūr al-Anṣārī, husband of the princess Hawwā'. 'Umar's scholarship was in great demand; he read al-Bukhārī's *Saḥīḥ* with Nūr, *ḥadīth* with the sultan and also taught various members of Mālik's family. The sultan gave him an *ḥākūra* on the western slopes of Jabal Marra, but the *faqīh* was not happy with the location, since the Fur on his estate could speak no Arabic and he no Fur, so he was assigned another *ḥākūra*.[26]

This happy picture of a learned sultan surrounding himself with scholars is misleading. The state presented two faces, one Muslim, one Fur, which uneasily co-existed; gradually the Muslim one began to predominate. The Islamic precepts had their impact on society, in, for example, a more restricted view of the woman's position, and in attitudes towards traditional beliefs.[27] Fifty years after 'Abd al-Raḥmān, a *malik* Sinji of *dār aba diima* was disgraced because he was discovered worshipping idols.[28] 'Abd al-Raḥmān is credited with various Islamically-inspired reforms. While still in Kordofan he abolished the seclusion ritual, part of the accession ceremonies.[29] Less successful was his attempt, in 1795, to prohibit the drinking of *marīsa* or beer, which despite the Islamic ban against intoxicants was and is widely drunk in Dār Fūr. Despite prohibition, *marīsa* continued to be drunk, even it was said in the sultan's *ḥarīm*.[30]

In judicial matters Islamic influence was very circumscribed. The ultimate judicial authority was the sultan, to whom from the Fur, at least, serious cases were referred by the local chiefs.[31] He heard cases, both in Fur and Arabic, in the courtyard of the *fāshir*.[32] Although *qāḍīs* were appointed by both Tayrāb and ʻAbd al-Raḥmān, their function seems to have been limited to the giving of advice.[33] ʻAbd al-Raḥmān was advised by various *fuqarā*', who included Mālik, ʻIzz al-Dīn, who is described by al-Tūnisī as head *qāḍī* (*qāḍī al-quḍāt*) and Ṭāhir Abū Jāmūs, a prominent *faqīh* from the Bornu community of Manawāshī.[34]

The sultans and their slaves

From about 1790 to 1804, the most powerful man in Dār Fūr and Kordofan was the slave eunuch, the *āb shaykh* Muḥammad Kurra.

Kurra, born a slave or enslaved later,[35] began his rise to power by entering the *kɔrkwa* guards of Tayrāb. He won promotion to the *somiŋ dogala*, but was later accused of interfering with one of Tayrāb's concubines and to show his innocence voluntarily castrated himself. The sultan, however, gave him to the *amīn* ʻAlī b. Jāmiʻ, in whose household he served. Apparently by the time of Tayrāb's expedition which he accompanied he was one of the sultan's *malik al-kōrāyāt* or masters of the royal grooms. At Bāra he was able to use his position as a court eunuch to play a part in the succession crisis of 1200/1786–7; his reward was the office of *āb shaykh*.

As *āb shaykh* to ʻAbd al-Raḥmān, Kurra seems virtually to have run Dār Fūr. In 1206/1791–2 he was sent by the sultan with the *abbo konyuŋa* Ibrāhīm b. Ramād to drive Hāshim and the Musabbaʻat once more out of Kordofan. This was successfully accomplished and Kurra, watched over by Ibrāhīm, remained in Kordofan, where he ruled in a manner calculated to reconcile the merchant communities there to Keira rule. His relationship with his master was not easy; on one occasion he was summoned back to al-Fāshir in disgrace to answer accusations of wanting to make himself independent.[36]

But he kept his master's favour sufficiently that before ʻAbd al-Raḥmān died he arranged with Kurra that his youngest son, Muḥammad al-Faḍl, then a boy of about fourteen, should succeed him. When the sultan died, Kurra, firmly in control of al-Fāshir, brought the boy out from the *ḥarīm* in order that the assembled title-holders could swear allegiance to him. With the aid of bribes all did so, although the aged Ibrāhīm b. Ramād is said to have disapproved of the choice. However, many of the *awlād al-salāṭīn* would not accept Muḥammad al-Faḍl and withdrew from al-Fāshir to their estates. They gathered their forces and marched on the capital, but were intercepted on the way by an army sent out by Kurra and crushed. Sixty of them were later executed on a field south of al-Fāshir known ever after as *qōz al-sittīn*, 'the *qōz* of the sixty'; a blood-letting which marked the end of the old-style opposition of the Keira claimants. Kurra was left to rule Dār Fūr unchallenged.[37]

Kurra, nicknamed *jābir al-dar*, 'tyrant of the land', ruled for about three years, but the opposition forces, who appear to have been mainly the old-established title-holders led by Ibrāhīm b. Ramād, began to gather around the young sultan now increasingly resentful of his slave's power. When the split finally came in Rajab 1219/October–November 1804, so strong was Kurra that it was the sultan and his partisans who had to withdraw from al-Fāshir to rally his forces.[38]

In the skirmishes that followed the sultan's forces had at first the worst of it, and al-Tūnisī records an unlikely tradition that Kurra planned to replace the Keira dynasty with his own by proposing his brother as sultan.[39] More probably he nominated the aged Ṭāhir b. Aḥmad Bukr as sultan. Eventually the *āb shaykh* was defeated and killed by the sultan's partisans led by Kurra's old enemy, the *abbo konyuŋa* Ibrāhīm.

No *āb shaykh* was ever again as powerful as Kurra had been, no slave ever achieved his position, no matter how influential he might become at court. A species of balance or compromise between slaves and title-holders was to continue until the end of the sultanate.

It was another slave eunuch, Musallim, who governed Kordofan in succession to Kurra, with the title of *maqdūm*, until the Keira lost the province to the Turco-Egyptians.[40] The loss of Kordofan was to be the first step in a process by which, as the nineteenth century progressed, the sultanate lost ground first to the Turco-Egyptian regime and then to the traders from the Nile. The economic basis of the state, essentially the slave trade, was eventually to be eroded both by the Turco-Egyptian stranglehold on its trade routes and by the pre-emption of its traditional slaving grounds by the Khartoum traders.

The first Musallim heard of the Turco-Egyptian invasion was when merchants from the Nile warned him of the advance of the forces of the *daftardār* Muḥammad Bey Kusraw, the general sent by Muḥammad ʿAlī, Viceroy of Egypt.[41] Neither Musallim nor the court in al-Fāshir appear to have appreciated the seriousness of the threat. The *maqdūm* made no attempt to utilize the very size of Kordofan to destroy the invaders – the strategy used so devastatingly by the Mahdi against Hicks Pasha sixty years later – but waited to receive them. At Bāra, on 19 August 1821, the Keira forces were crushed by the cannon and musketry of the Turco-Egyptians; Musallim, the *abbo daadiŋa* ʿAbd al-Qādir and many others died a hero's death and Kordofan was irretrievably lost to Dār Fūr.

The *daftardār* had apparently been commissioned by Muḥammad ʿAlī to conquer Dār Fūr as well, but the fierce revolt along the Nile that followed the initial conquest of Sinnār and its provinces diverted him. Dār Fūr was to be spared for another fifty years.[42]

Muḥammad al-Faḍl did mount an attempt to regain his lost province, but the expedition appears to have disintegrated before reaching the *daftardār*.[43] Thereafter the sultanate seems to have pursued a policy of cautious hostility towards the new colonial regime in Khartoum.[44] Muḥammad al-Faḍl closed the *darb al-arbaʿīn*, a measure which must have hurt him more than Egypt; Muḥammad ʻAlī banned the export of arms to Dār Fūr.[45] The viceroy also supported the pretensions of a claimant to the Dār Fūr throne, the sultan's brother Muḥammad Abū Madyan, who appears to have fled to Kordofan about 1837. Schemes to put Abū Madyan on the throne of Dār Fūr were entertained by Muḥammad ʻAlī at various times, but none materialized and the Keira prince languished as a pensioner in Cairo, where he met Dr Perron, the translator of al-Tūnisī's travels.[46]

On its western frontier Dār Fūr was less powerless to influence events. Under the strong Wadai sultan Ṣābūn (died *c.* 1230/1815–16), Dar Tāma was more firmly drawn into the Wadai sphere of influence, while an attempt by Muḥammad al-Faḍl to support a Wadai pretender came to nothing.[47] Later, however, Wadai fell into confusion and civil war, which Muḥammad al-Faḍl tried to exploit by sending an army to install another Wadai claimant, Muḥammad al-Sharīf, then living in Dār Fūr, as sultan. Muḥammad al-Sharīf was installed but soon after repudiated the agreement he had made to pay tribute and acknowledge the suzerainty of the Keira sultan; he proved to be one of Wadai's strongest rulers.[48]

When he felt his death approaching, Muḥammad al-Faḍl, like his father, turned to his slave confidant, Ādam Ṭarbūsh, to arrange the succession of the second of his sons, Muḥammad al-Ḥusayn.[49] The events leading to the accession of Muḥammad al-Ḥusayn were complicated; as the old sultan lay dying a conspiracy by a group of title-holders to put another son on the throne was foiled by Ṭarbūsh.[50] Once the sultan was dead, his eldest son, Abū Bakr, tried to seize the palace. This attempt at a *coup* was also foiled by Ṭarbūsh, who was eventually able with the aid of the *faqīh* Muḥammad Salāma to install Muḥammad al-Ḥusayn as sultan.

From Nachtigal's account and from oral sources, it would appear that by the time of the succession crisis of Ṣafar 1254/April–May 1838, something like two parties or factions had begun to emerge at court, roughly the slaves and the title-holders. Although the former controlled the *fāshir* and thus could put their nominees on the throne, the latter, with their estates, tribal followings and territorial commands, particularly the *maqdūm*ates, were strong enough to ensure that the slaves never completely took over. And the division was never rigid, alliances could be and were made across the party lines.

Although Muḥammad al-Ḥusayn may have been backed by Ṭarbūsh and the *fuqarā'* because of his piety and mildness, he was a poor choice in the threatening circumstances that soon faced the sultanate. Under his ineffectual rule, both the slaves and the title-holders ran riot in competing for estates and position, particularly after the sultan went blind in 1856 and his sister, the *iiya baasi* Zamzam, virtually ran the state.[51]

The sultans and the Arabs

Both Muḥammad al-Faḍl and his son were involved in campaigns against the Arab nomads to the north and south, but the campaigns led to very different results.

The *jammāla* or camel nomads of the north, operating in an ecologically marginal area and numerically small, were never a serious threat. Running from west to east the main tribes were the Maḥāmīd, Mahrīya, 'Irayqāt, Umm Jalūl and Zayādīya, the latter bordering Kordofan; all were nominally subject to the Keira. Some sources suggest the existence at one time in northern Dār Fūr and Kordofan of a confederation of tribes called Fazāra, but it seems to have broken up as a unit, if it ever existed, by the beginning of the nineteenth century.[52]

The Keira kept the nomads down by striking at their weakest point, their herds; Browne recorded that during his stay the Mahrīya and the Maḥāmīd fought between themselves. To punish them 'Abd al-Raḥmān sent a *malik* with about sixty horsemen, who seized half their camels and 'where they found five took three, as the fifth could not be divided'.[53] Nachtigal reported that the 'Irayqāt derided the rule of Muḥammad al-Faḍl because he was still so young. An expedition went north under the *baasi* 'Umar, who seized every fifth camel from the 'Irayqāt. But trouble continued and seven years later a larger force was sent, which met with disaster. Finally the *wazīr* 'Abd al-Sīd, the general who later successfully imposed Muḥammad al-Sharīf on Wadai, marched north and crushed the 'Irayqāt, seven of whose chiefs were executed in al-Fāshir before the sultan.[54] The camel nomads were more vulnerable to Keira reprisals and raids than their cousins in the south since they had nowhere to seek refuge save in the desert.

The raids against the camel-keeping nomads were small-scale affairs, part of the normal technique employed by Sudanic kings to quell the nomads. The series of campaigns that were waged in Muḥammad al-Ḥusayn's reign against the Baqqāra or cattle nomads, in particular the Rizayqāt, seem to have been much more serious. The southern campaigns were larger in scale, being fought over vast distances, they exposed the military deficiencies of the sultanate and finally they led to or coincided with the beginnings of the involvement of the Khartoum traders in Dār Fūr's affairs.

The relationship between the settled peoples and the nomads in the south was a complex one of interaction and exchange of products.[55] The relationship between the Fur and the Banī Halba along the Wādī Azum was particularly close; they paid the price when Muḥammad al-Faḍl objected to their wealth and independence and in 'the bloodbath of the Bani Halba' laid the tribe low for at least a generation.[56] There were probably several motives behind the punitive expeditions against the Baqqāra recorded from Tayrāb's time onwards; a defensive strategy of keeping the nomads from encroaching on the settled lands and a positive desire to share forcibly in the nomads' wealth in cattle. There was also the slave factor; the *ghazwa* parties had to pass through Baqqāra territory to get to their victims. Presumably, since we have little evidence, the nomads participated in and profited from the trade.[57]

The Rizayqāt and their allies the Habbānīya and Ma'ālīya were the particular object of Keira campaigning in the south. The Rizayqāt country in south-eastern Dār Fūr was poorly watered and not easily accessible and the tribe's nomadic cycle took them far south to the Baḥr al-'Arab. Tayrāb had campaigned unsuccessfully against the Rizayqāt, although later Muḥammad al-Faḍl's general, the *maqdūm* Sa'īd, had comparatively greater success.[58] Muḥammad al-Ḥusayn is said to have organized eighteen campaigns against the Rizayqāt; why is not clear, although Nachtigal recorded that the sultan found it a convenient method of disposing of some of his more dangerous servants.[59]

It would be tempting to postulate that these campaigns were caused indirectly by the opening up of the Baḥr al-Ghazāl by the Khartoum traders from the Nile and a consequent re-alignment of the slave trade routes to the disadvantage of the sultanate, but so far the evidence and chronology does not support this. The campaigns began over a decade before the penetration of the Baḥr al-Ghazāl from the Nile in approximately 1855,[60] although it is probable that *jallāba* were operating in the far south before then and thus beginning to cut out the Keira from their role as middle-men in the slave raiding/trading network.[61]

The campaigns initiated by Muḥammad al-Ḥusayn appear to have begun some time in the early 1840s and to have petered out inconclusively after 1856.[62] The sultan sent the *abbo somiŋ dogala*, 'Abd al-'Azīz, south to deal with the Rizayqāt. 'Abd al-'Azīz was at first successful in seizing large numbers of Rizayqāt cattle, but he was caught and ambushed by the nomads as he was returning north. The sultan was furious and the *abbo somiŋ dogala* was brought to court in disgrace and condemned to death. He saved his life by a judicious bribe to the sultan, who indeed commissioned him as *maqdūm* in southern Dār Fūr. Three years later the *maqdūm* was defeated and killed by the Rizayqāt in a tremendous three-day battle.

Following ‘Abd al-‘Azīz's death, the sultan ordered several of the leading title-holders, including the *āb shaykh* Raḥma Gomo, to concentrate their forces in the south under the leadership of Khalīl b. ‘Abd al-Sīd, a son of the general who had crushed the ‘Irayqāt in the north. The Keira forces set out in search of the Rizayqāt, but the expedition was a fiasco and the army had to retreat when their food ran out.[63]

In a further series of expeditions Ādam Ṭarbūsh, now *wazīr* to Muḥammad al-Ḥusayn, was no more successful than his predecessors, although he forced the Habbānīya to take refuge with their Rizayqāt allies. Finally he led a major force south into the marshy lands just north of the Baḥr al-‘Arab. Trapped in a marsh, Ṭarbūsh was killed along with fifty other notables, probably in 1856.[64]

Although Aḥmad Shaṭṭa, a son of the unfortunate ‘Abd al-‘Azīz, was appointed *maqdūm* in southern Dār Fūr, and was eventually able to impose some semblance of Keira rule in the south, the Rizayqāt remained outside his control as did the increasingly important trade routes northwards from the Baḥr al-Ghazāl along which the Khartoum traders sent their slaves and ivory. And the campaigns against the nomads had highlighted the inadequacy of Keira military organization.

The Fur tribal levies had given way to cavalry; a natural development as the state expanded beyond the mountains and conquest gave way to administration. Small forces of horsemen, wearing chainmail, armed with spears, swords and maces and mounted on imported war horses, were sufficient to curb the nomads and coerce the peasants.[65] Muḥammad Kurra had driven Hāshim and the Musabba‘āt out of Kordofan with only 200 such men,[66] and these bands, maintained by the sultan and the title-holders, fitted well into the political ethos of the state. But the long-range campaigns in the south and the earlier loss of Kordofan exposed the weakness of this haphazard style of warfare and attempts were made to introduce firearms. Both Muḥammad al-Ḥusayn and Aḥmad Shaṭṭa were reported to have brought in firearms and trained men in their use.[67] These attempts were probably made in imitation of the Turco-Egyptian soldiers or of the slave troops of the Khartoum traders. But this military revolution had not gone far before the end of the sultanate; ʻAbd al-Wahhāb, an envoy of the ruler of Egypt, Muḥammad Saʻīd Pasha, who visited Dār Fūr in 1862, reported that the Keira army consisted of about 3,000 cavalry, of whom 600 to 1,000 were heavily armed, and some 70,000 infantry, presumably tribal levies, who were badly armed and did not have firearms.[68] In the battles that led to the downfall of the sultanate, the Keira cavalry were to be destroyed by the rifles of al-Zubayr's slave troops.

The downfall of the first Dār Fūr sultanate

In 1856, the year of Ādam Ṭarbūsh's death at the hands of the Rizayqāt, a Jaʻalī trader from the Nile, al-Zubayr Raḥma, arrived in the Baḥr al-Ghazāl.[69] A man of outstanding ability and ambition, he rapidly took over the scattered trading stations in the Baḥr al-Ghazāl so that by 1865 he was virtual ruler of a vast trading empire. But as his empire grew he came into conflict with the imperial ambitions of the Khedive Ismāʻīl of Egypt; Turco-Egyptian anti-slaving measures and the Khedive's plans in the southern Sudan blocked al-Zubayr's outlets for his ivory and slaves through the White Nile. As a result the routes through Dār Fūr, along the peripheries of the sultanate, and Kordofan became vitally important to al-Zubayr and his trading partners.

Thus in Shawwāl 1282/February–March 1866 al-Zubayr made an agreement with 80 Rizayqāt shaykhs to secure the passage, on the payment of a toll, of his caravans through their lands, probably at the time when the *wazīr* Aḥmad Shaṭṭa at Dāra was beginning to put pressure on the nomads once more.[70]

Apart from involving himself the Rizayqāt, al-Zubayr, by

rationalizing the commercial network in the Baḥr al-Ghazāl, had struck a blow at the commercial basis of the Keira state, since he now controlled and drew his slaves and ivory from precisely the area, Dār Fartīt, which had supplied those commodities to Dār Fūr in the past. The collecting of the slaves and ivory and the revenues derived from them were now outside Dār Fūr's control, as were the routes along which the goods travelled.[71]

Slatin describes the result,

> The effect of this on the luxury-loving Darfurians was painfully evident. They saw their main source of ivory and slave supplies cut off, and to meet the Government expenditure increased taxation was enforced, which resulted in widespread discontent.[72]

What Slatin appears to mean is that the Keira and the title-holders in al-Fāshir could no longer pay, with slaves and ivory, for the imported goods that were an essential component in the ostentation and consumption that formed a basis of their power. And the revenues from their estates, mainly foodstuffs, were no adequate substitute.[73]

Meanwhile al-Zubayr had to deal with a rival in the Baḥr al-Ghazāl, Muḥammad al-Bulālāwī who arrived there in 1869 with the backing of the Turco-Egyptians.[74] Al-Bulālāwī was in origin a Bulāla *faqīh* from the lake Fitri region in what is now Chad who had spent some years at the court of Muḥammad al-Ḥusayn, who granted him an *ḥākūra*. But the *faqīh* quarrelled with Aḥmad Shaṭṭa, who coveted the *ḥākūra*, and with the *iiya baasi* Zamzam, who distrusted his influence over her blind brother, and he was forced to leave Dār Fūr. He then approached the Turco-Egyptians, claiming that he owned the copper mines at Ḥufrat al-Naḥās in southern Dār Fūr.[75] They sent him with a few regular troops to try to oust al-Zubayr, but the latter was too strong and three years later, in 1872, al-Bulālāwī was killed and his troops added to those of al-Zubayr.[76]

The precarious independence that the Keira sultans had been able to preserve since 1821 was now not only under pressure from the south but also from the east, since the Khedive had included Dār Fūr in his imperial plans. Propaganda aimed at a European audience depicted Dār Fūr as the last refuge of those slave traders driven out of the Egyptian Sudan by the zeal of the Khedive and his lieutenants; the exact opposite was the case.[77] In 1867 an Egyptian officer, Muḥammad Nādī Bey, was sent to al-Fāshir ostensibly on a diplomatic mission to the sultan, but in reality to spy out the land for an invasion attempt.[78] But the Khedive was to be forestalled by al-Zubayr.

Belatedly the old sultan and his court realized their danger and seem to have persuaded a section of the Rizayqāt to break their agreement with al-Zubayr and attack his caravans.[79] Al-Zubayr, before retaliating, wrote to the sultan in June 1873 to try to preserve the peace, but the letter was received not by the old sultan but by sultan Ibrāhīm.[80]

Muḥammad al-Ḥusayn died probably in April 1873; before he died, like his father, he tried to arrange with his slave confidants, the *amīn* Bakhīt, son of the former *wazīr* Adam Ṭarbūsh, and Khayr Qarīb, a Fartīt slave who ran the treasury, that his younger son, Ibrāhīm, should succeed him. But even with the threat of al-Zubayr developing in the south, Ibrāhīm's accession was disputed; a party, led by the *faqīh* Dardarī from Kordofan and Aḥmad Shaṭṭa, wanted as sultan the eldest son, Abu'l-Bashar who was married to the *wazīr*'s daughter. While still in Wadai Nachtigal heard rumours of the dispute which suggested that one faction, 'the genuine Fur', presumably the title-holders, opposed the slaves and their candidate. As the sultan lay dying, the *faqīh* Dardarī summoned Aḥmad Shaṭṭa back from Dāra, his capital in southern Dār Fūr, while Abu'l-Bashar entered al-Fāshir with 1,000 riflemen. But the *amīn* Bakhīt, like Kurra some twenty years earlier, as *abbo kɔrkwa* had the most armed men in the right place – the palace – and when the *wazīr* reached al-Fāshir, the *faqīh* was in prison and

Abu'l-Bashar's men disarmed. Ibrāhīm became sultan on 21 April 1873.[81]

Thereafter al-Zubayr began to close in on Dār Fūr, keeping up a correspondence with Ibrāhīm that became stiffer and stiffer in tone and ending with the demand, in November 1873, that the sultan should submit to the Khedive. Meanwhile he moved into Rizayqāt territory, brushing the nomads aside and occupying Shakkā on 26 August 1873. It seems that al-Zubayr decided he was strong enough to invade the sultanate from the time of his appointment as governor of the Shakkā region and the Baḥr al-Ghazāl.[82]

In fact the conquest of Dār Fūr was to prove a slow and complex affair; the vast distances and the difficulties of concentrating troops in an area of sparse grazing, water and food, made the campaigning very laborious. It was the Keira who took the initiative; Aḥmad Shaṭṭa, back at Dāra as *maqdūm* despite his role in the succession crisis, joined forceswith the *malik al-naḥās* Sa'd al-Nūr, son of the famous general Ibrāhīm b. Ramād, and attacked and defeated one of al-Zubayr's commanders. But while the *maqdūm*, despite his victory, felt it expedient to write a conciliatory letter to the trader, the sultan from al-Fāshir was urging on the Rizayqāt to attack al-Zubayr. Eventually the *wazīr*, goaded by the new sultan and compelled by his own men, attacked al-Zubayr near Shakkā in January or February 1874. In the battle that followed the *wazīr* and many other leading title-holders were killed.[83] This battle sealed the fate of the sultanate, in spite of a lull of a few months, since al-Zubayr began to bring up reinforcements from his camps in the south until he had some 7,000 men with him.[84]

The Turco-Egyptian authorities in Khartoum had been following al-Zubayr's progress anxiously and decided to move in. In February 1874 the Khedive Isma'īl declared war on the sultan and ordered the Governor-General, Ismā'īl Ayyūb Pasha, to concentrate his forces on the eastern Dār Fūr border.[85] But al-Zubayr was already on the move, having defeated another force and occupied Dāra.

To Dāra came the sultan with his title-holders and what was left of his army. After some delay, Ibrāhīm attempted an attack on Dāra, which failed. The demoralized Dār Fūr host retreated back towards al-Fāshir, but the retreat rapidly turned into a rout. Finally the sultan with only his title-holders and bodyguard made a stand at Manawāshī, where, on 23 October 1874, he was defeated and killed. On the orders of al-Zubayr, Ibrāhīm was buried at the Bornu mosque in Manawāshī. A week later al-Zubayr entered al-Fāshir where he was joined a few days afterwards by Ismā'īl Pasha.[86]

XII · Postscript

The Turco-Egyptian invasion of the Sudan in 1820–1 found the Funj kingdom ill-prepared to resist. Each of the feuding princes was individually and abruptly forced to choose between resistance and collaboration. The heir to the throne of Dongola, ousted by the Shāīqīya both from his capital and his place of honourable exile at Arqū, chose to collaborate; he was installed as the puppet governor of Arqū. The Shāīqīya princes resolved to fight, and were assisted, in some measure, by the Ja'aliyīn of al-Matamma. Two set battles between the horsemen of Sinnār and the Turks demonstrated the superiority of modern weapons; the defeated princes abandoned their provinces and took service with the invaders. The other riverain princes from Berber to Fāzūghlī, including the sultan, quietly capitulated.

As the invaders advanced they posted small garrisons at intervals along the Nile; the main force was decimated in the extreme south by disease and the determined resistance of the borderland hill peoples. The Sudanese were finding the taste of foreign rule bitter, and rumours of a general revolt among the erstwhile princes of Sinnār began to circulate. Sensing an impending crisis the Turkish commander marched back to Shandī, where he was assassinated. The timely arrival of reinforcements prevented the total collapse of the Turkish position and the rising was brutally suppressed. A few of the provincial lords not implicated in the revolt were permitted to retain a measure of local autonomy under Turkish overrule; these included the *makks* of the Blue Nile districts above Sinnār, Fāzūghlī and Arqū. Left in remote backwaters of the administrative and commercial system of the colonial regime, they gradually faded into genteel impotence and obscurity. In 1840 the Turks undertook the conquest of the eastern Funj provinces. In the heat of the bitterly-contested campaign for control of al-Takā the ranking Shāīqī dynast seized the opportunity to revolt, but failed. In short, almost every prince of Sinnār fought desperately against the Turks; they did so, however, in pathetic and ineffectual sequence.

By 1850 the only Funj province that retained its independence was Taqalī. The remote mountain stronghold became a refuge for slave soldiers escaping from the ranks of the Turkish army, who sometimes arrived carrying their rifles, and invariably an uncompromising hatred of the Turks. For at least fifteen years the kings of Taqalī threw back successive waves of invaders; in the end the fortunes of the little principality were submerged in the large political currents of the 1870s.

The colonial system had effectively decapitated the old Funj governmental system. The high rates of taxation, along with abuses associated with tax collection, gave the peasant cultivator a powerful incentive to abandon his vocation. Yet government commercial monopolies and favouritism closed the door to most opportunities for trade by ordinary Sudanese; only the nomadic groups who alone could supply desert transport profited. In these circumstances many found the frontier regions of the southern and western Sudan a land of opportunity. Beyond the effective control of Khartoum, yet accessible through many and devious channels to the demands of the Cairo slave market, merchants from the riverain Sudan forged commercial and political empires. With the rush of petty traders to the frontiers came also the religious and political organization that had served humble folk in the homeland, the Islamic brotherhood. One suspects that early brotherhoods on the frontier were branches of communities on the Nile. As wealth and power of the frontier merchants grew, however, it was natural that the southern orders should assume leadership in the far-flung network of brotherhood organizations. Among the younger generation of leaders who grew up in the immigrant community of the southern frontier was Muḥammad Aḥmad, the Mahdī.

The defeat of Manawāshī stripped away the superstructure of the Keira sultanate, whose territories were now incorporated into the Egyptian Sudan. Al-Zubayr went to Cairo to protest and was detained there, the Keira retreated into Jabal Marra, where they sought to maintain the Fur Kingdom, with some degree of success.

The Fur were still resisting when the Mahdist revolt broke out in 1881. Unlike the Baqqāra, the Fur and their chiefs were unresponsive to the Mahdī's message, and they largely supported the anti-Mahdist forces, particularly the revolt of the *faqīh* Abū Jummayza in 1888. The Fur under the Keira were fighting for their own conception of freedom.

After the defeat of the Khalīfa at Kararī in September 1898, a Keira claimant, 'Alī Dīnār b. Zakarīya, a son of Sultan Muḥammad al-Faḍl, hurriedly returned with a group of Fur and other chiefs to Dār Fūr and declared himself sultan; he was never formally enthroned. The newly established Condominium government in the Sudan had no immediate wish to annexe Dār Fūr, and from 1898 to 1916 'Alī Dīnār ruled the sultanate, reviving the old administrative system with some modifications, regranting the old titles and *ḥākūras*, driving back the Arab nomads who had encroached on the settled land during the chaos of the previous twenty years, and becoming increasingly nervous of the French advance from the west. His relations with the Condominium government deteriorated, mainly over the French issue, and in 1916, influenced by the Pan-Islamic propaganda of the Turks and the Sanūsīya in Libya, he declared war on the British. Dār Fūr was invaded, 'Ali Dīnār's army defeated at Birinjīya near al-Fāshir and he himself killed a few months later. Dār Fūr finally became part of the Sudan.

Notes

(*For full bibliographical details, see Bibliography*)

CHAPTER I

1. Much of the following is based on Barbour (1961).
2. Ibn Sulaym al-Aswānī in al-Maqrīzī (1853), 191.
3. Krump (1710), 235.
4. Trigger (1965), 156.
5. Brevedent in Crawford (1951), 294.
6. On the languages of Dār Fūr and Kordofan, see Tucker and Bryan (1956); ethnographic surveys can be found in MacMichael (1912) and (1922), I, 52–128 and Theobald (1965), 1–16.
7. Haaland in Barth (1969), 58–73.
8. Barbour (1961), 151.
9. On the Zaghāwa, see Tubiana (1964).
10. Asad (1970), 18–30.
11. Barbour (1954), 172–82.
12. On the economy of the mountain Fur Barth in Firth (1967), 149–74.
13. Greenberg in Sebeok (1971), 421–42.
14. Browne (1799), 300.
15. Yūsuf (1967), 166.
16. In only a few cases have we been able to supplement Professor Yūsuf Faḍl Ḥasan's survey of this literature as it concerns the Sudan (Yūsuf (1967), 182–203), but in some instances we have interpreted the evidence differently.

PART ONE

CHAPTER II

1. Egyptian expeditions against Makuria took place in 1276, 1288, 1289-90, 1304–5, 1323 and 1365–6; this list is not necessarily complete.
2. Yūsuf (1967), 110.

3. Ibn Faḍl Allāh (al-ʻUmarī) (1927), 49–50.
4. Though the Nubian dialects of Dongola and the Kenuz are distinct, they are similar.
5. Ibn Faḍl Allāh (1927), 49, n. 4; al-Qalqashāndī (1913–19), V, 278.
6. Monneret de Villard represents the former orientation, MacMichael the latter. Yūsuf (1967), 178 mentions the superficial character of Islam in Dongola during the transitional centuries, but does not call attention to the alternative set of beliefs.
7. Al-Bakāwī in Yūsuf Kamāl (1928–51), IV, fasc. 1.
8. Yūsuf (1967), 126–32.
9. Shinnie (1955), 76.
10. Al-Harrānī in Yūsuf Kamāl (1928–51), IV, fasc. 1.
11. ʻAbd al-Ẓāhir (1961), 144–5.
12. Ibn Khaldūn (1956–61), V, 922–3, gave a rather exaggerated account of the depredations of the Arabs in Nubia, perhaps as a case study illustrative of his theory concerning the role of nomads in the rise and fall of civilizations.
13. Alvarez (1961), II, 461. The emphasis on churches reflects the interests of the missionary Alvarez, and not necessarily those of the Nubians.
14. Kammerer (1929–52), XV, 75–80; Yūsuf (1967), 68–74.
15. Ibn Saʻīd in Yūsuf Kamāl (1926–51), IV, fasc. 1.
16. Lejean (1865), 5.
17. Ibn Baṭṭūṭa (1958), II, 362–3.
18. Al-Idrīsī cited in Yūsuf (1967), 73.
19. Ibn Jubayr (1907), 72.
20. Ibn Baṭṭūṭa (1958), II, 362–3.
21. Yūsuf (1967), 78–82.
22. Ibn Diqmaq in Yūsuf Kamāl (1926–51), IV, fasc. 2.
23. Ibn Faḍl Allāh in Yūsuf Kamāl (1926–51), IV, fasc. 2.
24. See Chap. IV.
25. Ibn Baṭṭūṭa (1958), II, 363.
26. Yūsuf (1967), 46–7.
27. Ibn Faḍl Allāh (1927), 16. The concluding *jīm* of the word 'Funj' is often omitted in Sudanese colloquial speech.
28. Lewis (1967), 157.
29. Crawford (1958), 127 and 143.
30. Penn (1934), 59–82; Aḥmad (1969), 14–26.
31. Aḥmad (1969), 14.
32. Penn (1934), 60.
33. Aḥmad (1969), 17.
34. ibid., 14–15, 20.

35. ibid., 16. The copper kettledrum was among the insignia of royalty.
36. Al-Dimashqī (1866), 268.
37. Aḥmad (1969), 21–5.
38. Penn (1934), 61.
39. *Makhṭūṭa* (1961), 4.
40. A discussion of the early Funj is to be found in Spaulding (1972), 39–53.

CHAPTER III

1. Crawford (1951), 331; *Makhṭūṭa* (1961), 129; Ḍayfallāh (1971), 39.
2. Bruce (1805), VI, 369–71.
3. The first ruler of Qarrī to be named ʻAjīb was a figure of the late sixteenth and seventeenth centuries.
4. Murray (1808), 416.
5. ibid., 425.
6. Bruce (1805), VI, 369–71.
7. Cailliaud (1823), II, 254.
8. Bruce (1805), VI, 369–71.
9. Hillelson (1935), 61–2.
10. Certain nineteenth-century Sudanese sources tell of an alliance between ʻAbdallāh Jammāʻ and ʻAmāra Dunqas to overthrow Soba, and describe a subsequent equal division of the kingdom between the two rulers. Reasons for rejecting this story are given by Holt (1960), 1–12, and Spaulding (thesis 1971), 87–97.
11. Barradas in Beccari (1905–17), IV, 108.
12. De Castro (1939–40), III, 80–4.
13. Villard (1929), 22.
14. Hartmann (1863), 224; Cadalvène et Breuvery (1841), II, 260.
15. Hillelson (1935), 61.
16. Russegger (1843), II, i, 18, 456; II, ii, 445, 514, 769.
17. Brun-Rollet (1855), 213.
18. Chataway (1930), 256; Crawford (1951), 152.
19. Celebi (1938), X, 895–6.
20. Russegger (1843), II, ii, 349, 477, 514, 769. Bruce (1805), VI, 372, also alluded to the language of the Funj, ʻAll that can be said with certainty of this term (Funj)', he wrote, ʻ*as there is no access to the study of their language* . . .'. (italics added).
21. See Chap. IV.

22. For a similar system in Wadai, see Nachtigal (1971), 170–1.
23. Cailliaud (1823), II, 273.
24. ibid., 274.
25. ibid.
26. Aḥmad (1969), 9.
27. Cailliaud (1823), II, 274.
28. ibid., 273.
29. ibid., 274.
30. ibid.
31. ibid., II, 406; Marno (1874), 68, 255.
32. Bruce (1805), VI, 371; Hoskins (1835), 201; Cailliaud (1823), II, 254; Aḥmad (1969), 19.
33. Hillelson (1935), 59.
34. Holt (1967a), 19–23.
35. ibid.
36. Aḥmad (1969), 19.
37. Bruce (1805), VI, 371.
38. *Makhṭūṭa* (1961), 4; De Castro (1939–40), III, 80–4; Villard (1929), 19–48.
39. Hillelson (1935), 59.
40. Aregay and Selassie in Yūsuf (1971), 70.
41. Russegger (1843), II, ii, 600 and 769.
42. Ibn Iyas (1932), V, 3; Wiet (1938), 115–40.
43. The bishop of Ethiopia was customarily selected by the Patriarch of Alexandria from among the Egyptian monastic community. Since he alone could ordain priests, the Ethiopian church could ill afford to be without a bishop for an interval approaching or exceeding the lifetime of one generation of clergy.
44. Castanheda (1924–33), Book V, Chap. 27.
45. De Barros (1628), Decada III, Book IV, Chap. 3.
46. Alvarez (1961), II, 449–50.
47. Ibid., I, 129.
48. Brother Antonio of Urvuar to Alessandro Zorzi in Venice about 1523 in Crawford (1958), 181.
49. Holt (1967a) 22.
50. Petti Suma (1964), 438.
51. Burckhardt (1822), 133–5.
52. Holt (1967a), 22.
53. Villard (1929), 47.
54. Penn (1934), 66–7.
55. Villard (1929), 47.

56. Cailliaud (1823), I, 394.
57. Crawford (1951), 331.
58. The long reign assigned by Funj tradition to the founder of the kingdom receives some corroboration from Reubeni's account, since he found him on the throne as late as 1523.
59. *Makhṭūṭa* (1961), 7 states that 'Amāra Dunqas was succeeded by his son 'Abd al-Qādir I, who reigned for ten years, when he was followed by Nāyil.
60. *Makhṭūṭa* (1961), 8 adds the comment that during the reign of 'Amāra II, 'Abdallāh Jammā' died and was succeeded by 'Ajīb the Great. This comment, lacking in earlier versions, should be rejected as a late 'Abdallāb-influenced attempt to conceal the sixteenth-century period of Funj hegemony throughout Sinnār.
61. According to *Makhṭūṭa* (1961), 8 Dakīn's regnal dates were 980–85/1572–3–1577; Dawra (or Dūka) was the brother rather than the son of Dakīn, and he reigned for eight years.
62. Crawford (1951), 329; *Makhṭūṭa* (1961), 8.
63. Ḍayfallāh (1971), 212.
64. *Makhṭūṭa* (1961), 8–9.
65. Aḥmad (1969), 35.
66. Penn (1934), 66. Penn's informant placed the whole episode during the seventeenth-century reign of the informant's last reigning ancestor, but it belongs properly to the reign of his earlier namesake.
67. Pereira (1892–1900), II, 374.
68. Ḍayfallāh (1971), 212.
69. Aḥmad (1969), 46.
70. Cailliaud (1823), II, 256.
71. Pereira (1892–1900), II, 78.
72. Penn (1934), 62; Aḥmad (1969), 47.
73. Ḍayfallāh (1971), 49–65.
74. Crawford (1951), 335, and with slight variations in Penn (1934), 64.
75. Krump (1710), 296–8; Bruce (1805), VI, 371.
76. The 'previous treaty' was spurious and 'Abdallāb propaganda designed to conceal the period of Funj domination. A typical version reads: "Amāra and 'Abdallāh were like two brothers but the rank of 'Amāra was higher than the rank of 'Abdallāh. So if they were together, 'Amāra would take precedence over 'Abdallāh, and if 'Amāra were absent, 'Abdallāh occupied his place. This custom continued to be followed . . . until the end of the kingdom.' Holt (1960), 6.

77. This may have been a nineteenth-century rationalization; Cailliaud's informants in Qarrī knew of no king before 'Ajīb, (1823), II, 96.
78. ibid., 236; Bruce (1805), VI, 369–71, 391.

CHAPTER IV

1. Poncet (1949), 103–4. The spelling has been slightly modernized.
2. Robinson (1929), 235.
3. Poncet (1949), 104.
4. Russegger (1843), II, ii, 489.
5. Poncet (1949), 103.
6. At the provincial courts, *mānjil*; the term used before the sultan is unknown.
7. Krump (1710); 301; Penn (1934), 68; Disney (1945), 38–9; Arkell (1932), 232, and plate 1, figure 1.
8. Poncet (1949), 100.
9. Hoskins (1835), 211.
10. Bruce (1805), VI, 349.
11. Krump (1710), 301.
12. Hoskins (1835), 45.
13. ibid.; Nalder (1931), 76–8.
14. Russegger (1843), II, ii, 462.
15. Poncet (1949), 103.
16. MacMichael (1922), II, 360.
17. Hoskins (1835), 209.
18. Cadalvène et Breuvery (1841), II, 338.
19. Krump (1710), 281, 313–14.
20. Brocchi (1843), V, 434; Holt (1969), 13.
21. Disney (1945), 38–40.
22. Brocchi (1843), V, 332–3, 434.
23. ibid., 434.
24. Bruce (1805), VI, 372; Brocchi (1843), V, 332–3, 434.
25. The *sīd al-qūm* was often the first and highest-ranking individual to sign 'Abdallāb documents. According to Funj dynastic practice, the 'Abdallāb *sīd al-qūm* would have been a member of the sultan's clan and an emissary from the central government.
26. Bruce (1805), VI, 272, 278.
27. Abu Selim (1967), 60, 66, 73, 76, 102, 106, 114, 119 and 136.
28. Bruce (1905), VI, 372.
29. Brocchi (1843), V, 434–5. The office of treasurer was mentioned

in the early account of Sinnār by Reubeni, Hillelson (1935), 59–60.

30. Krump (1710), 286; Bruce (1805), VI, 378; Hoskins (1835), 209; Hartmann (1863), 519.
31. Russegger (1843), II, ii, 505.
32. Holt (1963a), 50.
33. This practice among the Funj seems to be consistent with the royal succession system of the Meidob, a Nubian group in Dār Fūr whose institutions were not heavily influenced, until recent times, by either Christianity or Islam (Lampen (1928), 55–67). This correspondence between Funj and Meidob custom tends to confirm the hypothesis of the Nubian origin of the Funj.
34. Holt (1963a), 50.
35. Bruce (1805), VI, 381; Cailliaud (1823), II, 272.
36. Traditions collected by Robinson (1930–1), 364, suggest that the sultan was expected to repeat this ritual each year 'at the first sowing'.
37. Russegger (1843), II, ii, 609.
38. Bruce (1805), VI, 372; Russegger (1843), II, ii, 553, commented that the execution of a king could usually be considered 'simply as an expression of the dissatisfaction of the nobles with their king'.
39. Lepsius (1852), 212, 214–15; Russegger (1843), II, ii, 553; Arkell (1932), 231, n. 1; Whitehead (1934), 224.
40. De Lauture (1855–6), 82.
41. One may compare the *Funj Chronicle*'s treatment of the peaceful reign of the good sultan Nūl with that of either his predecessor or his successor. Nūl's reign was nicknamed 'the sleep', because nothing bloody and therefore noteworthy occurred (MacMichael (1922), II, 364).
42. Sinnār, concluded Crawford (1951), 173, was an anarchic tribal confederation with only the loosest sort of central authority. At best, according to Yūsuf (1967), 134, Sinnār was a league of tribal confederations, yielding merely 'a measure of political stability'.
43. Abu Selim (1967), 70, 124, 128.
44. Krump (1710), 295.
45. ibid., 286–7.
46. Penn (1934), 65.
47. Bruce (1805), VI, 391.
48. Disney (1945), 38.

49. Robinson (1929), 235. Funj marriage policy explains the unusual wording of article III of the treaty of Idrīs wad al-Arbāb, for 'if the daughter of the Fung Mek' were given in marriage to a ruler in the Buṭāna, it would bring him under the authority of the court of Sinnār.
50. Bruce (1805), VI, 295.
51. Nalder (1931), 80.
52. Krump (1710), 283.
53. Ibn al-Furāt (1936–42), VIII, 92.
54. Brocchi (1843), V, 434.
55. Russegger (1843), II, ii, 8.
56. Rüppell (1829), 107; Burckhardt (1822), 224.
57. Hoskins (1835), 90.
58. ibid., 59; Brocchi (1843), V, 106.
59. Cadalvène et Breuvery (1841), II, 336.
60. Rüppell (1829), 44.
61. Hoskins (1835), 90.
62. ibid., 37, 125, 211.
63. ibid., 89.
64. Brocchi (1843), V, 434; Abu Selim (1967), 76, 130; Holt (1969), 5, 6, 12.
65. Abu Selim (1967), 32.
66. Paul (1954), 23.
67. Burckhardt (1822), 61; Rüppell (1829), 27, 38.
68. Hoskins (1835), 207. By Hoskins' day the Turkish authorities had tried to replace the payments in kind characteristic of Sinnār with cash levies. Carradori's dictionary of medieval Nubian gave a term which he translated 'abacus', but perhaps such strings of beads were in fact intended (our thanks to Dr Edgar Gregerson for permission to consult his Carradori manuscript). Coarse clay beads were found in sets at Soba, and might well have served in calculation (Shinnie (1955), 57, and drawings on 55, figure 8, nos. 3, 6 and 18).
69. Bruce (1805), VI, 358, described a similar practice in regard to livestock collected as taxes from the nomads; at certain seasons, he said, most of the meat for sale in Sinnār came from stock taken as taxes.
70. Abu Selim (1967), 31–3; Paul (1954), 23.
71. Paul (1954), 23.
72. Hillelson (1935), 57.
73. Linant (1958), 54; Rüppell (1829), 22, 45–6; Cadalvène et Breuvery (1841), II, 331–2.

74. Krump (1710), 300.
75. Bruce (1805), VI, 370; Cailliaud (1823), II, 113.
76. Russegger (1843), II, ii, 581–2.
77. Hillelson (1920), 33–75.
78. Arkell (1956), 83–4.
79. Hartmann (1863), 524.
80. Holt (1969), 11.
81. Hartmann (1861, 206; – (1863), 293.
82. Abu Selim (1967), 49.
83. ibid., 90–1.
84. Brocchi (1843), V, 330–1.
85. Abu Selim (1967), 48, 60, 63, 66, 83, 97, 102, 114, 120, 136, 138. The meaning of the term may be tentatively derived from a comparison with Dār Fūr usage, where the *qawwārīn* were perhaps either 'collectors of horses for the sultan' (Arkell Papers[1], box 4, file 16, f. 61) or the collectors of customs dues (Kropáček (1971), 42, n. 45).
86. Brehm (1861), I, 171–2; Holt (1969), 6.
87. Polanyi (1968), 280–3.
88. Lapanouse (1802), 93–4.
89. Krump (1710), 289.
90. Browne (1799), 254–5, noted that the slave hunt in Dār Fūr was called 'selatea'; it seems reasonable to associate this term with the Funj officer.
91. Lapanouse (1802), 97.
92. The trade in more mundane items was left to private traders.
93. Krump (1710), 372.
94. Poncet (1949), 93–4; Norden (1757), II, 33; Sonnini (1799), III, 85–8.
95. Burckhardt (1822), 282.

CHAPTER V

1. All regnal dates given here are derived from the king-list of the *sīd al-qūm* Aḥmad, Crawford (1951), 331.
2. Bruce (1805), VI, 386.
3. Cailliaud (1823), III, 57–8.
4. Pereira (1892–1900), II, 154 ff.
5. Bruce (1805), VI, 377.
6. Lefèvre (1842), 262.
7 Pereira (1892–1900), II, 120–60; Crawford (1951), 180–7.
8. Bruce (1805), III, 312.

9. Poncet (1949), 110; Giamberardini (1963), 420, 422, describe the closing of the roads of Sinnār in similar circumstances at a later period.
10. Bruce's informants stated that the White Nile was the frontier between Funj and Shilluk in 1772 (Murray (1808), 420–1; Bruce (1805), VI, 270); this agrees with Westermann's Shilluk tradition that the Funj were not finally expelled from the east bank of the White Nile opposite the Shilluk country until their defeat by the Dinka leader Akwai Chakab in about 1775; (1912), lv.
11. When Sinnār fell to the Turks, the Shilluk resumed their northward expansion, occupying Alays (Russegger (1843), II, 2, 58, 347); this advance is discussed by Mercer (1971), 407–26.
12. Hofmayr (1925), 7 (freely translated).
13. Hartmann (1863), 545.
14. Hofmayr (1925), 77; Mohamed Riad (1955), 163.
15. Hofmayr (1925), 66.
16. Hartmann (1863), 433, 449; Brehm (1861), I, 246.
17. Cailliaud (1823), III, 84–5; Hartmann (1863), 473, 547, 559.
18. Ṣalāḥ (1967), 58.
19. Elles (1935), 7.
20. Ḍayfallāh (1971), 127–9. The shaykh had been a tutor to 'Ajīb the Great; perhaps he left Sinnār for Taqalī in about 1611, after his illustrious pupil's reversal of fortune.
21. Elles (1935), 3.
22. ibid., 5.
23. MacMichael (1922), II, 361–2; *Makhṭūṭa* (1961), 9–10; Hofmayr (1925), 74.
24. Hartmann (1863), 542; Elles (1935), 10 ff.
25. Peney (1883), 515.
26. MacMichael (1922), II, 362.
27. Bruce (1805), VI, 342–7.
28. ibid.
29. ibid.
30. ibid., 391–2.
31. ibid., 342–7.
32. Spaulding (thesis 1971), 183–4.
33. Ḍayfallāh (1971), 272–7.
34. ibid., 226–8; 272–7.
35. A colourful account of the battle as preserved in Shāīqīya tradition may be found in Buṣaylī (1955), 83–5 and Nicholls (1913), 10–4.

36. Ḍayfallāh (1971), 227.
37. Penn (1934), 65.
38. Hoskins (1835), 201.
39. ibid.
40. ibid.
41. Crawford (1951), 296.
42. Krump (1710), 256.
43. ibid.
44. Beccari (1905–17), XIV, 341–2.
45. ibid., 70–2.
46. Krump (1710), 287.
47. Bruce (1805), VI, 391–2; Burckhardt (1822), 225, 255–6, 320.
48. Krump (1710), 285.
49. Wansleben in Paulus (1792–8), III, 39.
50. The exchange of currency for gold by foreigners is documented from as early as 1700, Krump (1710), 288–9.
51. ibid., 242.
52. ibid., 288–9.
53. Poncet (1949), 105.
54. Krump (1710), 288.
55. ibid.
56. ibid.
57. Burckhardt (1822), 216.
58. Traditions originating after the fall of Sinnār have been excluded on the premise that they are less likely to contain accurate information about the sixteenth and seventeenth centuries than are the written documents of the Funj period.
59. Yūsuf (1967), 177, has argued that Arab nomads and Muslim traders were also important bearers of Islam. It may be suggested that whenever a nomad or merchant became known as a missionary, he would be considered one of the *fuqarā*'.
60. ibid., 180.
61. Accounts of early missionaries were collected by Trimingham (1949), 223, and MacMichael (1922), I, 248; II, 35, 82, 86. It seems doubtful that the existence of such illustrious individuals would have been ignored by the authors of the *Funj Chronicle* and the *Ṭabaqāt*; probably these accounts were late fabrications designed to glorify the ancestry of the narrators.
62. *Makhṭūṭa* (1961), 9; MacMichael (1922), II, 361; Yūsuf (1967), 179–80.
63. *Makhṭūṭa* (1961), 10.
64. Trimingham (1949), 119.

65. MacMichael (1922), II, 363.
66. Crawford (1951), 331.
67. Poncet (1949), 103.
68. Brevedent in Montano (1948), II, 438.
69. Krump (1710), 281.
70. Poncet (1949), 104.
71. Krump (1710), 335.
72. Crawford (1951), 294.
73. Montano (1948), II, 437.
74. Giamberardini (1963), 418.
75. Crawford (1951), 296.
76. Hoskins (1835), 201.
77. Buṣaylī (1955), 270–1.
78. Krump (1710), 335.
79. ibid., 270.
80. Beccari (1905–17), XIV, 72–3.
81. *Makhṭūṭa* (1961), 18.
82. Le Grand (1728), 437.
83. D'Albano (1961) 110, 120; *Makhṭūṭa* (1961), 18.
84. Le Grand (1728), 171; Beccari (1905–17), XIV, 400.
85. Ḍayfallāh (1971), 202–3.
86. Giamberardini (1963), 424–5.
87. ibid., 423.
88. ibid., 422.
89. Elles (1935), 13.
90. Hofmayr (1925), 74.
91. Hence his nickname 'the Shāīqī' in the traditions of Robinson (1929), 258.
92. ibid., 235.
93. Penn (1934), 65–6; Beccari (1905–17), XIV, 393.

CHAPTER VI

1. According to traditions published by Buṣaylī (1955), 256 ff, the founder of this dynasty was Shaykh Nūr, who came to power in 1507, which date is unlikely, since Shaykh Shanbū, grandson of the founder, was killed in 1780 (*Makhṭūṭa* (1961), 29–30). Probably the dynasty came to power about the second quarter of the eighteenth century.
2. MacMichael (1922), I, 347.
3. Krump (1710), 285; Poncet (1949), 107; Bruce (1805), VI, 396–7.

4. Bruce (1805), VI, 428–9; Burckhardt (1822), 192, 195–6, 218; Cailliaud (1823), III, 121.
5. Burckhardt (1822), 65.
6. ibid., 225–6.
7. Cailliaud (1823), II, 118.
8. Burckhardt (1822), 277, 395–6, 407.
9. ibid., 274–5.
10. Lapanouse (1802), 98, 116.
11. Cailliaud (1823), II, 100; III, 104–5.
12. Hoskins (1835), 160–3.
13. The sword was sometimes called a *djelebé*, roughly translatable as 'merchant's tool', Cadalvène et Breuvery (1841), II, 260.
14. Lejean (1865), 27.
15. Rüppell (1829), 65–6.
16. An immense genealogical literature of this character exists in the Sudan, both in the form of oral tradition and in writing.
17. Cailliaud (1823), II, 116–17.
18. For example, see Russegger (1843), II, i, 450 (general), 463 (Berber), 495 (Shandī); II, ii, 229 (Kordofan), 535 (Sinnār).
19. For example, Princess Naṣra, see Hill (1970), 116–20.
20. Hartmann, Marno and Cailliaud reported no examples of the practice south of the city of Sinnār, while Russegger (1843), II, ii, 535, specifically noted its absence in Ruṣayriṣ.
21. Hartmann (1863), 442–5.
22. *Makhṭūṭa* (1961), 17–18.
23. ibid.
24. Burckhardt (1822), 254; Bruce (1805), VI, 384; Crawford (1951, 252.
25. Pallme (1846), 13.
26. Burckhardt (1822), 235–42.
27. Krump (1710), 254; Abu Selim (1967), 90–1.
28. Bruce (1805), VI, 384.
29. Brocchi (1843), V, 326.
30. Spaulding (thesis 1971), 266–7, 271.
31. Brocchi (1843), V, 273; Arkell (1932), 207, 225, 227–8, plates I–VIII; Ḍayfallāh (1971), 133–47; Dr John Voll, personal communication.
32. Burckhardt (1822), 195, 204.
33. Cailliaud (1823), II, 114.
34. Hill (1970), 49, n. 2.
35. Rüppell (1829), 65–6.
36. Spaulding (thesis 1971), 260–73.

37. Buṣaylī (1955), 270–1.
38. Interview, shaykh Zubayr, Arqū, 20 January 1970.
39. Arkell (1932), 232.
40. Disney (1945), 40.
41. Penn (1934), 66.
42. Ḍayfallāh (1971), 234–7.
43. Nūl, according to the *Funj Chronicle*, was the son of a woman of the royal clan, but not in the line of the preceding kings.
44. *Makhṭūṭa* (1961), 19–20; MacMichael (1922), II, 364.
45. *Makhṭūṭa* (1961), 20.
46. Penn (1934), 66.
47. Abu Selim (1967), 138 (Rajab 1141/February–March 1729).
48. Holt (1969), 4, 6.
49. Brocchi (1843), V, 207–8.
50. The major sources for the war of 1744 are the *Funj Chronicle* (*Makhṭūṭa* (1961), 21–2; MacMichael (1922), II, 365), the chronicle of Iyāsū II (ed. Guidi (1910), 122–5), and various comments of James Bruce. Crawford (1951), 239–43, wrote an itinerary of the march of the Ethiopian army based upon his understanding of the geographical terms appearing in the sources.
51. *Makhṭūṭa* (1961), 22; Guidi (1910), 122, 125.
52. The *Funj Chronicle* stated that the Rās accompanied Iyāsū and was present at the decisive battle. Probably this was an editorial addition intended to increase the glory of Bādī's victory; the account of the Ethiopian chronicler may be preferred in this instance.
53. That Bishr walad Yūnus was probably the commanding *amīn* may be inferred from his signature on a charter from the period 1743–5 (Abu Selim (1937), 59–66). Both his predecessors and successors are known, and may be assigned to other periods (Holt (1969), 13).
54. The exact site is open to debate, see Crawford (1951), 241.
55. Guidi (1910), 122–5; Bruce (1805), IV, 123 ff.
56. Hartmann (1863), 440.
57. Guidi (1910), 125.
58. Bruce (1805), VI, 254.
59. ibid., 355.
60. *Makhṭūṭa* (1961), 20–1.
61. Cadalvène et Breuvery (1841), II, 200–3; MacMichael (1922), I, 203–6.

62. Abu Selim (1967), 60, 63–4, 66; *Makhṭūṭa* (1961), 24, where he is called *wazīr*.
63. See Chap. 9.
64. Abu Selim (1967), 106; Cadalvène et Breuvery (1841), II, 200–3, where the Funj sultan Bādī IV is confused with one of his earlier namesakes and assigned to the sixteenth century.
65. Abū Likaylik was from a family of the nobility among the Hamaj of the Blue Nile valley above Sinnār and the southern borderlands.
66. The version of MacMichael (1922), II. 365, stated that Abū Likaylik had commanded the Funj cavalry in the war against Iyāsū. If so, he did not particularly distinguish himself at that time, and probably the comment was merely intended to glorify the memory of his career, having no basis in fact.
67. *Makhṭūṭa* (1961), 22.
68. ibid., 23, and n. 1. Ḥillat al-'Akūra is an island village in the Blue Nile not far from the modern Wad Madanī.
69. ibid.
70. ibid., 23–4; MacMichael (1922), II, 366–7; Bruce (1805), VI, 354–5, 375.
71. *Makhṭūṭa* (1961), 20.
72. Peney (1885), 45–50.
73. Murray (1808), 423.
74. The *Funj Chronicle* commonly used the title of shaykh.
75. *Makhṭūṭa* (1961), 26; MacMichael (1922), II, 367.
76. MacMichael (1922), II, 386.
77. *Makhṭūṭa* (1961), 26.
78. He was the first strong 'Abdallāb leader to emerge after the disaster in Kordofan. Following the death of 'Abdallāh III and his brother Shammām, Mismar b. 'Abdallāh III was invested, but deposed after only two months in favour of Nāṣir b. Shammām (Ḍayfallāh (1971), 296). Nāṣir's reign was also short; by 1752 he had in turn been ousted by Muḥammad al-Amīn b. Mismār (Abu Selim (1967), 102).
79. Bruce (1805), VI, 416–17.
80. An indication of the early peaceful relations between Muḥammad al-Amīn and Abū Likaylik may be found in their joint signatures on charters dated 1762, 1763 and 1765 (Abu Selim (1967), 106, 86 and 97 respectively). Even long after the *mānjil*'s split with the Hamaj, Bruce found that he still 'spoke very respectfully of Adelan and Abou Kalec ('Adlān wad Ṣubāḥī and Abū Likaylik)'. Bruce (1805), VI, 416.

81. Bruce (1805), VI, 418; Murray (1808), 423.
82. Bruce (1805), VI, 423; for a discussion, see O'Fahey and Spaulding (1972), 325.
83. Cailliaud (1823), III, 106–7; O'Fahey and Spaulding (1972), 325.
84. Bruce (1805), VI, 436; Robinson (1925), 105.
85. Cailliaud (1823), III, 106–7; Bruce (1805), VI, 436 ff.
86. *Makhṭūṭa* (1961), 27; Robinson (1929), 243; Cadalvène et Breuvery (1841), II, 256–7.
87. Robinson (1929), 242.
88. Penn (1934), 70.
89. *Makhṭūṭa* (1961), 27.
90. ibid.
91. Westermann (1912), lv.
92. Elles (1935), 14.
93. *Makhṭūṭa* (1961), 27–8; Hillelson (1920), 33–75.
94. *Makhṭūṭa* (1961), 28–31; Penn (1934), 71.
95. Abu Selim (1967), 119.
96. *Makhṭūṭa* (1961), 31.
97. Cadalvène et Breuvery (1841), II, 209.
98. *Makhṭūṭa* (1961), 31.
99. ibid., 32–3; MacMichael (1922), II, 370–1.
100. ibid., 35–7.
101. Burckhardt (1822), 64, 66.
102. Spaulding (thesis 1971), 222–8.
103. Abu Selim (1967), 72–4.
104. Hoskins (1835), 201.
105. Burckhardt (1822), 66.
106. Rüppell (1829), 21; Spaulding (thesis 1971), 230, n. 2.
107. Petti Suma (1964), 443.
108. Nicholls, (1913), 8.
109. Holt (1967b), 142–57.
110. Burckhardt (1822), 66.
111. ibid., 45; Costaz (1823), 260.
112. Linant (1958), 164.
113. Cailliaud (1823), II, 183, 186, 195.
114. Ibid., 194.
115. Robinson (1929), 253, 259.
116. Burckhardt (1822), 248.
117. ibid., 65.
118. A Maḥasī told a French inquirer in 1799, 'this nation (Maḥas) is subject to the tribe of the Shāīqīya Arabs who, in their

raids, steal children from the Maḥas and incorporate them in order to increase the number of cultivators who work for their profit' Costaz (1823), 260.

119. Cailliaud (1823), II, 39.
120. Linant (1958), 63.

PART TWO

CHAPTER VII

1. Within the compass of this book, it is impossible to discuss all the traditions and their variants; most can be found in O'Fahey thesis 1972), 48–89.
2. Nachtigal (1971), 274.
3. Daju traditions can be found in Cadalvène et Breuvery (1841), II, 198–9; Nachtigal (1971), 272–4; MacMichael (1922), I, 71–6; Hillelson (1925), 49–71; Arkell (1952a), 62–70 and Balfour-Paul (1955), 9–10.
4. Tucker and Bryan (1956), 59–61.
5. Browne (1799), 280.
6. MacMichael (1922), I, 72; Arkell (1952a), 62–70, where the Arab geographical references are given.
7. Personal communication, R. Thelwall.
8. On the Tunjur today, see Temple (1922), 25; Lebeuf (1959), 35–7; Le Rouvreur (1962), 104–7; MacMichael (1922), I, 66–71, 122–8.
9. For the Tunjur traditions see Barth (1965), II, 846–7; Nachtigal (1971), 93, 158, 205, 207, 272–5; Carbou (1912), I, 74; Palmer (1928), II, 24–7, 32, and for the later history of the Tunjur in Kanem, Trimingham (1962), 213, n. 1.
10. Shuqayr (1903), II, 116, whose mid-eighteenth-century date for 'Abd al-Karīm is far too late; Tubiana (1960), 49–95.
11. D'Anania (1582), 349. We are grateful to John Lavers for this reference, which he is to publish in *SNR*.
12. But in some versions – including the earliest, Cadalvène et Breuvery (1841), II, 198–9 – he is called an 'Abbāsī, which, in the Sudanese genealogical convention, would suggest a link with the Ja'aliyīn.
13. Slatin (1896), 38–42.
14. Interview, Muḥammad Ibrāhīm, Zalingei, 27 May 1969, in O'Fahey (thesis 1972), 70–1.
15. Nachtigal (1971), 275.

16. Balfour-Paul (1955), 11; for a detailed description, Arkell (1946), 184–202.
17. Arkell (1952a), 129–55.
18. Doubt has been cast on the provenance of these fragments, Shinnie in Yūsuf (1971), 49, but Arkell is positive they came from 'Ayn Faraḥ (personal communication).
19. Arkell (1963a), 315–19; see also (1963b), 320–1, and (1959), 115–19.
20. Arkell (1961), 190–4.
21. Shinnie in Yūsuf (1971), 49.
22. Holt (1963a), 39–55.
23. Holt (1963b), 7–9.
24. Nachtigal (1971), 280–1; MacMichael (1922), I, 84–5; Abū Sinn (1968), 70–1.
25. Lampen (1928), 55–62; MacMichael (1922), I, 58–64, 77–80; Arkell (1947), 127–34.
26. MacMichael (1922), I, 66–7. This also is the impression of Arlette Roth-Laly from her recent investigations among the Tunjur (personal communication, M. J. Tubiana).
27. It is also difficult to accept the argument of Kalck (1972), 529–48, that Leo Africanus' 'Gaoga' is to be located in Dār Fūr, see our letter in *JAH*, XIV/3, 505–7. D'Anania (1582), 349, clearly distinguishes between the Uri state and Gaoga.
28. Barth (1965), II, 643, 'Wuwel-Banan the Jellabi'.

CHAPTER VIII

1. Neither Browne nor al-Tūnisī mention any ruler by name before Sulaymān. Cadalvène et Breuvery (1841), II, 198–200, list ten rulers between Daali and Sulaymān; Nachtigal (1971), 277, says at least ten ruled; Slatin (1896), 37, says Daali was Sulaymān's father, and Shuqayr (1903), II, 114, lists ten. Other king-lists in Dr Arkell's papers average around ten rulers.
2. Beaton, (1968). 10–12.
3. Nachtigal (1971), 208.
4. Description in Arkell (1937), 91–105; see also Wickens (1960), 147–51.
5. MacMichael (1926), 75–7.
6. Al-Tūnisī (1965), 95 (81) (in references to al-Tūnisī the figure in brackets refers to the French translation of Perron).
7. Nachtigal (1971), 338 and below, Chap. X.
8. Arkell (1952a), 131–5, but see Brenner (1973), 18–19.

9. Nachtigal (1971), 277, 369–70; he never saw the *kitāb dālī*.
10. Arkell (1952a), 145–6; some of the manuscripts are in Arkell Papers[1], file 17.
11. Arkell (1937), 91–105.
12. Nachtigal (1971), 277–9. On the Keira/Musabba'āt connexion, see O'Fahey and Spaulding (1972), 318–20.
13. Nachtigal (1971), 277–9.
14. We have no contemporary references. Browne (1799), 280, implies a date of roughly 1645–65; Cadalvène et Breuvery (1841), II, 198, give 1100–13/1688–9 – 1701–2; Nachtigal (1971), 274. 1596–1637; Shuqayr (1903), II, 113–14, gives dates for two Sulaymāns, 848–80/1444–5 – 1475–6, which seems too early on genealogical grounds, and 1106–26/1694–5 – 1714–5, which seems too late.
15. Wansleben in Paulus (1792–8), III, 45–6.
16. 'Kab' may be al-Kāb on the Nile near Isna, 'Dago' may be Daju or the Kharja oasis, the latter is more logical and 'Issueine' is probably to be identified with Suwaynī in northern Dār Fūr. We are grateful to Dr Arkell for the Kab and Dago suggestions.
17. D'Albano (1961), 47.
18. Krump (1710), 285, and Ḍayfallāh (1971), 137–8.
19. D'Albano (1961), 120–1, and above Chap. V.
20. Nachtigal (1971), 279–80; Shuqayr (1903), II, 113–14.
21. Ḍayfallāh (1971), 180, and Yūsuf (1971), 82.
22. Santandrea (1959), 115–90; O'Fahey (1973), 34.
23. Nachtigal (1971), 279; Shuqayr (1903), II, 113.
24. De Lauture (1855–6), 79.
25. Prov. Archives, DP. 66. b. 28, note by Keen, November 17 1930.
26. Prov. Archives, DP. 66. k. 1/31, Arari Dimligia, note by Aglen, 22 June 1948. There are extensive ruins at Arari.
27. MacMichael (1922), I, 198.
28. From the seal of Sultan Ibrāhīm, reproduced in Shuqayr (1903), II, 148.
29. Nachtigal (1971), 280.

CHAPTER IX

1. MacMichael (1922), I, 97–8.
2. From a letter of Sultan 'Abd al-Raḥmān to Bonaparte written in 1798, *Pieces Diverses* (1801), 187.
3. See letter (1245/1829–30) of Sultan Muḥammad al-Faḍl to the Viceroy of Egypt, Shuqayr (1903), II, 130–1.

4. Nachtigal (1971), 280–2. All dates for Bukr are guesses; Cadalvène et Breuvery (1841), II, 198, 1128–41/1715–16 – 1728–9; Nachtigal, *op. cit.*, 1682–1722, and Shuqayr (1903), II, 115, 1138–58/1725–6 – 1745–6.
5. Nachtigal (1971), 280; Arkell (1937), 103–4.
6. Nachtigal (1971), 280–1, but Abū Sinn (1968), 70–1, says that the conquest was under Sultan Muḥammad Tayrāb; this may mean that the latter consolidated Keira rule in Dār Qimr as is implied in Nachtigal (1971), 287.
7. MacMichael (1922), I, 84–5; Abū Sinn, *op. cit.*
8. Abu Selim (1967), 45–6.
9. Both Browne (1799), 188, and al-Tūnisī (1965), 54 (35), met Zaghāwa at the end of their journey from Egypt.
10. The Zaghāwa west of Kobe appear also to have been less influenced by Islam than those to the east, Tubiana (1967), 95–6.
11. Nachtigal (1971), 287; Tubiana (1964), 25–35.
12. ibid., 32, 195.
13. Arkell Papers[2], file 48, f. 222.
14. Arkell Papers[1], file 21, ffs. 84–94, note of a conversation with Melik Mohamedain Adam Sebbi, 1 February 1937; Nachtigal (1971), 324.
15. Arkell Papers[1], file 21, ffs. 84–94; MacMichael (1912), 109–12.
16. Al-Tūnisī (1851), 77–83, who says Ya'qūb invaded when Bukr was a boy; Barth (1965), II, 644, who places the invasion, or perhaps an earlier one, in the reign of Bukr's predecessor, Mūsā; Nachtigal (1971), 209–10, whose account is the most circumstantial and who dates the invasion to Bukr's old age.
17. Ḍayfallāh (1971), 200; Nachtigal (1971), 282.
18. There is no certainty in any of the dates given in the sources for the sultans until 'Abd al-Raḥmān, see O'Fahey (thesis 1972), 82–9. The order of succession is given in a land-charter of 1260/1844–5 (O'Fahey's collection, b. 17 Jadīd al-Sayl).
19. Al-Tūnisī (1965), 73 (55); Nachtigal (1971), 282.
20. Cadalvène et Breuvery (1841), II, 198; Nachtigal (1971), 283.
21. Shuqayr (1903), II, 115–16. A fourteenth-century ruler of Kano abdicated for similar reasons, Palmer (1928), III, 108.
22. Beaton (1941), 181–8; Al-Tūnisī (1965), 253 (256 and 439), describes a form of *levee-en-masse*, which he calls *gueldina.*
23. Arkell (1939), 251–68.
24. Nachtigal (1971), 283.
25. O'Fahey and Spaulding (1972), 321–3.

26. ibid.
27. Nachtigal (1971), 284. Sultan ʿAbd al-Raḥmān is said to have similarly given away Tayrāb's wives, al-Tūnisī (1965), 101 (89).
28. Cadalvène et Breuvery (1841), II, 204–5; Nachtigal (197), 284.
29. Cadalvène et Breuvery (1841), II, 206, call the Wadai sultan Jāmiʿ b. Yaʿqūb ʿArūs, who does not appear in any of the published Wadai king-lists. Nachtigal (1971), 210, says the invasion occurred in the reign of Yaʿqūb ʿArūs, whom he dates 1681–1707, which does not agree with his dates for ʿUmar, 1732–9.
30. Nachtigal (1971), 210.
31. ibid., 285.
32. ibid., 286; Slatin (1896), 42.
33. Nachtigal (1971), 286–7; Bruce is probably referring to the killing of Abu'l-Qāsim when he says, 'it is at Darfoor they put the king to death, with two razors, in a seshe, or handkerchief', Murray (1808), 39.
34. Nachtigal (1971), 286–7; interview, Riḥaymtallāh Maḥmūd al-Dādinqāwi, al-Fashir, 19 May 1970.
35. Al-Tūnisī (1851), 76–7; Nachtigal (1971), 238–9.
36. Al-Tūnisī (1965), 109 (98); Nachtigal (1971), 287, 330; personal communication, M. J. Tubiana.
37. Balfour-Paul (1955) 25, for a plan of Shōba.
38. Nachtigal (1971), 287.
39. ibid.
40. Interviews, *sharṭay* Muḥammad Ādam Yaʿqūb, Ghor Abeshei (Dār Birged), 26 June 1969, and Sabīl Ādam Yaʿqūb, al-Fashir, 4 June 1970, both descendants of Sulaymān.
41. Nachtigal (1971), 288; Slatin (1896), 46.
42. O'Fahey (1973), 31–2.
43. Al-Tūnisī (1965), 86 (68).
44. On these attempts, see O'Fahey and Spaulding (1972), 323–7.
45. Murray (1808), 425; Cadalvène et Breuvery (1841), II, 209.
46. O'Fahey and Spaulding (1972), 323–7.
47. Al-Tūnisī (1965), 86 (69); Shuqayr (1903), II, 117–18.
48. Al-Tūnisī (1965), 88 (70); Slatin (1896), 46.
49. This description of the succession crisis is based on al-Tūnisī (1965), 88–98 (76–85), who could well have derived his information from participants.
50. Al-Tūnisī (1965), 93–4 (77); Nachtigal (1971), 289.
51. Interview, Aḥmad Ādam Abbo, Kattāl (Kerio), 18 June 1970,

a descendant of ʻAlī; al-Tūnisī (1965), 99–100 (88–9); Shuqayr (1903), II, 121.

52. But he was probably not childless; his slave concubine, Umm Būṣa, appears to have given birth to the future sultan, Muḥammad al-Faḍl, about this time, Nachtigal (1971), 289.
53. Al-Tūnisī (1965), 95 (79).
54. ibid., 96 (83).
55. Nachtigal (1971), 289.
56. But Nachtigal (1971), 294, says he committed suicide some years later.
57. Al-Tūnisī (1965), 98 (84).
58. Nachtigal (1971), 289.
59. Al-Tūnisī (1965), 103 (91).
60. ibid., 104–11 (93–100); Nachtigal (1971), 290–2; Shuqayr (1903), II, 122. The civil war is discussed in O'Fahey (thesis 1972), 172–8.

CHAPTER X

1. Browne (1799), 239; al-Tūnisī (1965), 201 (194).
2. See Chap. VI.
3. Shuqayr (1903), II, 139–41.
4. ʻAlī Dīnār was the grandson of Sultan Muḥammad al-Faḍl, but he felt it necessary to call his father, Zakarīya, who never reigned, 'sultan' posthumously in his letters.
5. On the constitutional theory, Browne (1799), 277; Denon (1809), I, 167; Cuny (1854), 90–1; Slatin (1896), 42; Shuqayr (1903), II, 138.
6. Compare with the *ciroma* in Bornu, Cohen (1965), 97.
7. Al-Tūnisī (1965), 102 (89); Arkell Papers[1], file 14, ffs. 54–5.
8. Al-Tūnisī (1965), 167–8 (160–1).
9. Arkell Papers[1], file 14, ffs. 52–3.
10. Al-Tūnisī (1965), 168 (161).
11. Arkell Papers[1], file 14, ffs. 52–3.
12. Al-Tūnisī (1965), 198–9 (191), spitting and sneezing; 210 (203), veil; Shuqayr (1903), II, 124, eating.
13. Al-Tūnisī (1965), 348–9 (376–7); when Isḥāq was killed by an Egyptian musketeer, the latter was richly rewarded by ʻAbd al-Raḥmān and then executed.
14. Nachtigal (1971), 278.
15. ibid., 336–7; Arkell Papers[1], file 14, ffs. 52–3.
16. Nachtigal (1971), 288.

17. Browne (1799), 222–3, 229; al-Tūnisī (1965), 173–6 (165–8); Cuny (1858), 19–21; Combes (1846), II, 128–40 (a lurid account); Nachtigal (1971), 338–45.
18. Browne does not mention human sacrifice; al-Tūnisī does but without vouching for the story. Cuny says that Sultan Muḥammad al-Ḥusayn abolished it, but Nachtigal that it had disappeared by ʻAbd al-Raḥmān's time. See Tubiana (1964), 179–81.
19. Nachtigal (1971), 341–5.
20. Browne (1799), 222.
21. Prov. Archives, Western Darfur District Handbook.
22. Browne (1799), 283; Nachtigal (1971), 339; Felkin (1884–5), 225.
23. Al-Tūnisī (1965), 95 (81); MacMichael (1922), I, 93.
24. Balfour-Paul (1955).
25. Nothing remains of the nineteenth-century al-Fāshir palaces, which were built of wood and millet stalks, although the beautiful palace of ʻAlī Dīnār is used as the residence of the governor of Dār Fūr.
26. Al-Tūnisī (1965), 203–7 (197–201); Browne (1799) plan opposite 286 and 579–80.
27. Nachtigal (1971), 332.
28. Browne (1799), 579; Nachtigal (1971), 332. In a land-charter (O'Fahey's collection, b. 18 Jadīd al-Sayl) of Sultan Muḥammad al-Ḥusayn an estate is described as having reverted to the *bayt al-jibāya* upon the death of the grantee.
29. Al-Tūnisī (1965), 197–8 (189–90).
30. Browne (1799), 211.
31. MacMichael (1922), I, 91–103; Arkell (1951a), 61.
32. MacMichael (1922), I, 95.
33. Nachtigal (1971), 331–2; Arkell Papers[1], file 13, ffs. 38–43.
34. Al-Tūnisī (1965), 74–5 (56–7).
35. Nachtigal (1971), 329.
36. ibid.
37. ibid., 315–16; Shuqayr (1903), II, 133.
38. Nachtigal (1971), 287.
39. Browne (1799), 291; al-Tūnisī (1965), 103 (115).
40. Browne (1799), 296; Shuqayr (1903), II, 139–41.
41. Al-Tūnisi (1965), 179–84 (171–6); MacMichael (1922), I, 95.
42. De Lauture (1855–6), 95; Nachtigal (1971), 329–30. Many of the provincial chiefs had their own *ɔrreŋ duluŋ*.
43. Nachtigal (1971), 326–8; MacMichael (1922), I, 95–6. The title

was also used in Wadai, al-Tūnisī (1851), 364, and in Zaghāwa Kobe, Tubiana (1964), 49.

44. Nachtigal (1971), 332–4.
45. O'Fahey (1973), 29–43.
46. Interview, 'Abd al-Raḥmān Ādam Ṣāliḥ, al-Fashir, 15 May 1970.
47. Prov. Archives DP. 66. b. 6 vol. II Tribal affairs – General Zaghawa.
48. Browne (1799), 206–8, a *folgoni* summoned the traveller to al-Fāshir; al-Tūnisī (1965), 154 (140), when he visited Jabal Marra, two *falagna* went with him; Zayn al-'Abidīn (1847), 12.
49. Browne (1799), 213.
50. Nachtigal (1971), 334–5.
51. Prov. Archives DP. FD. 66 K. 1.5. Fasher District, Tawila Omodia; interview, Riḥaymtallāh Maḥmūd al-Dādinqāwi, al-Fāshir, 19 May 1970.
52. Nachtigal (1971), 337.
53. Al-Tūnisī (1965) 95, 116 (78, 105); Nachtigal (1971), 328.
54. *Sharṭay* possibly comes from a Daju word, *chorti*, meaning both 'drum' and 'chief'; *kiiso* bears the same twofold meaning.
55. Al-Tūnisī (1965), 143, 184 (132, 176); Nachtigal (1971), 324; Prov. Archives, Western Darfur District Handbook.
56. Beaton (1948) 5–6; there is some confusion as the exact position of the *dimlij* in the system.
57. Prov. Archives, Western Darfur District Handbook.
58. ibid.; on the prisons, al-Tūnisī (1965), 158 (146).
59. Nachtigal (1971), 324.
60. Al-Tūnisī (1965), 152, 182 (138, 173); Nachtigal (1971), 292, 324, 349.
61. MacMichael (1922), I, 84–5; Abū Sinn (1968), 70–1, 85; Le Rouvreur (1962), 153–62.
62. Al-Tūnisī (1965), 141 (130); Nachtigal (1971), 359.
63. For preliminary assessments, see Fourcade (1966), 35–53; Kropáček (1971), 33–50; see also Cuny (1854), 91–2.
64. Brenner (1973), 104–6.
65. Al-Tūnisī (1965), 143, 152, 184–5 (132–3, 137–8, 176–7).
66. Prov. Archives, Western Darfur District Handbook.
67. O'Fahey and Abdel Ghaffar (1972), 12–17.
68. Fourcade (1966), 45–7; see below Chap. XI.
69. Since al-Tūnisī does not mention the title, the first *maqdūms* probably came after *c.* 1810.
70. Nachtigal (1971), 326.

71. Browne (1799), 300.
72. Nachtigal (1971), 358.
73. Al-Tūnisī (1965), 106, 184, (93, 175); Nachtigal (1971), 331.
74. For descriptions, see Browne (1799), 180–215; Denon (1809), I, 280–1; al-Tūnisi (1965), 48–54; Hartmann (1863), 68–70.
75. Browne (1799), 253; Davies (1957), 172–9; see 'Umar al-Naqar in Yūsuf (1971), 98—108.
76. Petherick (1861), 266; Valensi (1967), 1267–88.
77. Browne (1799), 234–7; Slatin (1896), 108; Deherain (1904), 65–73.
78. Hartmann (1863), 69; Browne (1799), 57.
79. Browne (1799), 301.
80. ibid., 299.
81. Appendix in Denon (1809), II, ccl.
82. O'Fahey (1973), 32–6.
83. O'Fahey in Yūsuf (1971), 93; Baer (1969), 161–89.
84. Nachtigal (1971), 329.

CHAPTER XI

1. Although 1214/1800–1 is usually given as the date of his death, 1218/1803–4 appears on the seals of his son, presumably as an accession date.
2. Shuqayr (1903), II, 121.
3. Auriant (1926), 181–234.
4. ibid.
5. Brenner (1973), 89–103.
6. Tubiana (1964) is the only relevant work and that is concerned with the Zaghāwa in Chad.
7. Birged is virtually extinct, see O'Fahey (1969), 67–8.
8. Ḍayfallāh (1971), 105–6.
9. Arkell Papers[1], file 13, f. 47.
10. Bolton (1934), 229–41.
11. 'Umar al-Naqar in Yūsuf (1971), 98–108.
12. Nachtigal (1971), 280.
13. From a charter of Sultan Muḥammad al-Ḥusayn, dated 1260/1844–5 (O'Fahey's collection, b. 18 Jadīd al-Sayl).
14. See charter of 1263/1846–7 in Shuqayr (1903), II, 139, and translated in Kropáček (1970), 41–3.
15. See the sequence of charters from a later period for the descendants of Muḥammad Hadūj al-Kinānī, in O'Fahey and Abdel Ghaffar (1972), 19–47.

16. Shuqayr (1903), II, 137.
17. Trimingham (1962), 110.
18. Copy of charter in Arkell Papers[1], file 16, f. 61.
19. Copy of charter from Sultan Muḥammad al-Ḥusayn to the Barriyāb *fuqarā'*, Sudan Government Archives, Khartoum; see also Ḍayfallāh (1971), 293, n. 13.
20. Mosques were built at al-Fāshir, Jadīd al-Sayl, Azagarfa, Arari, Kerio and Manawāshī by 'Abd al-Raḥmān and his son; interview Sabīl Ādam Ya'qūb, al-Fāshir, 4 June 1970.
21. Nachtigal (1971), 293.
22. Al-Tūnisī (1965), 253–5 (255–7).
23. Interviews Aḥmad and Ḥāmid Ādam, Kattāl (Kerio), 17 to 20 June 1970.
24. Al-Tūnisī (1965), 126–7 (118–19).
25. Interview Aḥmad Amīn, al-Fāshir, 7 June 1970.
26. Al-Tūnisī (1965), 106–7 (116–17) and 67–9 (48–9), where the text of the charter is given; see also Kropáček (1971), 38–9.
27. Zayn al-'Abidīn (1847), 12–13.
28. Nachtigal (1971), 367–8.
29. Al-Tūnisī (1965), 102–3 (89–90).
30. Browne (1799), 291; al-Tūnisī (1965), 103 (90); Felkin (1884–5), 218.
31. Prov. Archives, Western Darfur District Handbook.
32. Browne (1799), 211. According to informants, Fur remained the principal court languages until and including 'Alī Dīnār's time.
33. Zayn al-'Abidīn (1847), 14, describes how a shakyh 'Abdallāh issued rulings (*fatwas*) for the sultan, who took little notice of them.
34. Interviews Aḥmad Amīn and Maḥmūd Tijānī, al-Fāshir, 7 and 31 May 1970; al-Tūnisī (1965), 117 (108).
35. Although al-Tūnisī (1965), 63 (45), denies he was of slave origin, oral informants said he was born a slave. The following account is based on O'Fahey (1973), 41–3.
36. O'Fahey and Spaulding (1972), 330–1.
37. Al-Tūnisī (1965), 129–30, 324 (122–4, 350); Nachtigal (1971), 298–9.
38. Al-Tūnisī (1965), 69–72 (51–4); Nachtigal (1971), 300–1; Shuqayr (1903), II, 124–5.
39. Although al-Tūnisī, as a boy, was in Dār Fūr at the time he may have misunderstood what he heard.
40. O'Fahey and Spaulding (1972), 331–3.
41. Cadalvène et Breuvery (1841), II, 214–31.

42. Al-Jabartī (1879), IV, 318; Consul Salt to Foreign Office, 30 June 1820, quoted in Marlowe (1972), 135.
43. Cadalvène et Breuvery (1841), II, 231; Shuqayr (1903), II, 130.
44. Kropáček (1970), 73–86.
45. Hill (1959), 30.
46. Al-Tūnisī (1965), 343–64 (370–96); Pallme (1946), 353–5.
47. Al-Tūnisī (1851), 110, 187–210.
48. Barth (1965), III, 533; Nachtigal (1971), 304–5; Shuqayr (1903), II, 129.
49. Nachtigal (1971), 305–8.
50. ibid. The conspirators included the *abbo daadiŋa*, the *ɔrreŋ duluŋ*, and the *abbo jabbay*.
51. Nachtigal (1971), 315–16.
52. Burckhardt (1822), 481: al-Tūnisī (1965), 139 (129); Yūsuf (1967), 166.
53. Browne (1799), 300–1.
54. Nachtigal (1971), 302; Slatin (1896), 45–6.
55. Haaland in Barth (1969), 58–73.
56. Nachtigal (1971), 301–2.
57. O'Fahey (1973), 31–2.
58. Nachtigal (1971), 301–3.
59. ibid., 308–13, is our main source for these campaigns.
60. Gray (1961), 58–9.
61. Barth (1853), 120–2; O'Fahey (1973), 34–6.
62. Neither Nachtigal, *op. cit*, nor Brun-Rollet (1885), 45, 129, give any dates. According to a dispatch to Muḥammad 'Alī Pasha in the Abdin Archives, 'Abd al-'Azīz was campaigning against the Rizayqāt in 1262/1846 (we are grateful to Richard Hill for this reference), and he is described as *maqdūm* in a charter of 1263/1846–7, Shuqayr (1903), II, 140.
63. Barth (1965), II, 675, refers to the village of *maqdūm* Khalīl in about 1854, just south of Nyala.
64. Cuny (1858), 11.
65. Pallme (1846), 352; Nachtigal (1971), 342.
66. Cadalvène et Breuvery (1841), II, 211.
67. Nachtigal (1971), 312; Shuqayr (1903), II, 132–3.
68. Heuglin (1863), 97–114.
69. Much of the following account of the end of the sultanate is based on al-Zubayr's autobiography, which appeared in various recensions; Shaw (1887), 333–49, 564–85, 658–83; Shuqayr (1903), III, 60–88; Jackson (1913).

70. Shaw (1887), 662–4; Shuqayr (1903), III, 67; Jackson (1913), 32; Shukry (1938), 222–3.
71. Gray (1961), 66.
72. Slatin (1896), 48.
73. Nachtigal (1971), 365–6.
74. This the 'al-Hilālī' of Holt (1970), 34.
75. Nachtigal (1971), 316–17; Slatin (1896), 48–9.
76. Shaw (1887), 658–62; Shuqayr (1903), III, 67–8, for al-Zubayr's version.
77. Shukry (1938), 222–3.
78. Hill (1959), 134.
79. Shaw (1887), 662–4; Nachtigal (1971), 319–20, says that the Wadai sultan urged the Dār Fūr ruler to take action against the traders.
80. This letter and others between al-Zubayr and the sultans are given in Shuqayr (1903), III, 68–77.
81. Nachtigal (1971), 70–1, 88, 319–20; Shuqayr (1903), II, 133–4, 147, gives the accession date; an eye-witness account in Arkell Papers[1], file 14, ffs. 54–5.
82. Shaw (1887), 664–5; Shuqayr (1903), III, 74.
83. Shaw (1887), 665–6; Shuqayr (1903), III, 75.
84. Gray (1961), 122.
85. Hill (1959), 137.
86. Slatin (1896), 53–5.

Sources and Bibliography

I. UNPUBLISHED

1. Prov. Archives. Archives of Dār Fūr Province held at Headquarters, al-Fāshir.
2. Arkell Papers. Deposited in two batches [1] and [2] (1967 and 1972) in the library, School of Oriental and African Studies, accession no. 210522.
3. Theses. R. S. O'Fahey, *The Growth and Development of the Keira Sultanate of Dār Fūr*. Ph.D. London 1972. J. L. Spaulding, *Kings of Sun and Shadow: A History of the 'Abdullab Provinces of the Northern Sinnar Sultanate, 1500–1800* A.D. Ph.D. Columbia 1971.

II. PUBLISHED

Abbreviations

BSG	*Bulletin de la Société de Géographie* (Paris)
BSOAS	*Bulletin of the School of Oriental and African Studies*
JAH	*Journal of African History*
SNR	*Sudan Notes and Records*

(A) Primary Sources, Travel and Geographical Literature

'Abd al-Ẓāhir, Muḥyī al-Dīn (1961) *Tashrif al-ayyām wa'l-'uṣūr fī-sīrat al-malik al-manṣūr*. Cairo.

Abu Selim, M. I. (1967) *Some Land Certificates from the Fung*. Occasional papers no. 2, Sudan Research Unit, Khartoum.

Alvarez, F. (1961) *The Prester John of the Indies*, ed. C. F. Beckingham and G. W. B. Huntingford. Cambridge.

Barros, J. de (1628) *Da Asia*. Lisbon.

Barth, H. (1853) Account of two expeditions in Central Africa by the Furanys, *Journal of the Royal Geographical Society*, 120–2.

—— (1965) *Travels and Discoveries in North and Central Africa*. London (centenary edition), 3 vols.

Beccari, C. (1905–17) *Rerum Aethiopicarum Scriptores Occidentales Inediti a saeculo XVI ad XIX*. Rome, 15 vols.

Brehm, A. E. (1861) *Reiseskizzen aus Nord-Ost Afrika: Egypten, Nubien, Sennahr, Roseeres und Kordofahn, 1847–1852*. Jena.

Brocchi, G. B. (1843) *Giornale delle osservazioni fatte ne' viaggi in Egitto, nella Siria e nella Nubia*. Bassano, 5 vols.

Browne, G. W. (1799) *Travels in Egypt, Syria and Africa*. London.

Bruce, J. (1805) *Travels to Discover the Source of the Nile in the Years 1768–1773*. Edinburgh, 2nd ed., 5 vols.

Brun-Rollet, M. (1855) *Le Nil Blanc et Le Soudan*. Paris.

Burckhardt, J. L. (1822) *Travels in Nubia*. London, 2nd ed.

Cadalvène, E. de and Breuvery, J. de (1841) *L'Egypte et la Nubie*. Paris, 2nd ed., 2 vols.

Cailliaud, F. (1823) *Voyage à Méroé, au Fleuve Blanc*. Paris, 4 vols.

Castanheda, F. L. de (1924–33) *Historia do Descobrimento e Conquista da India pelos Portugueses*. Coimbra, 4 vols.

Castro, J. de (1939–40) *Roteiros*. Lisbon, 3 vols.

Celebi, Evliya (1938) *Seyahatnamesi, Misir, Sudan, Habes, 1672–80*. Istanbul, Vol. X.

Combes, E. (1846) *Voyage en Egypte, en Nubie, dans le Desert de Bayouda des Bischarys*. Paris, 4 vols.

Costaz, L. (1823) Mémoire sur le Nubie et les Barabras, in *Déscription de l'Egypte*. Paris, 24 vols.

Crawford, O. G. S. (1958) *Ethiopian Itineraries circa 1400–1524*. Cambridge.

Cuny, C. (1854) Notice sur le Darfour. *BSG*, 4th series, VIII, 81–120.

—— (1858) Observations générales sur le Mémoire sur le Soudan de M. le Comte D'Escayrac de Lauture, from *Nouvelles Annales des Voyages*.

D'Albano, G. (1961) *Historia della Missione Francescana in Alto-Egitto-Fungi-Etiopia*, ed. G. Giamberardini. Cairo.

D'Anania, G. L. (1582) *L'Universale Fabrica del Mondo, Overo Cosmografia*. Venice.

Ḍayfallāh (1971) *Kitāb al-ṭabaqāt*, ed. Yūsuf Faḍl Ḥasan. Khartoum.

Denon, V. (1809) *Voyages dans la Basse et la Haute Egypte pendant les campagnes de Bonaparte*. London, 2 vols.

al-Dimashqī (1866) *Kitāb nukhbat al-ḍahr fī-'ajā'ib al-barr wa'l-baḥr*, ed. M. A. F. Mehren. St. Petersburg.

Felkin, R. W. (1884–5) Notes on the For tribe of Central Africa, *Proceedings of the Royal Society of Edinburgh*, XIII, 205-65.

Giamberardini, G. (1963) I viaggiatori francescani attraverso la Nubia dal 1698 al 1710, *Collectanea no. 8, Studia Orientalia Christiana*. Cairo, 363–437.

Guidi, I. (1910) *Annales Regum Iyasu II et Iyo'as*. Corpus Scriptorum Orientalium, Scriptores Aethiopici, VI, Paris.

Hartmann, R. (1861) Skizzen aus Aethiopen, *Globus*, IV, 202–6, 235–8.

—— (1863) *Reise des Freiherrn Adalbert von Barnim durch Nord-Ost-Afrika in den Jahren 1859 und 1860*. Berlin.

Heuglin, T. von (1863) Berichte und arbeiten über Ägyptischen Sudan und die Länder westlich und südlich von Chartum, *Petermanns Mitteilungen*, 97–114.

Hill, R. (1970) *On the Frontiers of Islam*. Oxford.

Hillelson, S. (1920) Historical poems and traditions of the Shukria, *SNR*, III/2, 33–75.

—— (1935) David Reubeni, an early visitor to Sennar, *SNR*, XVI, 55–66.

Hoskins, G. A. (1835) *Travels in Ethiopia*. London.

Ibn Baṭṭūṭa (1958) *The Travels of Ibn Baṭṭūṭa*, transl. H. A. R. Gibb. Cambridge, Vol. III.

Ibn Faḍl Allāh al-'Umarī (1927) *Masālik al-abṣār fī mamālik al-amṣār*, transl. Gaudefroy-Demombynes. Paris.

Ibn al-Furāt (1936–42) *Ta'rīkh ibn Furāt*. Beirut.

Ibn Iyās (1932) *Die Chronik des Ibn Iyas*, ed. P. Kahle. 2nd ed., Leipzig.

Ibn Jubayr (1907) *Riḥla*. Leyden.

Ibn Khaldūn (1956–61) *Kitāb al-'ibar wa-dīwān al-mubtadā' wa'l-khabar*. Beirut.

al-Jabartī (1879) *'Ajā'ib al-athār fi'l-tarājim wa'l-akhbār*. Cairo.

Jackson, H. C. (1913) *Black Ivory or the Story of El Zubeir Pasha, Slaver and Sultan*. Khartoum.

Krump, T. (1710) *Hoher und Fruchtbarer Palm-Baum des Heiligen Evangelj*. Augsburg

Lapanouse, J. (1802) *Mémoire sur les caravannes du Darfour et du Sennaar*. Paris.

Lauture, P. H. S. D'Escayrac de (1855–6) *Mémoire sur le Soudan*. Paris.

Lefèvre, L. (1842) Voyage au Sennaar et au Cordofan, *BSG*, 2nd series, XVII, 261–70.

Le Grand (1728) *Voyage historique d'Abissinie*. Paris.

Lejean, G. (1865) *Voyage aux Deux Nils*. Paris.

Lepsius, R. (1852) *Briefe aus Aegypten*. Berlin.

Linant de Bellefonds, L. M. A. (1958) *Diary*, ed. M. Shinnie. Khartoum.

Makhṭūṭa (1961) *Kātib al-Shūna fī-ta'rīkh al-sulṭāna al-sinnārīya wa'l-idāra al-maṣrīya*, ed. al-Shāṭir Buṣaylī 'Abd al-Jalīl. Cairo (*Funj Chronicle*).

al-Maqrīzī (1853) *Kitāb al-mawā'iz wa'l-i'tibār bī dhikr al-khiṭaṭ wa'l-āthār*. Būlāq.

Marno, E. (1974) *Reisen in Gebiete des Blauen und Weissen Nil in egyptischen Sudan und den angrenzenden Negerländer*. Wien.

Montano, G. M. (1948) *L'Etiopia Francescana nei Documenti dei secoli XVII e XVIII*. Rome.

Muḥammad b. 'Umar al-Tūnisī (1965) *Tashḥīdh al-adhhān bi-sīrat bilād al-'Arab wa'l-Sūdān*. ed. Khalīl Maḥmūd 'Asākir and Muṣṭafā Muḥammad Mus'ad. Cairo.

—— (1845) *Voyage au Darfour*, transl. Dr Perron. Paris.

—— (1851) *Voyage au Ouaday*, transl. Dr Perron. Paris.

Murray, A. (1808) *Life and Writings of James Bruce of Kinnaird*. Edinburgh.

Nachtigal, G. (1971) *Sahara and Sudan*. Vol. IV, Wadai and Darfur, transl. A. G. B. and H. J. Fisher. London.

Norden, F. L. (1757) *Travels in Egypt and Nubia*. London.

Pallme, I. (1846) *Travels in Kordofan*. London.

Palmer, H. R. (1928) *Sudanese Memoirs*. Lagos. 3 vols.

Peney, A. (1883) Mémoires sur l'ethnographie du Soudan égyptien, III – Daher et Tagala, *Revue d'Ethnographie*, II, 513–24.

—— (1885) Mémoires sur l'ethnographie du Soudan égyptien, IV – Le Fazoglou, *Revue d'Ethnologie*, III, 45–8.

Penn, A. E. D. (1934) Traditional stories of the Abdullab tribe, *SNR*, XVII/1, 59–82.

Pereira, F. M. E. (1892–1900) *Chronica de Susenyos, Rei de Ethiopia*. Lisbon, 2 vols.

Petherick, J. (1861) *Egypt, the Soudan and Central Africa*. Edinburgh.

Petti Suma, M. T. (1964) Il viaggio in Sudan di Evliyā Celebi (1671–1672), *Annali dell'Instituto universitario orientale di Napoli*, n.s. XIV/2, 433–52.

Pièces Diverses (1801) *Pièces diverses et correspondance relatives aux opérations de l'armée d'Orient en Egypte*. Paris.

Poncet, C. J. (1949) *The Red Sea at the Close of the Seventeenth Century*, ed. W. Foster, London.

al-Qalqashandī (1913–19) *Kitāb ṣubḥ al-a'ashā*. Cairo.

Rüppell, E. (1829) *Reisen in Nubien, Kordofan und dem Petraischen Arabien*. Frankfurt am Main.

Russegger, J. von (1843) *Reisen in Europa, Asien und Afrika.* Stuttgart.

Ṣalāḥ Muḥyī al-Dīn (1967) Makhṭūṭa ta'rīkhīya 'an mulūk al-'Abdallāb, *al-Kharṭūm*, December, 56–60.

Shaw, F. L. (1887) The story of Zebehr Pasha, as told by himself, *The Contemporary Review*, 333–49, 564–85, 658–83.

Shuqayr, N. (1903) *Ta'rīkh al-Sūdān al-qadīm wa'l-ḥadīth wa-jughrāfiyatuhu.* Cairo, 3 vols.

Slatin, R. (1896) *Fire and Sword in the Sudan.* London.

Sonnini, C. S. (1799) *Voyage dans la Haute et Basse Egypte.* Paris, 3 vols.

Wansleben, M. J., in Paulus, H. E. G. (1792–8) *Sammlung der Merkwurdigsten Reisen in den Orient.* Jena, Vol. III.

Whithead, G. O. (1934) Italian travellers in Berta country, *SNR*, XVII/2, 217–29.

Yūsuf Kamāl (1928–51) Youssouf Kamal, *Monumenta Cartographica Africae et Aegypti.* Cairo and Leyden.

Zayn al-'Abidīn (1847) Zein el-Abdin, *Das Buch des Sudan*, transl. G. Rosen, Leipzig.

(B) Modern Works

Aḥmad 'Abd al-Raḥīm Naṣr (1969) *Ta'rīkh al-'Abdallāb, min khalīl ruwāyātihim al-simā'īya.* Khartoum.

'Alī 'Abdallāh Abū Sinn (1968) *Mudhakira ta'rīkhīya 'an mudīrīya Dār Fūr.* Khartoum.

Arkell, A. J. (1932) Fung origins, *SNR*, XV/2, 201–50.

—— (1937, Darfur antiquities, II, *SNR*, XX/1, 91–105.

—— (1939) Throwing sticks and throwing knives in Darfur, *SNR*, XXII, 251–68.

—— (1946, Darfur antiquities, III, *SNR*, XXVII, 185–202.

—— (1947) The Baza festival in Jebel Meidob, *SNR*, XXVIII, 127–34.

—— (1951a and b, 1952a and b) History of Darfur, A.D. 1200–1700, *SNR*, XXXII/1 and 2, 37–70 and 207–38; XXXIII/1 and 2, 129–53 and 244–75.

—— (1956) The making of mail at Omdurman, *Kush*, IV, 83–4.

—— (1959) A Christian church and monastery at Ain Farah, Darfur, *Kush*, VIII, 115–19.

—— (1961) *A History of the Sudan from the Earliest Times to 1821.* London, 2nd edition.

Arkell, A. J. (1963a) The influence of Christian Nubia in the Chad area between A.D. 800–1200, *Kush*, XI, 315–19.

—— (1963b) A Persian geographer throws light on the extent of the influence of Christian Nubia in the 10th century A.D., *Kush*, XI, 320–1.

Asad, T. (1970) *The Kababish Arabs*. London.

Auriant, A. (1926) Histoire d'Ahmed Aga le Zantiote. Un projet de conquete de Darfour, *Revue de l'histoire des colonies françaises*, XIV, 181–234.

Baer, G. (1969) *Studies in the Social History of Modern Egypt*. Chicago.

Balfour-Paul, H. G. (1955) *History and Antiquities of Darfur*. Khartoum.

Barbour, K. M. (1954) The Wadi Azum, *The Geographical Journal*, CXX, 172–82.

—— (1961) *The Republic of the Sudan: A Regional Geography*. London.

Barth, F. (1967) Economic spheres in Darfur, in R. Firth, *Themes in Economic Anthropology*, 149–74. London.

Beaton, A. C. (1941) Youth organization among the Fur, *SNR*, XIV, 181–8.

—— (1948) The Fur, *SNR*, 1–39.

—— (1968) *A Grammar of the Fur Language*. Sudan Research Unit, Khartoum (mimeograph).

Bolton, A. R. C. (1934) El-Menna Ismail: Fiki, *SNR*, XVII, 229–41.

Brenner, L. (1973) *The Shehus of Kukawa*. Oxford.

Buṣaylī, al-Shāṭir (1955) *Ma'ālim ta'rīkh sūdān wādī al-Nīl*. Cairo.

Carbou, H. (1912) *La Région du Tchad et du Ouaddai*. Paris, 2 vols.

Chataway, J. D. P. (1930) Notes on the history of the Fung, *SNR*, XIII/2, 247–58.

Cohen, R. (1965) The dynamics of feudalism in Bornu, *Boston University Papers on Africa*, II, 85–106. Boston.

Crawford, O. G. S. (1951) *The Fung Kingdom of Sennar*. Gloucester.

Davies, R. (1957) *The Camel's Back*. London.

Deherain, H. (1904) *Etudes sur l'Afrique*. Paris.

Disney, A. W. M. (1945) The coronation of the Fung king of Fazoghli, *SNR*, XXVI/1, 37–42.

Elles, R. J. (1935) The kingdom of Tegali, *SNR*, XVIII, 1–35.

Fourcade, J. F. (1966) Documents arabes interessant l'histoire du Dār-Fūr, *Dossiers de la R.C.P. no. 45, 1*, C.R.N.S., Paris, 35–53.

Gray, R. (1961) *A History of the Southern Sudan, 1839–1889*. London.

Greenberg, J. H. (1971) Nilo-Saharan and Meroitic, in T. A. Sebeok (ed.), *Current Trends in Linguistics*, VII, 421–2. The Hague.

Haaland, G. (1969) Economic determinants in ethnic processes, in F. Barth (ed.), *Ethnic Groups and Boundaries*, 58–73. London.
Hill, R. (1959) *Egypt in the Sudan, 1820–1881*. London.
Hillelson, S. (1925) Notes on the Dagu, *SNR*, VIII, 59–71.
Hofmayr, W. (1925) *Die Schilluk*. Mödling.
Holt, P. M. (1960) A Sudanese historical legend: The Funj conquest of Soba, *BSOAS*, XXIII/1, 1–12.
—— (1963a) Funj origins: a critique and new evidence, *JAH*, IV/1, 39–55.
—— (1963b) *A Modern History of the Sudan*. 2nd edition. London.
—— (1967a) Sultan Selim I and the Sudan, *JAH*, VIII/1, 19–23.
—— (1967b) The sons of Jābir and their kin, *BSOAS*, XXX/1, 142–57.
—— (1969) Four Funj land-charters, *SNR*, L, 2–14.
—— (1970) *The Mahdist State in the Sudan, 1881–1898*, 2nd edition, Oxford.
Kalck, P. (1972) Pour une localisation du royaume de Gaoga, *JAH*, XIII/4, 529–48.
Kammerer, A. (1929–52) *Le Mer Rouge, L'Abyssinie et l'Arabie depuis l'antiquité*. Memoires de la société royale de géographie d'Egypte, Vols. XV–XVII, Cairo.
Kropáček, L. (1970) The confrontation of Darfur with the Turco-Egyptians, *Asian and African Studies*, Bratislava, VI, 73–8y.
—— (1971) Title-deeds in the fief system of the Sultanate of Darfur, *Acta Universitatis Carolinae*. Prague, Philologica IV, 33–50.
Lampen, G. D. (1928) A short account of Meidob, *SNR*, XI, 55–62.
Lebeuf, A. M. D. (1959) *Les Populations du Tchad au nord du dixième parallèle*. Paris.
Le Rouvreur, A. (1962) *Sahariens et Saheliens du Tchad*. Paris.
Lewis, B. (1967) *The Arabs in History*. New York.
MacMichael, H. A. (1912) *The Tribes of Northern and Central Kordofan*. Cambridge.
—— (1922) *A History of the Arabs in the Sudan*. Cambridge, 2 vols.
—— (1926) A note on the burial place of the Fur sultans at Tura in Jebel Marra, *SNR*, IX/2, 75–7.
Marlowe, J. (1972) *Perfidious Albion*. London.
Mercer, P. (1971) Shilluk trade and politics from the mid-seventeenth century to 1861, *JAH*, XII/3, 407–26.
Mohamed Riyad (1955) Of Fung and Shilluk, *Weiner Volkerkdl. Mitteilungen*, III, 138–66.
Nalder, L. F. (1931) Tales from the Fung Province, *SNR*, XIV/1, 67–86.

Nichols, W. (1913) *The Shaikia*. Dublin.

O'Fahey, R. S. (1969) On Nubian problems: a brief note on the Birged language, *Bull. Inter. Comm. on Urgent Anthropological and Ethnological Research*, XI, 63–4.

O'Fahey, R. S. and Spaulding, J. L. (1972) Hāshim and the Musabba'āt, *BSOAS*, XXXV/2, 316–33.

O'Fahey, R. S. and Abdel Ghaffar Muhammad (1972) Documents from Dār Fūr, fascicle 1, University of Bergen, Norway (mimeograph).

O'Fahey, R. S. (1973) Slavery and the slave trade in Dār Fūr, *JAH*, XIV/1, 29–43.

Paul, A. (1954) Some aspects of the Fung Sultanate, *SNR*, 17–31.

Polanyi, K. (1968) *Primitive, Archaic and Modern Economies*. Garden City, N.Y.

Robinson, A. E. (1925) Nimr, the last king of Shendi, *SNR*, VIII, 105–18.

—— (1929) Abu el Kaylik, the kingmaker of the Fung of Sennar, *American Anthropologist*, n.s. XXXI, 232–64.

—— (1930–1) The regalia of the Fung Sultans of Sennar, *Journal of the Royal African Society*, XXX, 361–76.

Santandrea, S. (1959) A Ndogo-kindred group, *Annali Lateranensi*, XXI, 115–90.

Shinnie, P. L. (1955) *Excavations at Soba*. Sudan Antiquities Service, Khartoum.

Shukry, M. F. (1938) *The Khedive Ismail and Slavery in the Sudan*. Cairo.

Spaulding, J. L. (1972) The Funj: a reconsideration, *JAH*, XIII/1, 39–53.

Temple, O. and C. L. (1922) *Notes on the Tribes, Provinces, Emirates and States of the Northern Provinces of Nigeria*. London.

Theobald, A. B. (1965) *'Alī Dīnār: Last Sultan of Darfur, 1896–1916*. London.

Trigger, B. G. (1965) *History and Settlement in Lower Nubia*. Yale University Publications in Anthropology no. 69, New Haven.

Trimingham, J. S. (1949) *Islam in the Sudan*. London.

—— (1962) *History of Islam in West Africa*. London.

Tubiana, M. J. (1960) Un document inédit sur les sultans du Waddai, *Cahiers des études africaines*, 11, 49–112.

—— (1964) *Survivances préislamiques en pays Zaghawa*. Paris.

Tubiana, M. J. and J. (1967) Mission au Darfour, *L'Homme*, VII/1, 89–96.

Tucker, A. N. and Bryan, M. A. *The Non-Bantu Languages of North-Eastern Africa*. London.

Valensi, L. (1967) Esclaves chrêtiens et ésclaves noirs à Tunis au XVIIIe siècle, *Annales*, XXII/6, 1267–88.

Villard, U. de Monneret (1929) La prima esplorazione archaeologica dell'Alto Egitto, *Bulletin de la société de géographie d'Egypte*, XVII, 19–48.

Westermann, D. (1912) *The Shilluk People*. Berlin.

Wickens, G. E. (1970) A brief note on the early history of Jabal Marra and the recently discovered Tora city of Kebeleh, *SNR*, L1, 147–51.

Wiet, G. (1938) Les relations égypto-abyssines sous les sultans mamlouks, *Bulletin de la société d'archéologie copte*, IV, 115–40.

Yūsuf Faḍl Ḥasan (1967) *The Arabs and the Sudan*. Edinburgh.

—— (1971) *Sudan in Africa: Studies presented to the First International Conference, Khartoum 1968*. Khartoum.

Index